Karen Lury is a reader in Film and Television Studies, University of Glasgow. She is the author of *British Youth Television: Cynicism and Enchantment* (2001) and *Interpreting Television* (2005).

THE CHILD IN FILM

TEARS, FEARS AND FAIRYTALES

KAREN LURY

I.B. TAURIS

LONDON · NEW YORK

1006410274

Published in 2010 by I.B.Tauris & Co Ltd
6 Salem Road, London W2 4BU
www.ibtauris.com

ISBN: 978 1 84511 967 6 (HB)
        978 1 84511 968 3 (PB)

A full CIP record for this book is
available from the British Library

Printed and bound in Great Britain by
CPI Antony Rowe, Chippenham

FSC
Mixed Sources
Product group from well-managed
forests and other controlled sources
Cert no. SGS-COC-002953
www.fsc.org
© 1996 Forest Stewardship Council

Contents

List of Illustrations vii

Acknowledgements ix

Introduction
Tears, Fears and Fairytales and Other Stories of
Childhood 1

Chapter One
Hide and Seek: Children and Ghosts in
Contemporary Japanese Film 17

Chapter Two
Dirty Little White Girls 53

Chapter Three
Mud and Fairytales: Children in Films about War 105

Chapter Four
The Impropriety of Performance: Children
(and Animals) First 145

Notes 191

Bibliography 199

Index 205

Illustrations

1. 'The broken threads of childhood': Nikolay
   Burlyaev as Ivan in Ivan's Childhood   9

2. 'Hide and seek': Toshio (Yuya Ozeki) plays
   in Ju-On (The Grudge)   18

3. 'Whose hand is this?': Yoshimi (Hitomi Kuroki)
   holds the ghost's hand in Dark Water   35

4. Ikuku (Rio Kannu) is reborn, in Dark Water   36

5. Toshio (Yuya Ozeki) as a ghastly and ghostly
   'Peter Pan', in Ju-On (The Grudge)   39

6. 'Dancers for money': Virginia (Shirley Temple)
   and Uncle Billy (Bill Robinson) dance in
   Littlest Rebel   68

7. 'And so to bed': Lloyd Sherman (Shirley Temple)
   and Walker (Bill Robinson) as partners in the famous
   'staircase dance' in The Little Colonel   72

8. 'Who is holding whose hand?': at the drive-in
   in Lolita   79

9. 'Dancing around the subject': Humbert
   (James Mason), Dolores (Sue Lyon) and Tom
   (John Harrison) in Lolita   82

10. Iris (Jodie Foster) and Sport (Harvey Keitel),
    dancing in Taxi Driver   91

11. Creasy (Denzel Washington) teaches Pita
    (Dakota Fanning) to swim, in Man on Fire   100

12. Creasy's (Denzel Washington) damaged hands,
    in Man on Fire   102

13. Creasy's (Denzel Washington) white gloves,
    in Man on Fire   103

14. Creasy (Denzel Washington) and Pita
    (Dakota Fanning) embrace, in Man on Fire   104

15. 'The burning barn', in Mirror   128

16. Isobel leaps through the flames, in Spirit
    of the Beehive   129

17. Jamie (Christian Bale) and the fire, in
    Empire of the Sun   131

18. Ofelia (Ivana Baquero) in the bowels of the
    tree, in *Pan's Labyrinth*   132

19. Jamie (Christian Bale) in the mud, in
    Empire of the Sun   132

20. 'The sheep', in *Padre Padrone*   169

21. Gavino (Fabrizio Forte), in *Padre Padrone*   169

22. Jamie (Stephen Archibald) cowers in a corner,
    in *My Ain Folk*   174

23. Maddalena (Anna Magnani) and Maria
    (Tina Apicella) in the projection booth, in
    Bellissima   183

24. 'Crying with laughter', in *Bellissima*   185

25. Maria's (Tina Apicella) screen test – bad acting
    or good crying?, in *Bellissima*   187

Acknowledgements

This book has been an ongoing obsession for some time and I would like to thank and acknowledge many people who have helped in different ways. To begin, I must start with my colleagues in the Department of Theatre, Film and Television Studies at the University of Glasgow, including: David Archibald, Karen Boyle, John Caughie, Minty Donald, Ian Garwood, Ian Goode, Michael McCann and Philip Schlesinger. Particular thanks go to colleagues who read with discrimination, and sometimes a little bemusement, different chapters in preparation – Dimitris Eleftheriotis, Katie Gough, Philippa Lovatt, David Martin Jones and Simon Murray. I would also like to single out Dee Heddon, who invited me to present at a day symposium she hosted at the Tramway in Glasgow which inspired the chapter on child performance, and who further helped me as I made my way in (and out) of the forest. And, as always, Christine Geraghty acted as a wonderful – and much abused – sounding board for some of my wackier ideas. I hope she knows how grateful I am.

Outwith Glasgow, I would also like to thank Robin Nelson who read – at almost the last gasp – a chapter I was particularly anxious about and who responded with his characteristically ready generosity and sensitivity. I am also grateful to Jackie Stacey, who invited me to a symposium that allowed me to test out my thoughts in a friendly but stimulating environment. Along the way, informal conversations, suggestions and observations from a host of siblings, friends and colleagues have helped me more than they might have guessed: thanks to Eylem Atakav, Caroline Beven, Adrian Howells, Karin Lesnik-Oberstein, Adam Lury, Celia Lury, David Lusted, Rob Maslen, Nick Millar, P.A. Skantze, Sara Thomas, Evie Pryde, and Rachel and Zoe at Offshore. Final thanks here must go to Philippa Brewster at I.B.Tauris, who never wavered in her enthusiasm or patience. The research and the writing of the book were supported by a research leave grant from the AHRC.

None of this would have been possible without Tim Niel, and none of it would have been worthwhile without Delilah, Alice and Edie.

Introduction

Tears, Fears and Fairytales and Other Stories of Childhood

> If endings are what History deals in, then its mode of beginning always suggests a wayward arbitrariness: 'once up on a time' is the rhetorical mode: the unspoken starting point of written history.[1]

I have a problem with beginnings; and with the endings that they inevitably promise to the reader. This is probably because my curiosity about the figure of the child in film is not driven by the belief that I will reach a confident conclusion or even a series of conclusions about what this child means or 'does' to cinema, or to the body of the films in which he or she appears. I am more interested in thinking about, thinking with, worrying and speculating about this child, and undertaking a mode of questioning that is akin to the child's accelerating queries of 'but why?' As we know, that question can never be satisfactorily answered, since it originates and is generated by the pleasures of the give and take of knowledge, on a testing that is ultimately irrational and peters out (unending) in 'just because'. Consequently, the reader should be aware that I have not written a book that satisfactorily details a history of the child in film, although I have, at different points, used history as a way of contextualising and interpreting the films I discuss.[2] My approach is to work my way out from the middle, assessing different appearances and performances of children in a range of films. The inspiration for my investigation and selection of films was the sense that the child and childhood, and indeed children themselves, occupy a situation in which they are 'other': other to the supposedly rational, civilised, 'grown up' human animal that is the adult. The films I focus on were not made for a child audience, or at least not exclusively; rather, the child characters I discuss feature in a variety of films aimed at adult audiences and address issues such as children's abandonment and murder, children's sexuality, their experience of the trauma of war and their exploitation in ways that might be deemed inappropriate

1

for a child audience (ironic as that may be). It is how these child characters are seen to participate, react and perform in an adult's world that interests me. In describing the child as other I am not suggesting that there is something wrong with the child, or that it is completely alien or unknowable. Instead, my approach is closer to that of the geographer Owain Jones, who in a series of essays has demonstrated how:

> Otherness...does not just mean simple separation and unknowability. It is a more subtle idea of the knowable and unknowable, the familiar and the strange, the close and the distance, being co-present in adult-child relations...otherness is not only healthy for children and for child-adult relationships, it is essential to what children are. It should be central to ideas of childhood too.[3]

Throughout all the chapters in the book, but perhaps most provocatively in the chapters on the figure of the Japanese child in J-Horror films and in my examination of the sexuality of the character I have called the 'dirty little white girl', I have used otherness as a way of conceptualising the child in film. In my chapter, 'Hide and Seek: Children and Ghosts in Contemporary Japanese Film', I suggest that in the J-Horror genre of films, the child functions as the kind of spectre identified by Jacques Derrida and is therefore an inhuman entity, acting as an irruption of repressed mythic, or pre-modern temporality into the present day. Following Colin Davis's reading of Derrida and his exploration of the associated study of 'hauntology', I suggest that the ghastly children of J-Horror – Toshio, Sadako and Mitsuko – articulate the concerns of a spectre that cannot be answered, that is irrational.[4] These child demons are thus distinct from the more familiar Western inflection of the child as ghost, in which the ghost is understood as a residue of the human who may still be saved or redeemed (and thereby contained) once their unresolved demands are understood and named. Drawing on anthropological and historical accounts of the child's symbolic importance to Japan as a modern nation state, I suggest that it is not surprising that the child as demon, as inhuman, as a traumatised yet simultaneously threatening other, lurks and surprises in these films. I have further contextualised my analysis by exploring a range of different Japanese films that are not horror stories but which similarly examine the abandonment, sadness and endurance of children, but this time from their own, rather than the adult's, perspective. In films such as *Dare mo shiranai* (*Nobody Knows*), *Eureka*, and *Kichijuro* it is the child's perspective and the child itself that become the focus for the narrative. In pushing what are marginal, background figures in the horror genre to the foreground – literally by changing our point of view – these films represent the child's desires, struggles, and trials. These child characters act as a response to the un-presence of the scary children who play their unnerving games of 'hide and seek' in J-Horror films such as *Ringu*, *Honogurai mizo no soko kara* (*Dark Water*) and *Ju-On* (*The Grudge*). Whilst my analysis in this chapter is sustained by a formal reading of the films themselves, I was directly inspired by the elegant and poignant acknowledgements which preface Susan Honeyman's book on children's literature, *Elusive Childhood*.[5] In closing her brief acknowledgements, Honeyman reflects on a eulogy given at the funeral of a friend, Anne Turner. In his speech, Turner's brother recalled an incident from their shared childhood in which they were accused of biting and leaving teeth marks on the corner of their parents' dresser.

> Left with only one other possible suspect, my parents confronted Anne, believing that they had apprehended the guilty party…During the interrogation my parents informed Anne that they knew that one of us had committed this infraction. In one of her earliest feats of dizzying logic and self-assurance, Anne replied, 'How do we know that one of you didn't do it?'[6]

Although Honeyman's book is a model of literary criticism and offers a variety of fascinating insights, it was this emotive trigger that inspired my analysis. It represents so clearly the significance of the child's point of view and the way in which adults presume to know and understand the world from only their own perspective. In the Japanese films, the apportioning of blame and the question of point of view (the child's versus the adult's) became increasingly important in understanding how the children might function: not only as terrifying harbingers of death but as interruptions, disturbing the apparent homogeneity of time and experience in contemporary Japan.

In the second chapter, 'Dirty Little White Girls', I trace or chase the figure of the 'little white girl' across a number of American films, from Lillian Gish – an adult performing as a 'little girl' in *Broken Blossoms* – to characters played by real little girls such as Shirley Temple, Jodie Foster and Dakota Fanning. My focus in the chapter is the way in which these little white girls expose a raced historical narrative in which the problematic otherness and supposedly playful and primitive sexuality of children is associated with a stereotypical representation of black male sexuality as similarly uncontrollable and uncivilised. Following arguments made by Toni Morrison in her critique of the racism inherent within certain canonical texts in American literature, I examine how the black male figures in these films serve to emphasise the apparent vulnerability, the littleness and, emphatically, the 'whiteness' of the girl child. The most symptomatic text is probably *Lolita* (and I focus on the relationship between Nabokov's novel and the film adaptation directed by Stanley Kubrick) but, as I demonstrate, nearly all the films are dominated by white male adults desperate to shore up their hetero-normative masculinity, and specifically their 'whiteness', and that they choose to use and abuse the sexuality of the little white girl in order to do so.

If the recurrent concerns of these films – innocence, purity and white masculine identity – are continually informed by the alliance of the little white girl and the adult black or coloured man, this is an alliance which must ultimately be usurped or marginalised so as to restore the status quo. Yet the little girl is, as my title suggests, not always or necessarily the passive, uninterested object that these films apparently depict (and their white male protagonists require). The excessive formal qualities of the films I discuss – in their melodramatic and increasingly Gothic tone – suggest that there are desires, emotions and a form of 'wanting' that is being repressed. This repression can only be glimpsed through the presence of shadows, the use of music and via small and apparently naïve gestures – such as mimicry, holding hands and in the exchange of smiles. I am not suggesting that the little girls' desires are the same as those expressed via an adult's sexuality but there are elements of these little girls' interactions with their favoured adult partner – touching, flirtation, the expression of a 'crush' – which are erotic even if they are not (and should not be) entangled in the goal-oriented, penetrative ambitions of adult male heterosexuality. Underpinning my analyses lie a range of studies within queer literary theory which have increasingly associated what Freud suggested were the 'polymorphously perverse' qualities of children's sexuality with queer sexual identity. This literature suggests that queer sexuality and the sexual or erotic impulses of children might be aligned, since they exist 'to one side' of the conservative heterosexual romance and its interest in the closing off, or in the resolution of desire. In particular, I was drawn to the complex but compelling arguments of Kathryn Bond Stockton in her essay, 'Growing Sideways, or Versions of the Queer Child: the ghost, the homosexual, the freudian, the innocent and the interval of animal'. Although her texts (drawn mostly from modernist literature) and her theoretical ambitions are different from my own, her provocative stance and the inclusion of the animal, with its simultaneously curious yet somehow natural alignment with the child, provoked a series of associations that recur at different points in my arguments. In the following passage, Bond Stockton pursues a series of questions that I found useful:

> Not uncommonly, children are shown as having a knack for metaphorical substitution, letting one object stand for another, by means of which they reconceive relations to time. Given that 'the child' is often defined as a point in time, how are children depicted as conceiving their relation to the concept 'growing up'? Are they shown as unwittingly making strange relations ('my dog is my wife') when they anticipate how they will participate in adult time? Must they turn their relations sideways (fantasizing having a baby with their parent, or even with a playmate) in order to imagine themselves growing up?[7]

The strange and unconsidered relations managed by children and her suggestion that children might grow 'sideways' instead of, or as well as, 'up' seemed to me to offer a playful and productive way of trying to envisage the 'what if' of childhood. That is, what if children don't (want to) grow up at all? What if they prefer the messiness, the ambivalent relations, confusing associations and excitable passions that are allowed in childhood but which are conceived as perverse in adulthood? I therefore draw on some aspects of this queer perspective but I reconfigure it to understand how the heterosexual romance between (or the sexual exploitation of) the little white girl and the adult male is played out in a range of films, including The Baby Burlesks, Lolita, Taxi Driver and Man on Fire. Despite the predictable closing down of the unruly and perverse desires of the little girl engineered by each film's resolution, I remain invested in the middle of these narratives in which the active and illegitimate wanting of the (dirty) little white girl resonates so strongly.

In these chapters certain themes preoccupy me and emerge with varying inflection: the nature of embodiment, the rupture of everyday modern temporality and the recognition that childhood and the child's presence offer opportunities for transgression which usurp or ignore conventional modes of identification and expressions of sexuality. These qualities suggest that the child figure is a more complex and powerful agent than might otherwise have been expected, and this focus is sustained in the last two chapters of the book. In the third chapter, 'Mud and Fairytales: Children in Films About War', I investigate how a number of films articulate the relationship between witness, memory and history through the character and presence of the child. In rejecting the more common assessment of the child symbolically representing the nation, I choose to concentrate on the way in which the child in films about war influences the manner in which history or the stories of the war are told and re-imagined on screen. I argue that the presence of the child allows film-makers to reflect on what can and cannot be said and to create filmic worlds in which the child's perspective is orchestrated via the representation of different embodied encounters and the adoption of an alternate mythic temporality, specifically the 'once upon a time' of the fairytale.

I am interested in the way in which the child must work with and against their imperfect ability to *speak* of their experience. In doing so, I draw on ideas originating in the work of the Italian philosopher, Giorgio Agamben, and specifically his book *Remnants of Auschwitz: the witness and the archive*. In this controversial text he advocates and describes a figure which he identifies as the only possible 'true' witness of the trauma of war, and in his book, specifically of the Holocaust. He suggests that this true witness is characterised, perversely, by their inability to speak, and that they exist solely as what remains after the destruction of their humanity, thus forcing us to confront the inhuman, stubborn remnant of what was once the civilised human subject. Only this 'animate corpse' can provide irrefutable testimony as to the horror of the Holocaust. Agamben's identification of this figure characterises it as an entity that must communicate its experience as being 'beyond or before' the constraints and traps of narrative and even of language itself. I suggest that the child's apparent inadequacy in relation to language (or deliberate retreat from language) aligns it with this figure. This means that the child's presence creates an opportunity for film-makers to articulate the trauma and experience of war not primarily through speech or a coherent chronological, historically accurate narrative; instead, in films such as La Jetee (The Pier), Mirror and El Espiritu de la Colmena (The Spirit of the Beehive) the perspective of the child allows for a confusing, often stuttering temporality and the dislocation of sound from the image. Equally, in these and other films – such as Idi I Smotri (Come and See), Empire of the Sun and El Laberinto del Fauno (Pan's Labyrinth) – the child's experience is represented through a series of embodied encounters that resonate within but do not faithfully reproduce the most familiar form of narrative and aesthetic that the child has access to – the fairytale. It is not that fairytales contain the child's experience, rather that the temporal ellipses, economic and symbolic density of the fairytale world are employed to represent the child's point of view. The world in these films is animated: it comes alive as a nightmarish fairytale, and the importance of the elemental aspects of this world (mud, fire, forests and rain) is played out in a series of encounters between the body of the child and its environment. The children in these films are covered in mud, starved, rained on, and stare in terror and awe at the fires which burn in forests, which burn buildings and people. Subjected to the indifference of a natural world exposed through the catastrophe of modern warfare, these child characters are forced to accept a non-anthropocentric perspective on events. The child figure does not, or cannot, provide authority on the facts of war, yet the representation of its experience as visceral, as of and on the body, demonstrates how the interweaving of history, memory and witness can be powerfully affective.

The text which lurks underneath my analyses in this chapter is Georges Perec's autobiography/novel *W*. *W* is a twisted partnership of two competing stories. One details Perec's apparently imperfect rememberings of his wartime experience. As a young child of Jewish and Polish parents in France during the Second World War, Perec went into hiding in the French countryside and was orphaned; his father was killed as a soldier in the war itself and his mother was deported and killed in Auschwitz. The other story is a fantastical, fictional history of the island 'W', in which the Olympian ideal of sport has evolved in to a version of the death camps. In this novel Perec articulates – ironically through the word-play and innocent sophistication of his written language – the peculiar and affective otherness of a child's experience of war. In this novel and in many of the films about war featuring children, the child's perspective, or the adult's memory of its experience as a child in war time, is determined by the child's comprehension of events, and this is represented as patchy, partial and potentially over-determined. Characterised, like Perec's novel, by 'holes' in the story, aspects of the child's experience are frequently revisited or imagined in fantasy rather than as a straightforward reconstruction of the original events. In these stories, real events are important but they exist in constant tension with what is being imagined and with what remains unsaid, producing a framework in which the child's experience is glimpsed, inferred and felt from the gaps in between. In the preface to *W*, Perec writes:

> One of these texts is entirely imaginary: it's an adventure story, an arbitrary but careful reconstruction of a childhood fantasy about a land in thrall to the Olympic ideal. The other text is an autobiography: a fragmentary tale of wartime childhood, a tale lacking in exploits and memories, made up of scattered oddments, gaps, lapses, doubts, guesses and meagre anecdotes. For it begins to tell one tale, and then, all of a sudden, launches into another. In this break, in this split suspending the story on an unidentifiable expectation, can be found the point of departure for the whole of this book: the points of suspension on which the broken threads of childhood and the web of writing are caught.[8]

Perec's description of the imperfect overlapping of history, memory, fantasy and personal experience allowed me to understand the motivation for the fantastic situations and images that were seemingly conjured up by many of the children in these films and their strange co-existence with the blunt realities of war. Similarly, Perec's insistence on the significance of the gaps and lapses in the narrative revealed how these films also evoke fragile webs of experience (the 'broken threads of childhood'), as they attempt to replicate the perspective of their child protagonists.

In the final chapter of the book 'The Impropriety of Performance: Children (and Animals) First', I examine the context for the child's performance on screen, locating it initially in terms of risk: the risk to the child in the exploitation of its labour and the controversy concerning the 'quality' of children's performances in film. The central concern of this chapter is to try and consider whether or not children – who apparently have limited experience and understanding – can be said to be acting. This is particularly problematic in relation to acting for film,

Figure 1 'The broken threads of childhood': Nikolay Burlyaev as Ivan in *Ivan's Childhood* (Dir. Andrei Tarkovsky, 1962)

since film acting itself is frequently undermined as a professional skill. First, it is argued that the nature of film production does not allow for a sustained, authored performance from the actor, and second, it is frequently suggested that the most effective performances (particularly from children) are nothing more than 'captured actuality'. This would suggest that many of the most acclaimed performances from children in film emerge when they are not 'acting' at all. Yet if children performing in films are not acting then what is it that they are doing? In addition, if many children are not trained or professional actors, why are many of their performances so compelling? My suggestion is that it is precisely this uncertainty (about whether or not they are acting) which makes them so troubling, yet so appealing. In fact, it refers directly to a central problem of the book – how can children's subjectivity, their emotions, their experiences and their thoughts be represented on screen? If, as I have suggested in other chapters in the book, the child figure is frequently over-determined by the priorities of interested adults – of the director, of the writer, of the other adult actors and the adult audience – when is it ever possible to identify the 'childish-ness' of the child at all? Surely the essential child-ish attributes of the child ought to be located (to some degree) in their performance and presence – in their body, gestures, behaviour, voice and cries – since the child inhabits and possesses a real body and its behaviour is presumably under the child's control. Yet to assume this places us in a curious double bind: first, if we are watching a film in which the child is simply 'being' (not acting) then we read a performance onto something that is not a 'performance' at all. Second, if the child is acting (seeming) then we may be confronted with an individual that might be regarded as a 'freak', a child who must possess adult-like qualities which allows it to act in a child-like rather than child-ish manner. And it is the case that many successful child actors are frequently identified as odd, miraculous or unique, as having or being 'It'; as possessing extraordinary, contradictory, qualities and abilities. Then the question becomes whether these marvellous individuals are really children – or children as we would normally understand them to be. In neither of these versions of the child on screen does the performance of the child actually offer or establish what it is to 'be' a child, only what we think or perceive that children may be 'like'. This 'impropriety' on the part of the child actor therefore challenges the nature of what proper adult performance is believed to do – that is, to show us what it is to 'be' human.

To try and come to terms with this impropriety, I concentrate on two aspects of the child's performance. First, I explore the alliance of the child actor to the (non-human) animal on screen. As performing children and animals can be categorised as equivalent – in the risk they pose to the production process, in their appeal and in the fact that they don't act 'properly' – then it may be that one function of these performers is to act as the ground for the proper performance of the adult. A 'proper' performance is the conscious, intended acting of adult human actors. When we see (or believe) that adult actors are orchestrating a set of behaviours that refer directly to their status as not just 'living entities' but as conscious intending subjects (as human), then their performances function not just to express fictional characters but also allow us to recognise how the humanity of the human, its performativity, produces a subjectivity that is self-conscious, coherent and legible, in contrast to the unconsciousness, incoherence and illegibility of the 'something else' that is manifested by the animal and in the child.

To explore this argument I look first, in some detail, at sequences from two autobiographical films – Padre Padrone and My Ain Folk – to consider how in both these films there seems to be an overt transition for the child actor (which parallels that of the child character) from a position as other to a performance of human-ness, of personhood, and that this is often at the expense of their previous alliance with the animal. I argue that while this transition may be important and unavoidable, it necessarily lessens the child performer's affective power and therefore its fascination for the film audience. Second, I consider the significance of tears and crying as a key activity within different children's performances in a number of films. The contradictory and messy evidence that tears provide seems to me to express the central confusion of child performance – when a child cries, on film, or in everyday life, are they 'seeming' or 'being'? The way in which we routinely determine whether or not someone is 'really' crying (and the fact that we are so often duped) makes the blurry status of tears – existing perilously between, or as both real *and* performed behaviour – explicit. What is more remarkable or awful: that a child on screen may be really crying (and not acting) or that the child can cry at will and can act without feeling, or act self-consciously and therefore not 'like a child'? If, on film, we are never sure whether we are getting one thing or the other, then this must demonstrate that we accept the myth of the miraculous, freakish child performer who can cry convincingly on cue, or that we acquiesce in the exploitation of an ordinary child who must have been made, or have made themselves, cry for our pleasure. By concluding with an analysis of a key scene from Luchino Visconti's *Bellissimma* I demonstrate how the peculiar presence of the child performer, and the way in which it can convincingly perform 'real' tears, allows Visconti to critique (and ironically replicate) the authentically freakish behaviour, as well as the probable exploitation of the child actor in film.

The origins for my interests in this chapter are difficult to identify. Initially, I think they stemmed from the apocryphal story that continues to circulate in relation to Margaret O'Brien – one of the most successful child stars of the 1940s – who is perhaps now best known for her role as Judy Garland's little sister, 'Tootie' in the musical *Meet Me in St. Louis*. It is generally claimed that not only could she cry on cue, but that she would even ask 'how far down' her tears should fall on her cheeks. I first heard this as a child from my mother and even then I was conscious that this would be a pretty miraculous physical and/or emotional feat. More concretely, I was driven by the cumulative effect of watching so many child performers over the period of my research and the way in which it seemed that so many directors seemed happy simply to follow the child performers, to focus on their bodies as they moved. In Robin Wood's well-known discussion of the child in Italian neo-realist films, he comments on the way in which, at the end of *Germany Year Zero*, Rossellini simply allows the camera to follow his boy protagonist – Edmund – on a walk through Berlin. We are interested in this 'performance' even though we are unsuspecting (at least on first viewing) that this walk will lead to Edmund's apparent suicide. Even in retrospect there is perhaps nothing – but somehow everything – to be read from Edmund's movements, his gait and aimless play. Similarly, in the critical writing on the Spanish actor, Ana Torrent, as a young child, there is a fascination – an adoration – of her presence on screen even when, perhaps particularly when, she is doing nothing at all. What is it, I wanted to know, that is so fascinating, so appealing, yet sometimes and simultaneously, disturbing, about the child's performance, about its presence on screen? I began to feel that it was not simply an erotic or narcissistic fascination, that it was a regard not driven by the need for identification but rather, as Lorri Nandrea might have it, an 'objectless curiosity'. One can understand 'objectless curiosity', she suggests, 'as a mode of apprehending otherness, one that may sidestep dynamics of identification and permit an interestingly non-appropriative relationship to the phenomenal world.'[9]

In her essay on this expression of interest (this kind of looking), Nandrea insists that it is not necessarily innocent: related to the staring or 'rubbernecking' of crowds at disasters or accidents, 'objectless curiosity' is scandalously without purpose, as it is neither scientific nor diagnostic. Rather, it suggests:

> a mode of attention that differs from the active, essentially teleological investigation that progresses, through space and time, toward comprehension. Instead, the crowd's curiosity seems to rest with what is, in a sense, ahistorical in the present: what is out of sync, aberrant, disruptive, unexpected or inexplicable; the aspect of the present that is new and different by virtue of not being 'same old, same old'.[10]

This attitude seems to me to chime so well with my interest in the child's performance and perhaps with the child figure throughout the book. I have not sought to diagnose or champion this child; instead I have – as my opening paragraph implies – found myself 'wondering'. This is not perhaps a respectable pursuit (you might legitimately ask, so what? Or, what's the point?), but respectability is not my concern. In fact, to make my interest respectable and the research apparently legitimate would be to stamp out or to resolve the otherness that I find so intriguing about the child in the first place. As Nandrea writes:

> If 'motivated' curiosity ultimately seeks to explain the strange, and thus to rob it of its strangeness, bringing about the return

of the same, objectless curiosity is invested in the strange as such; that is to say, in difference or the return of the new.[11]

This methodology – if it can be called that – brings me perilously close to a variety of fantasies about the child. Is this wonder at the child's otherness really another way of romanticising and essentialising the child figure? To be invested in the strangeness of childhood must surely depend upon the impossible – for it is impossible that the child will not be (eventually) the same as the adult and, equally, all children are inevitably – obviously – human. But I might put it the other way around: thinking about children has suggested what is strange about being human, about adult subjectivity. Simply and literally, by watching films that represent and employ children I have had the opportunity to explore a different point of view. I don't mean, exclusively, that it is another way of looking – although several writers have commented usefully and extensively on the importance of the child's gaze in cinema – rather, I have been interested in the way in which children in film manage not their apparent strangeness, but how they can reveal the strangeness of the world in which they live.

The (not quite) child figure that loiters behind these thoughts is the twelve-year-old, eponymous hero of Russell Hoban's novel, *Riddley Walker*. This book, which as far as I know has yet to be adapted for film, presents a world that we guess is an apocalyptic future in which human society has returned to, or evolved into, a mess of chaotic, primitive communities and which subsists on half-remembered and much mangled stories from the past – stories that are from the reader's present. These stories are fictional (Punch and Judy), religious (The Legend of St. Eustace) and scientific (nuclear fission). Famously, the book is apparently written by Riddley Walker himself, and he writes in a consistent, but crazy, phonetically determined language, that reads, feels and sounds plausible to the English reader, yet which also remains elusive – just beyond full comprehension. Riddley tells us at the very beginning of his story that, at twelve, he has become a man; yet he is only just a man, and still in a sense a child. The reader feels this all the more acutely because he speaks in a language that is almost but not quite our own.

Riddley is a 'wunnerer', a 'connexion man' who tries to make sense of his world. *Riddley Walker* thus manifests many of the central concerns of my own work, which is interested in the effects the child figure has on story-telling and how the presence of the child forces some radical readjustments to what we see and hear on screen. In *Riddley Walker* the child speaks, but not in a language we completely understand; the child occupies a temporality that may be the past or the future, yet which simultaneously feels un-synched, somehow 'out of time'; and the experience of the child is visceral – demanding the representation of not just what can be seen and heard, but what may be smelt and touched. On Riddley's journey he establishes a relationship with a dog pack which replicates the way in which many of the children I discuss forge an uneasy alliance with the natural, animal world in a manner that usurps a conventionally anthropocentric position. *Riddley Walker* is about discovery (although we may not be quite sure what is discovered) but it is also about the quality of imperfect rememberings and suggests that mis-remembering can be as significant as 'the truth'. Most importantly, early on in the novel Riddley identifies an understanding of subjectivity that recognises that a person is both someone and something else:

> Wel I cant say for cern no mor if I had any of them things in mynd befor she tol me but ever since then it seams like they all ways ben there. Seams like I ben all ways thinking on that thing in us what thinks us but it dont think like us. Our woal life is a idear we dint think of nor we dont know what it is. What a way to live.

And like Riddley I might suggest:

> Thats why I finely come to writing all this down. Thinking on what the idear of us myt be. Thinking on that thing whats in us lorn and loan and oansome.[12]

Chapter One

Hide and Seek: Children and Ghosts in Contemporary Japanese Film

At the door of her kindergarten a little girl waits and waits and waits in the pouring rain for her mother. But who is she: the mother, the daughter, or the ghost?

In the house, on the stairs, just behind you, glimpsed from the window of a lift, reflected in a glass door, a little boy plays hide and seek. Under the table, in a cupboard, on your bed, he curls up tight, his chin on his knees, anxiously drumming his fingers. Is that him, there, in the corner of the room as you turn your head? Does he look at you while you sleep?

The naked feet of a little girl can just be seen from under the hem of her plain white dress. We never see her face which is always just out of sight, or covered by the veil of her long dark hair. Is she victim or demon?

Black hair swinging, the tiny girl clambers crab-like out of the locker, creaking and groaning, striking terror into the college students who scuttle back on all fours in ghastly mimicry of the little figure before them. There is no escape: she will scare them to death.

These four scenes are played out in a series of films produced since the late 1990s in Japan, marketed in the West as 'J-Horror'. *Dark Water, The Grudge* 1 & 2, *Ring, Ring 2, Ring 0: Birthday* and *The Locker* 1 & 2 are part of an escalating series of filmed stories, told and retold in a variety of different media (novels, manga, television series, films) for the original Japanese and later for the American market. The films, which borrow various themes and motifs from traditional Japanese ghost stories and earlier classic films (*Kwaidan, Ugetsu Monogatori*) also incorporate a range of non-Japanese influences, from American horror films of the 1970s and 1980s (*Nightmare on Elm Street, The Evil Dead*); British Gothic films from the 1960s (*The Haunting, The Innocents*); and European art-house films (*Don't Look Now, Dekalog*).

The prefix 'J' is understood in the Western context as a reference to the Japanese origin of the films (although increasingly this is often merged or confused with Korean and Taiwanese films). In a more precise definition of 'J'-culture

Figure 2 'Hide and seek': Toshio (Yuya Ozeki) plays in *Ju-On* (*The Grudge*) (Dir. Takashi Shimizu, 2002)

the Japanese critic, Tomiko Yoda, represents this mode of production as a 'subculturation of the national'.[1] That is, whilst the form (the borrowings, what she calls the 'patchwork of citations') of 'J' culture may be global in its scope and potential dissemination, the 'content', the symbols, objects, props of the mise-en-scene are recognisably local or national (Japanese), producing a sense of 'visceral proximity' for their target audience. As she notes, when such forms are marketed (or remade) for a non-Japanese audience, these symbols and props can be replaced with objects familiar to the new local/national context. Or they may be reconfigured: one such symbolic figure in these films that enacts a specialized function is the child – the child who can variously appear, as I have indicated, as ghost, monster and victim. Whilst the child remains and performs a broadly similar function in these stories, whether the films are initially made for a Japanese or American market, there is something distinctive about the use of the child in the Japanese versions of the stories. My argument is that the child figure is used so frequently and resonates so tremendously in these films because it represents a particular preoccupation for Japanese national identity.

Ghostly Thoughts

First, a brief detour to investigate the nature of the ghost: in the West, ghosts have been predominantly represented as visions of dead people who return seeking justice or acknowledgement from the living. Often the ghost betrays or serves to reveal a secret (a murder, a wrongdoing) that must be solved before he/she can properly and finally 'pass over'. As Colin Davis notes, this presents the ghost as a symptom which can be solved via a method akin to the psychoanalytic process, where once the ghost (secret) has been uncovered, acknowledged and finally 'spoken' it will no longer haunt or terrify the living. Many well-known films which feature haunted children, such as *The Sixth Sense*, *Poltergeist* and *The Exorcist*, follow this model: the child is only safe once the ghosts or demons which terrorise them are named or acknowledged. In some films, as in *The Others* (where the children finally learn that it is they who are the ghosts), the 'naming' and speaking to – or for – the ghost is more ambiguous in terms of its redemptive effect. Equally, is it an act of love, therapy or violence that causes the governess in *The Innocents* to scream; 'Say his name! Say his name!' at Miles, the little boy in her care, who is apparently haunted by a malevolent male spectre? Tragic certainly, since the shock of being forced to speak the ghost's name results in Miles collapsing and dying in her arms.

Davis goes on to outline an alternative understanding of the ghost by following Jacques Derrida's investigation of haunting in his *Spectres of Marx*. Here, Davis claims, Derrida represents the ghost as not so much a return from the past, but more as a representation of something 'other', something that precisely *cannot* be spoken. Contrasting this 'spectre' with the psychoanalytic model which restores the ghost to its proper place (to the 'other side', to eternity or elsewhere), Davis suggests that:

> Derrida wants to avoid any such restoration and to encounter, what is strange, unheard, *other*, about the ghost. For Derrida the ghost's secret is not a puzzle to be solved ...The secret is not unspeakable because it is taboo, but because it cannot

(yet) be articulated in the languages available to us. The ghost pushes at the boundaries of language and thought.[2]

Further, he claims: 'Derrida's aim is not to reveal the content of the ghost's secret, rather he aspires to learn to attend to its mystery, to hear within it the rumbling of what has yet to be understood.'[3]

It seems to me that it is this kind of spectre – an unknowable, persistent un-presence (as opposed to a 'presence from the past') – which is closest to the ghosts found in J-Horror. In *Ring*, for example, there is a false ending which plays exactly on the audience's pre-existing understanding that the ghost in a horror story is a problem that can be solved and thus escaped from. At a climactic point in *Ring*, the central female character, Reiko, is desperately seeking a way to protect her son (Yoichi) from the curse of a malevolent female ghost – Sadako. Reiko and her ex-husband (Ryuji) have successfully uncovered Sadako's story and ultimately locate her unburied remains (she had been entombed in a well). Having found Sadako's body and rescued it, both characters and audience believe that the curse will now be lifted and that Yoichi and Ryuji (who is also in danger) must now be saved. However, the following day Ryuji dies (clearly a victim of Sadako) and it is clear that this ghost cannot be stopped or resolved simply by an acknowledgement of past wrongs. In fact it emerges that the curse can only be escaped by being transferred or passed on like a virus to another victim. Sadako's ghost – or the un-presence that is Sadako – is therefore not a secret to be revealed but is something other, inescapable and unknowable. Intriguingly, like many of the ghosts in this genre, she never speaks and simply creaks and groans (rumbles?) whilst confronting her victims, thus uttering or speaking in a way that cannot be translated.

Equally, in *The Grudge*, uncovering the identity of the little boy (and his mother) does nothing to release their victims from their terrible, inevitable deaths. Indeed, there is apparently no logical rationale for the selection of the ghosts' victims (who include police officers, social workers, school girls and a teacher); they simply seem to have necessarily, or accidentally, inhabited the same 'space' as the ghosts. This random malevolence is repeated in *The Locker*, where the girl-ghost is understood to be the manifestation of an abandoned baby (who had been left in the locker to die). Despite the acknowledgement by the students of this tragedy and the enacting of several attempts to resolve it through a quasi-religious ritual – they rebuild a damaged idol and light incense in her memory – she continues to pursue her victims.

DarkWater might at first seem to be the exception here: it does appear that the mother's ultimate sacrifice (she allows herself to become the mother of the dead, abandoned little girl) serves to protect her actual daughter (Ikuku) from the ghost's evil intent. However, as the film's epilogue reveals (when we see, ten years later, Ikuku now a high school pupil, returning by chance to find her mother still living apparently unchanged in the haunted apartment), the ghost has not gone away, rather the mother and the ghost are now in a kind of terrible, melancholy limbo where nothing ever changes, but in which the ghost now has a mother who 'will never leave her alone again'.

Ghosts as relentless, a-temporal others are also discussed by Bliss Cua Lim in her essay, 'Spectral Times: the ghost film as historical allegory'. Here she states:

> The hauntings recounted by ghost narratives are not merely instances of the past reasserting itself in a stable present, as is usually assumed; on the contrary, the ghostly return of traumatic events precisely troubles the boundaries of past, present, and future, and cannot be written back to the complacency of a homogenous, empty time.[4]

Cua Lim's argument, which I build on here, also refers directly to Derrida and suggests that ghosts act as un-presence, disturbing our sense of what is possible, and remain fundamentally untranslatable. Furthermore, she suggests that one of the ways in which this is played out is that the ghost disturbs our (modern) sense of temporality. The 'empty homogenous time' she refers to here is the concept of a modern, historical temporality in which events proceed in a linear, teleological manner, allowing for a rational interpretation of events, and thus underpinning and naturalising the ideology of the modern narrative which is committed to presenting as inevitable the idea of development or progress. The time of modernism, therefore, organises a world that is necessarily disenchanted, since both gods and ghosts (who manifest time as eternal or cyclical) cannot be incorporated. Since gods and ghosts cannot be assigned a 'place in time' in the time of history, there will necessarily be, as Dipesh Chakrabarty has argued, a tension between the 'general secular time of history and the singular times of gods and spirits'.[5] What I am suggesting is that the relentless ghosts of J-Horror are akin to the gods, demons and spirits excluded from the time of history/modernity. Their presence is therefore not simply about the representation or re-emergence of the past in the present, instead their activities, demands and desires actually threaten the apparent coherence or unquestioned naturalness of the now that we understand as the present. This is perhaps particularly pertinent in relation to Japan since its adoption and adaptation to the construction of a historicized time was relatively recent and spectacularly rapid. As Stefan Tanaka observes:

> By the end of 1873, the government had completely transformed the calendar. This was a terrific opportunity: not only did it introduce the possibility that the past is old and must be changed, but it reconfigured time markers to shift attention from the spirits and gods to the emperor, the centre of the emerging nation-state.[6]

Like other nation states, Japan adopted a universal, rational mode of time-keeping (moving from a lunar to a solar calendar) so that it could become a recognisably modern nation state, organised and interpreted via a historical, rational and disenchanted time. As Tanaka suggests, it is now difficult to imagine what effects – social, emotional and cultural – this change might have incurred, but is probable that:

> The time of the solar calendar was completely alien to the inhabitants, unsettling the knowledge and customs that revolved around the lunar calendar. Those inherited ideas and customs that explained the connection of humans to humans and to the environment now became anachronistic...The significance of this new time is that it is abstract; it opened up the possibility for the transformation of myriad communities that had somehow coalesced in a 'Japan' into a unified nation-state that is rational, scientific, and efficient.[7]

Thus the beliefs, forms of knowledge and rituals associated with pre-modern Japan were effectively reinvented as tradition which, once reified, could become the history of 'before'. Of course these forms of belief did not disappear – indeed they served to illustrate, in part, what it meant to be Japanese. Yet, since it is firmly located in the past, the concept of tradition also (safely) identified those beliefs and rites as *other* to the new modernising nation state. The previous 'heterogeneous worlds of temporalities' were now confined to one time, and thus to one space, the homogenous and unified nation state. Under this new homogenising temporality it was now possible to track Japan's development along a linear path from pre-modern, to modern, to post-modern. Japan's phenomenally successful passage along this trajectory became a fundamental aspect of its national self-identity. Yoda writes:

> For over a century the ruling elites of Japan, the nation reputed to be the most successful latecomer to modernity, had been intensely self-conscious about their relation to the West, measuring themselves against the time lag to the dominant Other ... The challenge that Japanese economic advances posed on Eurocentric history and the mapping of the world in other words, was perceived as the nation's triumph over modernity and over history itself.[8]

Japan's tremendous economic success after the Second World War was therefore seen as both a challenge to, and in effect a surpassing of, Eurocentric dominance and the modernist narrative of development. Japan in the 1980s and early 1990s was represented by many commentators in Japan and elsewhere as the epitome of the giddy symbolic density and inflated economics of post-modernism. However, by the late 1990s, Yoda points out:

> The self-congratulatory exuberance that accompanied the bubble economy and the boom of post-modernism in Japan had fizzled by the mid-1990s, replaced by the debilitating air of anxiety (*fuan*). The structure of feeling of posthistory has remained, but in the 1990s it became associated with unbearable fragmentation, opacity, and paralysis. Japan in

the recessionary decade seemed arrested in the seemingly paradoxical state of unending and entrenched present coexisting with momentous instability.[9]

In this time of anxiety, of paralysis, of an unending, entrenched but threatened present, there is an obvious context in which ghosts – as indicators of other temporalities and as traumatic remainders or reminders – are likely to surface. The question I will next pursue is why, in these films, these ghosts so often manifest as children.

The Modern Child

The category of childhood and the figure of the child are caught up in and enact the ambitions and ideology of modernity in the West and elsewhere. In her book, Strange Dislocations: childhood and the idea of human interiority, 1780–1930. Carolyn Steedman eloquently details how, at the end of the nineteenth century, in the West, the child figure came to represent in a variety of discourses (education, history, psychology, anthropometry and biology) a symbol of both the 'interiorised self' and the historicity of the individual. Thus, certain narratives which might be said to characterise modernity – those of the self (psychoanalysis), of the human race (evolution), of the necessity and inevitability of development and progress (history) – could be illustrated by the evidence provided via the apparently natural being and development of the child. The usefulness of children within these forms of discourse necessarily led to an increasing desire to map out and control their apparently natural and universal attributes. Thus, different forms of progressive social policing – such as mass schooling, specialist children's hospitals, curbs to children's labour and the development of special societies for the prevention of cruelty to children – might all be understood as ways in which the child and childhood were increasingly distinguished and fixed. As Steedman suggests, this meant that 'The late nineteenth century fixed childhood, not just as a category of experience, but also as a time-span'.[10]

Set apart in terms of time and experience, the child and childhood became paradoxically other to adult human life – childhood was a special, if restricted, time period in which children were different from adults and should be treated accordingly. Yet the child also served as both evidence and ground for the interpretation of everybody's individual self, in that what happened to you 'as a child' determined how you would act and think as an adult. In addition, by mapping out a narrative of progress and a series of developmental milestones for the normal child, it also became possible for the child to act as the personification of development itself, whether this was applied to the individual or the human race. As Stefan Tanaka observes:

> Childhood...becomes a temporal category with specific meanings, a category that cuts across spatial divisions and experiential categories and facilitates the unity of previously disparate categories into a whole. It is seemingly universal because it is tied to the body and 'experienced' by everybody (i.e. it is a period through which all adults pass).[11]

This process identified by Steedman and others as occurring in the West was also adopted in Japan and, as both Tanaka and Andrea Arai attest, was tied specifically to the project of nation-building, or 'national identity formation'. In terms of a national project the child provided a way in which national identity could be both essentialized (Japanese children were inseparably *all* 'children' and *all* 'Japanese') and programmed (through the social organization and educational programming of actual children). As Tanaka states:

> Here childhood becomes a political tool; it is part of the effort of a nation-state to monopolize those mnemonic devices that reinforce its vision of what society should be – in the case of Japan, the marginalization of dissatisfaction and restlessness in favour of obedience and loyalty.[12]

In the context of Japan, the infantilization of the national self might be seen to have had disastrous consequences in relation to the cult of the Emperor, where the extension of the concept of family in terms of loyalty, hierarchy and obedience might seem to have engineered a particularly unfortunate playing out of the child-nation dynamic. As Norma Field writes: 'As the family became conflated with the patriarchal, indeed, fascistic, family state, the only role left for the child was of miniature instrument to be moulded in the service of that state.'[13]

It might be thought that in the post-war period the relationship between 'child' and 'nation' as mutually consolidating myths might have receded. Yet this was not to be the case; indeed, one of the most famous Japanese films from the early post-war period – *Nijushi no hitomi* (*Twenty-Four Eyes*) – tracks the changing fortunes of a group of children from the pre- to post-war period. Whilst the inevitably traumatic events they encounter mean that the children's progress to adulthood is not always happy (or indeed reached), the concluding sequence of the film, in which the children's elementary school teacher returns to teaching and is confronted with the daughter of one of her original children, would seem to underscore the film's investment in the child as a way of sustaining a Japanese self, as a perpetually renewing figure that can connect past and present. As Tanaka claims:

> Each period is set apart from others to show both change – a change in which there is a strong connection between the past and the present – and continuity. Childhood provides the structure for ensuring that the bodies understand those ideals; it facilitates the constant reproduction of the national ideals through the education of the child.[14]

Via education, the body and the mind of the child can be moulded to ensure a coherent and visible national identity. More than this, the figure of the child can be used to represent the continuation of the nation state itself. The child acts to stabilize the inherent instability of modernism. Children are at once a link to the past (as the offspring of their parents and thus inheritors of their history and traditions) while simultaneously (by growing up) vehicles to the future, and seemingly embody the potential for progress.

In the later post-war period, the apparent success of the Japanese education system in producing active and loyal workers and consumers was seen as a fundamental part of Japan's economic triumph. Arguably, the schooling of Japanese children in the post-war period prepared and produced a population of regulated, Japanese bodies that could be put to service in both the production and consumption activities required by advanced capitalism. And as Yoda argues, the success of this process became part of the myth which suggested that Japan could take part in the global economy without losing its own individuality, since by establishing itself as an economic superpower it could confirm the exceptional and supposedly essential national character of the Japanese.

Yet the experience of the actual children who were to carry this burden of over-investment indicated that the stress of conformity, of overwork and the relentless struggle of living up to the ambitions of their anxious parents became increasingly impossible to bear, meaning that the process of becoming 'compatible' with the constraints of the Japanese society and economy was not necessarily easy or straightforward. In her essay, 'The Child as Laborer and Consumer', Norma Field identifies numerous forms of physical and psychic malaise experienced by Japanese children in the mid-1990s. Physical problems such as chronic constipation, high blood pressure, ulcers and hair loss as well as the psychological suffering related to the effects of bullying, along with the continuing problem of 'school refusal', seemed to be endemic in the school population. By the mid-1990s, the prevalence of these medical, social and psychological problems had become visible enough for Field to argue that childhood and children were under threat. Furthermore, she suggests:

> The normalization of dysfunction among Japanese children is striking precisely because, as I have emphasized, it is taking place in an orderly, prosperous society. It is likely, therefore, that had the children's bodies not begun to register (made visible like prodigious spectacle) their suffering, it would have continued to be officially ignored.[15]

By the mid-1990s, children were understood as victims, providing evidence that the national project was questionable, even malign. Thus, it is not surprising that the child as victim (the dead child, the traumatised child, the abandoned child) might be prominent in popular fictional narratives addressed to a Japanese audience.

However, as I have indicated, in the series of films I am discussing, the child is not unambiguously a victim and he or she may equally (or even simultaneously) act as a threat. The child figure in these films is contradictory. This might be understood in relation to the fact that the category of child as inhabited and expressed by actual children is inherently unstable. As Tanaka observes:

> Children are natural beings, clear for everyone (with the proper knowledge) to see, that become the metonym for a childhood that seeks monopoly over experience itself. But children also embody instability; like ghosts who constantly threaten to create mischief or conflagration, children constantly pose the threat that they might rebel or not mature and turn into productive citizens.[16]

The categories of the child and real children are evidently not equivalent. The real child's potential to 'fail' and thus meet the pre-determined norms of childhood, or the possibility that it might act in a way that is 'not natural', threatens not just the category of childhood but, because of the child and childhood's dominant position within the national imaginary, the self-identity of the nation.

In the period of social crisis following the collapse of the bubble economy and the consequent recession in Japan in the 1990s, the child emerged as a figure that could embody victimhood and simultaneously act as a threat. Real children were suffering and real children could – and would – act in ways that threatened the accepted model of childhood and its promise of a seamless trajectory that led to becoming a responsible adult-citizen and effective worker/consumer. The fact that this had always potentially been possible – that this trajectory was a socially constructed myth and not natural or inevitable – could not be imagined until the supposed relation between the model of childhood and the success of the economy broke down. Yet for many commentators, because this conception of the child was so central to the coherence and maintenance of national identity, the economic and social problems were not blamed on outside factors but rather on the failure of the child, or on the child's guardians and educators. It was the nature and education of the child rather than external influences that were to blame for Japan's economic and social crisis.

What or who the child actually 'was' became a focus of concern. In her thesis, 'Recessionary Effects: the crisis of the child and the culture of reform in contemporary Japan', Andrea Arai outlines how one prominent Japanese social commentator, Kawakami Ryoichi, identified and speculated on a new child figure, the 'strange-changed child' (kodomo ga hen da) whom he saw as different from previous generations. He argued, for example, that:

> The student movement and the inner-school violence (konai boyoku) of the 80s were preferable to the 90s strange (hen da) child. We can't get through to these children, they're incomprehensible (tsujinai; wakaranai), and we don't have a clue what they're thinking. The recent (juvenile) crime is unbelievable. We can't feel at ease. Killing used to be out of need, for money. Now the idea of killing is for fun, pleasure, a game.[17]

Kawakami's reference to 'killing for fun' is directly connected to a major incident that took place in 1997, involving a Japanese high school student. Arai explains:

> Known as the, 'Kobe wounding and murdering of children incident', 'Shonen A' ['boy' or 'youth' A] was a third-year junior-high student at the time, wounding and murdering a series of elementary-aged children, decapitating the final victim. Youth A accompanied his heinous deeds with chilling taunts to the authorities ('hey, the game starts now' – sa gemu no hajimari desu) and explanations of his monstrous transformation ('I just want to kill' – koroshite mitai) that indicted the education system for the invisibility of his existence (tomeina sonzai).[18]

In the UK, the murder of the toddler James Bulger by two young boys similarly instigated a series of popular articles in the press and elsewhere, debating the nature of childhood, the impoverished state of the community and the moral inadequacy of society. The fact that by the late 1990s Japan provided a context in which the notion of children undergoing a 'monstrous transformation' appeared plausible would seem to indicate – perhaps all too neatly – why the malevolent or ambiguous child-ghosts in J-Horror are so prevalent. The recurring appearance of the child as ghost or demon in these films could be understood as a response to contemporary social and political anxieties, about childhood and about national identity. Unfortunately, these anxieties are often, as Arai and others have pointed out, used as evidence in conservative polemics and as triggers for regressive social policies. Yet I want to take on board Arai's own expressed belief that the figure of the malevolent child can also open up possibilities. To do so, I will look more closely at the role children play in J-Horror and how their ghostly existence, or close alliance with ghosts is supported by the distortion and manipulation of time in the films. This narrative play, I suggest, makes evident the child-ghost's potential to disrupt the apparent naturalness of a homogenous, disenchanted present. These child-ghosts, as Tanaka argues, hint at:

> the possibility of multiple temporalities: like the ghosts that haunted pre-Meiji Japanese society (and continue to today through a much less public presence), the past is not stable and constantly shifts, threatening to destabilize the certainty of the known world.[19]

As an over-determined symbol of modern Japanese identity, the child's ambivalent presence exposes the contradictory, fragile aspects of the national imaginary. Their appearance also reveals the dislocation (in Steedman's terms) between the experience of actual children and the category, or personification of the child in contemporary Japan. This latter claim can be consolidated via reference to a number of films which can be seen as the inverse of the J-Horror genre (specifically in terms of their representation of the child). In *Nobody Knows*, *Eureka*, *Kikujiro* and *Kichiku* (*The Demon*) the fates of the children in what might be seen as their 'hiding places' are explored in detail. In these films, rather than children being glimpsed at the edges of the frame (or from the corner of the eye) their marginal presence, their desires and fears and their struggle for survival, is the focus of the film. In these films, the child is sought out and retrieved from his or her marginal or invisible existence.

Time Out of Joint: Fractured Narratives in J-Horror

The *Ring* series is characterised by an eerie mixture of temporalities. While, as previously stated, numerous versions of the story have been produced (in Japan and elsewhere), the three Japanese cinema releases (*Ringu*, *Ring 2* and *Ring 0: Birthday*) provide a loosely chronological story expressing the origins of the demon figure, Sadako, and the terrible vengeance she wreaks on a young family and their acquaintances and relations. The films were not produced or released chronologically, and we begin the story in the middle (some 30 years after Sadako's apparent murder) and move forwards (in the relatively conventional sequel Ring 2) only to retreat to the origins of Sadako in the last film, Ring 0. The first American version of the story, The Ring condenses some of the plot from all the films and thus erases the overarching temporal confusion of the Japanese series. Since the American film necessarily condenses so much of the story it also removes much of the sense of dislocation between the 'uncanny time' of Sadako and her embodiment of an urban myth, and the ongoing yet curiously empty, banal sense of time-passing in the apparently bleak urban environment of present-day Japan. It is this juxtaposition that creates the peculiar mood, or the unsettling temporality, that distinguishes the Japanese films.

Ring begins with a date on screen; initially for the watching audience, this has little significance until it becomes evident that this is the 'deadline' for Sadako's first victim, Reiko's niece, Tomoko. Later on, when a date reappears on screen we recognise it as ominous because it confirms that Reiko herself is now being forced to submit to the compressed count-down time of the curse. Once the video has been seen, the victim has only seven days to live and Reiko's days are literally numbered. Ironically, her inability to control time (to fit the regimes of modern time-keeping) has already been evident. In an earlier scene, before she has been cursed, we see her arriving home late from work, flustered and unprepared for Tomoko's wake. Curiously, once she has been cursed, despite the increased pressure on her time that Reiko experiences, many of the film's scenes continue to manifest an emptiness where time acts as a drag on the characters' activities and desire for progress. In Ring and Ring 2 (both directed by Hideo Nakata) a contemporary, urban Japan of dull colours and liminal, uniform spaces – such as hospital corridors, streets, commuter trains and minimally furnished apartments – embody the mundane and often frustrating passage of time, and necessitate the 'wasting of time' by the characters as they move about the city or large institutions. In Ring, while following the progress of all three protagonists as they travel – with some urgency – to the countryside, and then by ferry to the island where Sadako lived, there is still a surprising amount of uneventful time captured on screen. As the sea itself is such a prominent motif in the films, it is perhaps not too fanciful to suggest that the characters seem, at points, to be subjected to a kind of nightmarish temporal undertow, which drags at their heels as they try to move forward to a resolution.

Reiko's inability to control her own time also seems to get worse rather than better as the seven days slip by. Desperately seeking a solution, she works late in the office and in libraries, and twice has to phone her young son, Yoichi (who is home alone) to apologise that she will be late. As time passes, she seems increasingly unable to maintain a coherent temporal presence for herself. Her experience of psychic 'flashbacks' present her not just as seeing the past (as is in a dream or vision) but as actually experiencing the past as it happens. For example, when she 'sees' the incident in which Sadako is supposed to have murdered a reporter at a public exhibition of her mother's psychic powers, Reiko is herself incorporated into the grainy black and white of this vision from the past. Further demonstrating her physical connection to this past, once she 'returns' from this vision she continues to carry a physical mark – a handprint on her arm – from Sadako. The past is not simply 'remembered' in the present but is literally taking place and, in effect, overlapping and contaminating the 'now'. (This is a temporal confusion that Nakata reproduces to an even greater degree in DarkWater.) In this way, the films take on some of the qualities of the cursed video itself, with its strange montage of images that refer to Sadako, but which do not tell her story. By refusing to tell her story properly (they do not provide a beginning or an end, nor do they tell 'what happened, when'), the video and the films themselves refuse temporal coherence or a clear chronology for Sadako. Ultimately, the irrelevance of the regimes of modern temporality – where time is passed meaningfully, or kept (by meeting deadlines and noting dates) – is revealed as inadequate as a way of containing the increasingly mythic monster that is Sadako. As Ring 2 reveals, the successful passing of their deadlines by both Reiko and Yoichi does not release them from Sadako's malevolent influence. Even the noted continuity error between the two films – in *Ring* it is claimed that Sadako died after seven days in the well, whereas at the beginning of *Ring 2* it is suggested that she may have been alive in the well for 30 years – is simply a further manifestation of the irrelevance of ordinary (non-mythic) temporality for Sadako, who as a demon/spirit inhabits her own, singular time.

At first, in *Ring*, the adults' preoccupation and inability to manage their own time is contrasted with the child Yoichi's sense of purpose and control. For example, when Reiko arrives home late to prepare for Tomoko's wake, not only is Yoichi dressed and ready, he has also found her an appropriate dress and laid this out. Although a lonely little boy, his initial adherence to routines (such as going to school) relate to the organisation of everyday, ordinary modern time. However, these routines are ultimately disrupted and abandoned once he is taken away from the city, to the country house of his grandfather, where he (illicitly) sees the cursed video. As he becomes detached from the time-based routines of modern life, he is presented as an increasingly liminal or a-temporal figure. Associated more and more closely with Sadako (he also begins to experience visions that suggest a connection between them) and her mythic time, he is no longer an innocent victim: so much so, that in *Ring 2* he seems increasingly possessed by her. This is made evident when he seems to gain some of her telekinetic powers and in a sequence where the ghost of Reiko's father tells her that Yoichi is no longer her son. Yoichi's desire to return to normality, to the 'everyday time' of the modern world, is hinted at in an early scene in *Ring 2*, where we see, via pieces of paper in their apartment, that he has been writing – in mute frustration – to his mother, insisting that he wants to go to school: to return, perhaps, to an institution where time is strictly controlled and thus made safe.

In *Dark Water*, the inability of parents (mothers) to meet the regime of institutional time-keeping is a narrative thread that links the fate of all three female protagonists. At different points in the film we witness Yoshimi Matsubara (the mother), Ikuko Matsubara (her daughter) and Mitsuko Kawai (the dead little girl) waiting to be picked up by their mothers at the end of the kindergarten day. Yoshimi and Ikuko will eventually be picked up by their fathers, but Mitsuko, it emerges, will walk home alone, and drown, accidentally – but implicitly as a result of this neglect – in the water tower of her apartment block. The coincidence of the waiting scenes is underlined by the fact that in all three instances it is raining heavily. Water – as puddles, leaks, steam, sweat or rain – not only signals the presence of Mitsuko, but also links the three characters across and within time. The most obvious manifestation of this is the leak from Mitsuko's supposedly empty apartment through Yoshimi's ceiling, represented by a water stain that grows ominously and drips more intensively as the narrative progresses. Whilst superficially the film's narrative coincides, in part, with a bureaucratic time-period (the ongoing divorce proceedings undertaken by Yoshimi), the infiltration of Mitsuko into the relationship between Yoshimi and Ikuko exposes the cyclic temporality at work within the peculiarly intense and reciprocal relationship between mother and daughter. For example, Ikuko is, at certain points in the film, presented as a miniature version of her mother – they are doubled in the frame (one behind the other) as they share bath-time together, and doubled again as they practice Ikuko's self-introduction for her new kindergarten in the bathroom mirror. Fragile and affectionate, Yoshimi confesses that she needs Ikuko as much as Ikuko needs her ('as long as you are with me, I can manage anything'). This circle of attachment between mother and daughter is at first threatened and then usurped by Mitsuko, who wants to take Ikuko's place. That this is her intent is first hinted at in an early scene in the film. Travelling up in the lift in the apartment block (which is marked by a small puddle of water on the floor), Yoshimi takes what she thinks is Ikuku's hand to step out on to the landing. Yet Ikuko runs out in front, excited: it is the ghost's, not Ikuku's hand that Yoshimi holds. In a climactic sequence at the end of the film, this incident is replayed dramatically as Yoshimi is again tricked into taking the wrong daughter into the lift; this time she does not let go, and to save Ikuku she submits willingly to the ghost's embrace (saying, 'I am *your* mother'). The motif of water as a connection between past, present and future is later deployed with almost ridiculous emphasis as a great gush of water pours down on Yoshimi and Mitsuko, effectively consolidating their union. Simultaneously, with an inevitable suggestion of 'waters breaking' and of the birth process itself, the gush of water also expels Ikuku who, once the doors close and her mother disappears, is left, drenched and sobbing, on the landing by the lift, at once abandoned and saved.

Abandoned as a child by her own mother, Yoshimi is desperate not to replicate the trauma of her childhood. Inadvertently, however, she does seem to be inadequate as a mother – she fails to pick Ikuko up on time, and Ikuko (due to the influence of Mitsuko) also falls seriously ill. By agreeing, at the end of the film, to act as Mitsuko's mother (for what may be eternity) she is thus ensuring that she will *always* be a good mother: she has effectively saved Ikuko, and since she is now trapped or becalmed in limbo, she will never run out of time (since time is meaningless) and will therefore always be there for her daughter. This sequence at the end of the film is eerily reminiscent of the much maligned epilogue to Steven Spielberg's *A.I.*, in which David, the robot-child, has one 'perfect day' with his human mother engineered for him by an alien race after the end of the world. David is also an abandoned child and simply wants confirmation that his mother, after all, does love him and wishes to be there for him always. In relation to *A.I.* some critics felt that David's perfect day an unnecessarily sentimental happy ending: in *Dark Water*

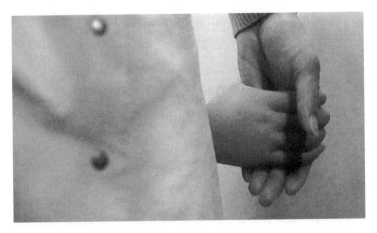

Figure 3 'Whose hand is this?': Yoshimi (Hitomi Kuroki) holds the ghost's hand in *Dark Water* (Dir. Hideo Nakata, 2002)

this day is perhaps re-imagined as nightmare. Yet, *Dark Water* also offers a happy ending of sorts: by entering a place where time does not pass, Yoshimi prevents the traumatic past – a series of broken attachments between mother and daughter – from repeating itself. Yoshimi's sacrifice effectively cements the circle of attachment that binds mother and daughter to each other. At the end of the film, despite the fact that she knows she will never see her mother again, Ikuku also realises that her mother did not abandon her – and that she never stopped (can never stop) loving her. Thus, whilst the film is frightening and suspenseful – drawing explicitly on films such as *The Shining* (in its use of lifts and corridors) and *Don't Look Now* (a child figure in a hooded raincoat) – the ending might, curiously for a horror film, be seen as upbeat.

Conversely, *The Grudge* films offer no possibility of escape, and of all the J-Horror films their narrative structure is the most overtly fractured and superficially incoherent. The story is effectively told via a series of episodes that are not presented chronologically but which often go back in time or leap-frog into the future; as well as, increasingly, overlap with one another, to the extent that characters from one episode witness, impossibly, other characters (or even themselves) at another time. Characters

Figure 4   Ikuku (Rio Kannu) is reborn, in *Dark Water* (Dir. Hideo Nakata, 2002)

may also appear as cameos in other episodes that may take place either before or after their story has been told. Whilst in the first film this confused chronology and overlap is, to an extent, contained within the space of the haunted house, in the second film this temporal confusion extends to any environment that the contaminated characters inhabit.

One particularly effective example of this temporal confusion occurs in The Grudge 2, in an episode featuring a young television journalist, Tomoka, and her boyfriend Nori. Whilst working on a television programme about the paranormal, Tomoka takes part in the filming of a reputedly haunted house. Unwittingly, she becomes infected by the curse. The first indication that she may be cursed comes in the series of loud thumps that she hears emanating from a wall in her apartment. The sounds are particularly eerie since they come from the external wall in her flat, meaning that there is no neighbour on that side and thus no rational origin for the sound. Second, as she demonstrates later to Nori, the thudding sounds are also peculiar in that they occur at exactly the same time each night (12.27 a.m.). The temporal instability of the narrative and the increasing temporal confusion of the characters is first indicated when Tomoka comes home late one evening to her apartment. Once inside, she sees Nori's shoes at the door, and as she moves into her flat she can just glimpse a shadowy figure through the curtains of her living room. At this point she calls out to Nori, asking what he is doing. At that same moment her mobile phone rings and it is Nori telling her that he is just coming – so who, or what, is in the living room? When she looks up from her phone, the figure in her living room has gone. When Nori finally arrives, he stays with her and also hears the thudding sounds at 12.27 a.m. One morning (which may be the next morning but we cannot be sure), we see Nori phoning Tomoka, explaining that he will come up and keep her company that evening. Speaking into her answer phone, he is puzzled by a strange creaking or groaning sound (the film audience will know that this is the sound of the ghost). The film then cuts to the evening and we see Nori walking up to Tomoka's lighted apartment. Strangely, once he is at the door, there appears to be nobody in. Using his key to enter, he is confused to find that the lights are, as he had initially thought, on. Puzzled, he takes off his shoes and moves towards the lighted living room; only to see – through the curtain – that Tomoka is already there, apparently terrified and scuttling backward on all fours away from something he and we do not see. He begins to chide her for being unnecessarily scared by the noise. Yet at the same moment, his phone rings and now it is Tomoka explaining that she is just coming. When Nori looks up from his phone he finds that the apartment is now in darkness. At this point he goes into the living room and, as he looks up, an expression of horror comes over his face and we watch as a length of black hair falls (or grows down) behind him and then curls up around his neck to strangle him. The film then cuts to Tomoka arriving at her apartment, which is now (once more? Has always been?) in darkness. Taking off her shoes, she is surprised to see that Nori's shoes are already there. In her living room there is – as before – a dark shape. This time she enters the room and switches on the light to see that it is Nori, hanging, strangled by a noose of long black hair. A young boy (who we know already as Toshio) is pushing Nori's corpse so that it swings and the feet thud against the wall. Falling to the floor, Tomoka backs away from this terrifying sight in a series of movements that we have already seen (from Nori's perspective) and which we are reminded of, from his perspective, in a brief flashback. As she moves backwards, the time on the clock is revealed and it is, of course, 12.27 a.m., the time at which they have always heard the strange knocking sound. Tomoka is ultimately strangled in the same way as Nori, and finally both corpses swing, their feet thudding against the wall, as they are suspended from the ceiling by a mass of dark hair emanating from the ghost-mother. The characters have not only shared an experience of psychic precognition (hearing the sound of the feet knocking on the wall before it has happened), they have also, impossibly, glimpsed – in their present – a future in which they are already dead, or about to die. This tricky mixture of future glimpses and flashbacks pepper the narratives of The Grudge films, and the story constantly circles back on itself allowing noone a reprieve. Only Toshio and his mother – the original victims of the crime and the bearers (or perhaps heralds) of 'the grudge' – seem unaffected by the multiple and overlapping temporalities they inhabit. Their a-temporal status is confirmed through the fact that Toshio has not aged, although it is discovered in another episode that he has been missing for over ten years. His lack of growth clearly marks him as a being outside of 'normal' teleological time, a ghastly Peter Pan – a child who will never grow up.

Toshio as a perverted child figure resonates with many of the children found in other J-Horror films: the stunted 'double' of Sadako in *Ring 0*; Mitsuko in *Dark Water* who will never age; and the little girl ghost in *The Locker* films. In these films, this unnatural lack of growth on the part of the child is contrasted with the perversely *excessive* growth of dark hair: the mother in *The Grudge*, Sadako in the *Ring* series and the little girl ghost in *The Locker* all have hair which grows rapidly and alarmingly. Equally, at one point in *Dark Water*, the uncanny appearance of Mitsuko's long dark hair in a glass of water chokes Yoshimi as she drinks. The ambiguously erotic and malevolent appearance of long dark hair is a feature of several Japanese ghost stories. One famous cinematic example is the episode, 'Black Hair' from *Kwaidan*. In the J-Horror films, the excessive and at times ridiculous growth of hair can also be understood in relation to the child. The unnatural growth of hair is perhaps directly connected to the distortion of the normally controlled maturation of children. The fantastic and disgusting growth of hair refers to bodily changes that would be understood, in other circumstances, to be natural.

Figure 5 Toshio (Yuya Ozeki) as a ghastly and ghostly 'Peter Pan', in *Ju-On* (*The Grudge*) (Dir. Takashi Shimizu, 2002)

Indeed, the managing and mapping of childhood is, in part, about containing and explaining the child's biological and physical development. Despite the continued efforts of psychology, medicine and education to 'explain away' or reduce the anxiety associated with growth, changes to the body – the appearance of hair in 'odd places' during puberty, the pain, confusion and mess of menstruation – are often experienced by individuals as strange, uncomfortable and frightening. It is not surprising that if these changes, or the energy associated with 'growth' itself, become detached from the normal and expected trajectory of development, and are redirected elsewhere, (other than the child's body), this process might seem peculiarly disturbing. For many of the children in J-Horror, the temporal sequence of development – from an asexual child to a mature, sexualised adult – has been upset, and it may be that the energies that would normally have been related to the changes in their own bodies have been displaced – with horrific consequences.

The terrible deeds they commit and the secrets they know mean that we can no longer consider these ghastly figures as children, as they surely know too much and are no longer innocent. Yet, disturbingly, in terms of their external appearance, it remains evident that they have not grown up. At once child-like in terms of their physique but not children in terms of their behaviour and knowledge, they enter the category of the freak. Indeed, both Sadako and Yoichi are called freaks. As such, their presence creates a crazy 'excess' of energy and puts time – literally – out of joint. As Arai suggests:

> As long as the child is on its way, in the sense of ensuring a sequence of development, and confirming a punctuality and singularity for meaning, it does not disturb; its difference stands purely as a sign of how far we have progressed. However, as Stefan Tanaka has poignantly argued, 'when the child does not develop that full interiority, childhood becomes an exteriority that threatens'.[20]

The temporal disorder associated with and represented by these threatening child-ghosts not only challenges the category of childhood, but inevitably and palpably disturbs the supposedly coherent, stable, homogenous and empty time of modernity. As bodies that suffer and are also associated with unruly and uncanny change, these children are arguably representatives of the 'strange-changed' children described by Kawakami. From the perspective of the horror film, the consequences of this change are catastrophic for adults.

Yet the films present only one side of their story. What if we were to experience the world from the perspective of the children themselves?

Ghostly Children: Tales from the 'Other Side'

The films I will discuss in this section do not relate to one another in the same way as the J-Horror films. Made by different directors at different times, the links between the films and my suggestion that they open up a kind of dialogue with the J-Horror cycle is more speculative. Nonetheless, I find it compelling that it is relatively easy to find a number of Japanese films that respond so directly to the fluctuating un-presence of the child evoked so chillingly in J-Horror. While these films also represent the traumatised, abandoned child – children living on the margins, all but invisible to adult society – they are not simply disturbing, ghostly figures that threaten adults' composure and lives. Rather, the films investigate the child's story and world. It is as if these films go 'back stage' into the children's lives and examine not their brief interruptions into the adult world but instead explore, without judgement, their 'hiding places' and strategies for survival. As Kore-eda Hirokazu suggests, in relation to the abandoned children which feature in his film, Nobody Knows:

> I am confident that the world they inhabited was more than a grayish hell. There must have been a kind of richness in their lives different from the richness of material abundance ... Do we not have a responsibility to imagine the richness they must have known, instead of condemning them, in our ignorance of their experience, to hell?[21]

The story of Nobody Knows follows the fate of four children: Akira (the oldest boy, twelve years old), Kyoko (the oldest girl, ten years old), Shigeru (another boy, seven years old) and lastly Yuki (a girl, four years old). All four have different fathers, and at the beginning of the film are looked after by their mother. The film begins as the family moves into a new apartment; strictly speaking however, it is only Akira and his mother who are seen to move in – at least by the other adults in the apartment block. The other children are smuggled in later: Yuki and Shigeru literally so, as they are 'unpacked' from large suitcases. Kyoko waits all day in the streets of Tokyo until she is taken to the flat, under the cover of darkness, by Akira. The mother insists that the three younger children hide as the landlord has made it a condition of the tenancy that there are to be no young children. Thus, whilst Akira is free to come and go, the younger children are confined to the apartment and are not even allowed to venture outside on to the small balcony. None of the children is registered for school – hence 'nobody knows' they exist. The film begins harmoniously, even charmingly; the mother is clearly feckless but affectionate, and, though cramped, the children seem happy enough. Kyoko, for example, expresses her delight in the smell of the fresh tatami mats that cover the apartment's floor. Unfortunately, the mother soon disappears, and it later emerges that she has gone to live with a new man, without telling him of her existing children. She insists that Akira, using a small (and rapidly decreasing) allowance, look after his younger half-siblings ('I'm counting on you'). The bulk of the film concentrates on the experience of the four abandoned children, living alone, where, at first, the younger three are effectively isolated from the outside world.

One distinctive aspect of the film is the delicacy with which the children are pictured. The documentary style of the camera work caresses the children, inhabiting their space with them and focusing on their concerns. There is, however, a sharp contrast between the way the children are seen inside and outside of the flat. Outside, Akira is frequently framed in long shot, sometimes almost lost in the crowd, a figure that we have to actively seek out and locate. In the cityscape the children are represented as marginal figures. Inside the flat, the camera comes much closer to the children, travelling over their faces and bodies as they draw, sleep, read and play. There is almost an obsession with representing touch: we watch the children's fingers stroking wax crayons as they decide which colour to choose; trace stick figures with them on steamed up windows; watch as fingers anxiously count out money; and look again and again at Kyoko's fingers as she attempts truncated melodies on her treasured toy piano. Their business is curious, delicate and sensitive. The bodies – and particularly the hands and feet – of the children thus carry the story. The film slowly reveals the changes to the children as they react to the environment around them; season by season as we pass through winter, spring and to the hot and humid days of summer; incrementally, as their bodies grow (out of their clothes and shoes). They become gradually filthy and dishevelled, and their hair grows more and more unruly. Time here is both full – of small incidents, meals, concentrated and distracted play – and empty. Nothing much happens and there is a great deal of silence and boredom, periods of waiting and hoping, until a catastrophic accident towards the end of the film forces a change to their family dynamic. As Linda C. Ehrlich notes in her review of the film:

> For children in such an extreme situation, happiness resides in small thing – the smell of fresh tatami mats upon moving into the new apartment, seeds gathered from a discarded plant that germinate in empty ramen cups and grow on the verandah. One of the plants falls off the ledge, foreshadowing more serious accidents to follow. The passage of time is marked by small changes – the deepening of Akira's voice, the switch from frozen hands in winter to skin streaked with sweat in summer.[22]

The foreshadowing of tragic events by small incidents is played out at several points in the film. Yuki's accidental death as a result of falling off a chair is hinted at earlier at several points in the film – most explicitly, as Ehrlich points out, when one of the plant pots falls off from the balcony, smashing onto the ground below. At other times, the camera lingers tenderly on fingers stroking Yuki's hair as she falls asleep. These moments are poignantly revisited in the later and hesitating caress of Yuki's hand by Akira once Yuki has died (or, as the children say – once she has fallen asleep and won't wake up). Appropriately, and movingly, once Yuki has died we never see her face, only close-ups of her hands and feet. As the children finally move her body into a suitcase so that Akira can take her and bury her (he chooses to take her on the monorail to the airport so that she can see the planes), the painfully tragic-comic aspects of their lives are exposed as they place her favourite squeaky slippers on her feet. The slippers have been seen once before as Yuki chose to wear them for her birthday treat: earlier in the film, accompanied by Akira, Yuki is finally taken out of the apartment under the cover of darkness, her footsteps squeaking along the corridors and stairs as they walk. What is significant about this sequence is that this sound – the squeaky sound of children's footsteps in plastic slippers – would be an occasion for fear in J-Horror. Sounds that are apparently of place (thumps, running feet, dripping water) are heard in the horror films from the adult's perspective, as odd, spooky interruptions, which infiltrate from another world into the real world and indicate a ghostly presence for which there seems to be no rational origin. In *Nobody Knows*, what might be heard by adults as impossible sounds (the squeak of a child's slipper heard on the stairs at past midnight when there are not meant to be any children in the building) are relocated, attached to the children as a significant part of their (and not the adults') story. What makes the film so distinctive is that children are seen *and* heard in the film. Yet, as Ehrlich suggests,

> ...to listen to childhood is not always to listen for what one expects to hear, or even for what one wants to hear. Kore-eda is rigorous in his willingness to listen to childhood's silence, to the silence that surrounds the flood of words and the flurry of everyday actions.[23]

In the film, young children are apparently banned from the apartment block as they will make too much noise. Ironically, the film audience has to strain to listen to the children, who don't tell their story directly but via the evidence carried by their bodies, through the implied senses of touch and sometimes of smell, and from their barely audible sighs and the squeak of small slippers on the floor.

While the children are undoubtedly the centre of attention for the viewing audience, they are marginal presences for most of the adults in the film. For instance, a tense early moment takes place as Akira has to move quickly to hide Kyoko around the corner from the landlord. Later, we watch (from a low angle set at his eye level) as Shigero slips unnoticed by the legs of unidentified 'education mamas' as they discuss their children's test results at the front of the apartment block. The children's only constant friend and visitor is another (slightly older) girl who, whilst clearly cared for at her own comfortable home, is also a marginal figure. This is Saki, a high school student, who we see being bullied and who therefore avoids school. During the day she hides with the children and it is she who ultimately helps Akira to bury Yuki. If we were to re-imagine the film from the adults' perspective, all of the children would appear in a similar way to the liminal, marginal and elusive child figures in J-Horror, glimpsed and heard at odd moments only as they appear briefly 'out of place'. Nobody Knows' effectiveness lies in the reversing of this perspective; and instead it provides a drawn out, careful revelation of the richness, tenderness and tragedy of the children's relationships and experience that takes place on the fringes of the adult's world.

The minutiae of children's experience in relation to traumatic events is also the central premise of Shinji Aoyama's film Eureka, which focuses primarily on the experience of two middle-school children, a boy Naoki and his younger sister Nozue, who survive a violent bus-jacking where everyone (apart from the bus driver) is killed. Subsequently, they are effectively orphaned, as their mother leaves and their father dies in a car accident. As in Nobody Knows, we spend time with them as they initially attempt to survive on their own in their parents' house. More fortunate than the abandoned children in Nobody Knows, they are ultimately cared for by the bus driver, Makato, who, similarly traumatised, seeks them out and works with them towards a kind of resolution. This is achieved, in part, when he takes the siblings and an older cousin of theirs on a long bus journey. The film, shot almost entirely in sepia, is remarkable for its length (it runs for three hours and twenty minutes), a running time that is perhaps justifiable since it attempts to demonstrate – in a way similar to Nobody Knows – both the importance and the experience of time as it is passed by the children. Time in the film has a bloated quality, and the passing of time is probably the film's real subject. The film's length means that we witness numerous sequences in which the children do nothing: they doze, fidgeting in their sleep, on sofas and cushions, stare out of windows, fetch food from the supermarket on their bicycles, eat and watch TV. As in *Nobody Knows*, silence surrounds their activities; for most of the film, both children are effectively mute. Aside from the few interested adults – Makato, who recognises his trauma in theirs, and an older cousin Akihiko, who comes to check on the children on behalf of their extended family (although Akihiko is a benign figure, the relatives, we discover, are really only interested in the insurance money) – The children and their experiences are, almost invisible to the outside, adult world. This is made clear in relation to a developing sub-plot involving the activities of a serial killer who has been murdering young women in the area. Both the police and the viewing audience's initial suspicion is that it must be Makato; in fact the killer turns out to be Naoki, who is finally caught and confronted by Makato and then taken to the police. As a result of his murderous acts, Naoki is akin to one of the avenging child-ghosts from J-Horror, yet in this instance we see his deeds in context, as part of his tragedy and from his point of view. The fact that neither the viewing audience nor the police initially suspect him, partly and presumably because he is still a child, only reveals how little children normally register as active agents, as people that are significant from the adult's perspective.

An additional aspect of the film's power is that it merges the everyday, almost interminable, passage of time with a sense of legendary, fairytale time. At the end of the film, after their long bus journey has taken them to the coast and ultimately to a religious site, Makato tells Kozue, 'Let's go home'. As Aoyama notes, this is the same as the line spoken to Debbie (Natalie Wood) by Ethan (John Wayne) in John Ford's epic Western *The Searchers*, another film in which a journey is undertaken to rescue an orphaned girl child but happens too late, so that the girl has no home and no childhood to return to. Yet *Eureka* re-imagines this, less ambiguously, as a moment of hope, for as the film switches at this point from sepia to colour, we are reminded inevitably, of another mythical, fairytale journey, The Wizard of Oz, (and another orphaned girl looking for home). An important difference in Eureka is that the colour change implies that it is the real world, not some 'fantastic land' that can now be seen in colour, and it is therefore the return of the characters to the real, everyday world which opens up the possibility of future adventures.

Another journey to find a home, and specifically a mother, is undertaken by a young boy, Masao, in Takeshi Kitano's Kikujiro. Employing a more episodic narrative structure than either Nobody Knows or Eureka, the film still conforms to a child's understanding of time as it is organised via a 'photo diary' apparently constructed by Masao, pasted into a typical children's scrapbook bearing the title 'What I did last summer'. The strangely retrospective temporality of the film (a story that has already happened, unfolding as if it were in the present) is implied by the fact that the first sequence of the film is actually the end of the story, as we watch Masao run across a bridge wearing a back-pack with angel wings. As we see Masao being given this bag in the course of the film, this run across the bridge must actually take place after the events we are yet to see. Episodes begin with chalk titles superimposed over 'snapshots' of key scenes and are identified simply and sometimes obliquely, by names such as 'Scary man', 'Angel Bell' or 'Octopus man'. In terms of its cinematography, the film mimics the photograph in its extensive use of long shots, still camerawork and long pauses, during which we simply watch the characters wait, standing still and often isolated within the frame. The film follows the adventures of Masao and Kikujiro; the latter is played by Kitano himself and is known, for most of the film, as 'Mister'. Kikujiro, a truculent, comic and gangsterish figure, has been paid by his wife to accompany Masao from Tokyo to Toyohashi to visit Masao's mother. Masao cannot recall living with his mother and lives with his grandmother, who tells him that his father died in an accident and that his mother has to work elsewhere in order to provide them with money. Masao discovers an address for, and a photograph of, his mother by accident. In a key sequence in the film, Masao and Kikujiro finally reach the street and house where Masao's mother lives. Approaching the house first, Kikujiro is confused, as the sign by the house identifies it as belonging to the 'Yoshimura Family', and he suggests to Masao, who is waiting some distance away, that it may be the wrong house. Yet, at that moment, we see Masao's mother come out of the front door – we recognise her from the photograph – followed by what must be her husband and young daughter. It is clear that the father is taking the little girl to the beach; we watch as Masao's mother waves them goodbye, and returns to her house. She does not appear to see either Masao or Kikujiro. The sequence – which confirms that Masao has, in fact, been abandoned by his mother who evidently has a new family that does not include him – is perhaps not entirely unexpected, but it is moving. It provides another instance where the experience of the abandoned child is represented from the child's perspective. In this scene Masao is apparently unseen by his mother, and our point of view is entirely with him, but if we were to view the scene from the mother's perspective, it might be that Masao would hover just at the fringes of her vision, as a shadowy (ghostly) figure that is glimpsed and disappears. Masao, from his mother's point of view, would be out of place and potentially threatening in relation to her new family set-up.

Yet as in Eureka, the child is offered some hope and Masao's journey does not end here: in fact it begins – again like Eureka – at the beach. It is here, as Masao's photo diary asserts, that his relationship with Kikujiro reaches a real turning point: the episode title states, 'Mister played with me'. Kikujiro, who has been distinguished up to this point mainly by his own selfish (and childish) interests and desires – he loses the money for the trip by gambling, makes a detour to a luxury hotel in order to try and learn to swim – now concentrates on Masao, ensuring that the return trip is pleasurable.

Masao is normally sad looking and slightly chubby; he is earlier referred to, semi-affectionately, 'little mule'. With his glum demeanour and strange bow-legged walk, Masao is obviously physically doubled with Kikujiro. The adult and the child are doubled psychologically too, as it emerges that Kikujiro has also 'lost' his mother. As Kikujiro now makes his living as a low-ranking Yakuza (suggested by the distinctive tattoo on his back), he also provides a hint as to what the boy's future might be. Yet the film does not end on a bleak note; Masao's friendship with

Kikujiro cemented, he runs home across the bridge, and whilst we do not see him running (this time), we know that the angel wings on his back-pack will be flying in the wind.

Yoshitaro Nomura's The Demon was made in 1978 and relates to a different generation of children than the other films I have described. It is neither an art film (as both Nobody Knows and Eureka clearly are) nor a director's pet project (which Kikijuro appears to be). It is melodramatic in tone and while the events that take place might be said to be horrific, it is more akin, as several critics have noted, to a suspense film by Alfred Hitchcock (in particular, the music refers directly to much of Bernard Herrmann's work for Hitchcock's films.) The film follows the fate of three children – Riichi (the oldest boy, six years old,) Yoshiko (a girl, three years old) and Shoji (another boy about eighteen months old) – who are abandoned by their mother at the house of their father and his wife. Their mother had been their father's mistress, while his wife knew nothing of the other woman and has no children of her own. Angry and resentful, the wife soon makes it clear that she wishes the children would disappear. One day she catches Shoji slowly making a mess with the remnants of a lunch and in her fury she grabs him and stuffs the remaining food into his mouth, causing him to choke. Shoji is so ill that he is taken to a doctor who warns the father that, whilst it is only severe indigestion, he should take care of the boy, as young children can easily die from this kind of problem. Later, Shoji lies sleeping, while the wife is tidying up, or searching for something in shelves nearby. Around this time – accidentally (perhaps) – a heavy mat falls on Shoji's face. He is subsequently found dead under the mat, though whether this is through accidental suffocation or as a result of his chronic indigestion is not made entirely clear.

From this moment on, it is made explicit that both the father and his wife are determined to get rid of the remaining children by whatever means necessary. To that end, the father takes Yoshiko to Tokyo and deliberately abandons her at the viewing level in the Tokyo Tower; as she is so little it is presumed by the father that she will be too young to know his name and his address and, as it turns out, we never see her again. Events then take an even darker turn, as the father and his wife plot to murder Riichi, who is evidently too old and too smart simply to be abandoned.

After an abortive attempt to poison him, the father takes Riichi on a trip to the coast, and at a remote cliff edge, whilst Riichi is sleeping in his arms, the father throws him on to the rocks and sea below (beaches and the coast, it is clear, are key geographical sites for the Japanese). Yet Riichi miraculously survives. Whilst he then refuses to speak to the police and his rescuers and refuses to reveal the name and location of his father, the father is ultimately discovered and brought face to face with his son.

In terms of its plot – abandoned children and a series of traumatic and murderous events – *The Demon* is certainly close to some of the J-Horror films I have discussed, yet the film is particularly significant for the way it anticipates, in several sequences, an understanding of the child's point of view which features more explicitly in the other films I have discussed in this section, particularly *Nobody Knows*. For example, the opening sequence of the film pictures, with a mixture of hesitancy and intimacy, the three children at play in much the same way as the children are filmed in *Nobody Knows*. Yet significantly, after a few minutes, the perspective changes; the camera effectively moves its point of view so that it is now behind, instead of in front of, the children. Now, we see the children and their play from their mother's anxious and frustrated point of view. From here, the scene, which had initially appeared to represent a contented, busy and aimless harmony, is revealed (from the adult's point of view) as an irritating mess of sweaty, fidgeting children on a hot summer's day. This move articulates the change in perspective between the J-Horror films – which present the children from the adult's perspective – and the films discussed in this section, which aim to present the world from the child's point of view. In *The Demon*, this contrast between different points of view – in which the children can be seen as charming or as monstrous – is frequently revisited. For example, in one scene set at a public playground, the children delight in making grotesque figures of themselves in a series of distorting mirrors, a process which explicitly exposes the children to their father as both children at play and simultaneously, in their reflections, as disturbing, monstrous intrusions into his life. As the narrative progresses, the children become increasingly threatening and uncanny figures; Shoji's musical box, for example, starts playing and is discovered inside the house, after his death, when it was meant to have been already thrown away. Equally, Riichi, once his brother and sister have died or disappeared, becomes increasingly sullen and mute. In another effective sequence, Yoshiko features as a ghostly presence, a reminder of her father's guilt. Riding on an express train to the coast, Riichi and his father pass through Tokyo and can therefore see the Tokyo Tower from their window; as they pass through the city, the tower appears and disappears from behind different buildings. Riichi points this out to his father: 'Now I see it...now I don't. There it is again.' As this is the tower where the father abandoned Yoshiko, from the adult's guilty perspective this game acts as a form of torture. It mimics the spooky appearances and disappearances of the ghosts of the traumatised and abandoned children in J-Horror (or their unnerving games of hide and seek). Even more explicitly, in the final scene, in which Riichi is forced to confront his father, the possibility of children haunting their parents is directly referred to. In this sequence, Riichi barely looks at his father and only speaks out to deny him, saying, 'He's a stranger'. Since Riichi will not speak for himself, the policemen admonish the father on his behalf: 'How will you apologize to him? Nothing you say will be enough!', but perhaps most eerily they also suggest: 'This will come back to haunt you!'

What *The Demon* reveals is that the child as an ambiguous presence – as victim and possibly a demonic ghost – has a history, and that it is not an entirely new phenomenon. *The Demon's* production history reveals that the problem of child abandonment may stretch even further back than the film's production: made in 1978, it is from a story originally written in 1957, and was apparently based (like *Nobody Knows*) on real events. Additionally, within the film itself it is made clear that the father's inadequacies may stem from his own abandonment and effective slavery at an early age in a printing apprenticeship. Therefore, whilst the director of the orphanage who comes to collect Riichi at the end of the film blames the failure of young parents *today*, it is evident that earlier generations were not necessarily any better.

Seen in dialogue with one another, the J-Horror films and the other Japanese films I have discussed reveal a complex picture of Japanese childhood. As heavily invested symbols of national identity and as vehicles of modernity, Japanese children are seemingly idolised but burdened with responsibility. In addition, parents themselves often seem inadequate in relation to their own responsibilities. Children are therefore abandoned, victimised and murdered. The threat posed by these complex and frequently suffering children is not just to the idea of childhood but also to an understanding of 'how the world is'. More than fantasies and semi-factual tales of child abuse, these films reveal a tension between a linear, teleological history – an empty and homogenous time – with other enchanted temporalities, inhabited and expressed by children, apparently, but never completely, repressed. In these films, we witness and experience these other temporalities inhabited by children as they overlap, or interrupt the everyday time of modern life. The singular time of childhood itself, the powerful, cyclical bonds of mothers to daughters, of fathers to sons, and the mythic temporality of fairytales and epics are imagined and represented in all their complex strangeness.

Chapter Two

Dirty Little White Girls

John Wayne lifts and holds her at arm's length. No matter how often I've seen *The Searchers* before, I do not know, at this very moment and for a split second, whether he will kill her or fuck her. (Lesley Stern, commenting on her reaction to the climactic scene of John Ford's Western, in which Ethan Edwards, played by white screen legend John Wayne, finally locates Debbie [Natalie Wood] his niece, a little white girl who was captured seven years before by a Native American Tribe.)[1]

I noticed when you was checking in you had a lovely pretty little girl with you. She was really lovely. As a matter of fact she wasn't so little, come to think of it. She was fairly tall little. What I mean is taller than little, you know what I mean. But, uh, she was really lovely. Gee, I wish I had a lovely, pretty, tall, lovely, little girl like that, I mean. (Quilty [Peter Sellers], talking to Humbert Humbert [James Mason] in Stanley Kubrick's adaptation of *Lolita*.)

The substitution of the white daughter for the coloured one is, then, a historical necessity: despite the irony of her married name, Shirley Temple can never be black. (Ann duCille.)[2]

This chapter is marked, first, by a series of disturbances: disturbing activities, presences and responses. One aspect of this disturbance is obvious, signaled by the quote from Stern, that when we least expect it to, cinema has the ability to evoke the potentially disturbing nature of the relations between adult male characters and the children they pursue – here a little white girl, Debbie. The narrative motif of the little white girl being lost and found, or stolen, repossessed and revenged, haunts many of the films I discuss. That this narrative is also simultaneously imbued with violence, sex and race will also become evident. This chapter is also coloured by an absence. The peculiar history of American film-making in the twentieth century demonstrates a lack, an almost complete absence of the little black girl as major character or as star. While there have been successful black child performers in popular music and television (mostly boys), the little black girl, it seems, has been lost and nobody is looking for her. This chapter is therefore about the privileging of the little white girl, and about what that whiteness seems in conflicting ways to signify, and how in a series of films the coalescence of little, white and girl produces and seemingly legitimates an extraordinary range of emotion – sentiment, anxiety, melodrama and desire.

The historical scope of this chapter is wider and more ambitious than other chapters in the book. It is not, however, a historical account of 'little white girls' and their appearance in American film. So, while I begin with a film from the early period of cinema and conclude with some observations about films from the present day, the argument is not secured by its chronology or historical evidence. It is instead an attempt to describe the sounding out of a disturbance that echoes – forward and back, around and around – circling on the concerns and signification of little girls, race and sexuality. My approach is heavily indebted to Lesley Stern's book *The Scorsese Connection*, in which she also employs another recurring element that features in the films and in this chapter – touch. In the observation I cite below, she indicates how touch – whether this is 'being touched' through sentiment, seeing characters touch, or imagining touch – informs our response to film. It is, she suggests, how we as viewers generate memories, or a corporeal archive of feeling:

> As viewers we experience a kind of 'physical contact' though it is not necessarily or exclusively an identification with the protagonist's act of touching. It is more like the return of the image, its registering in our body. What takes place is something like the cinematic equivalent of Proustian 'involuntary memory', and it is crucially dependent on an associational register, on a relation between sensations, between images (it is not about the affect an image may induce in total isolation). It 'takes place', of course, in time, but here time is contracted, two different instances are superimposed, so that we move out of the logic of narrative.[3]

In one sense, this chapter is about the way in which instances in different films touch upon others, a touch that some readers may feel unnecessarily contaminates my view of earlier films and distorts my response to contemporary ones. It is also about touch because touch is so central to childhood and to sexuality. In the contemporary language of child sexual abuse, for example, there is the division between, and the interpretation of, the 'good touch' and the 'bad touch'. The distinction – it is hoped – is made clear to the child, but it remains the case that in most children's day-to-day experience there is also a mundane routine for children and their adult carers of touching taboo parts of the child's body. Children are washed, dressed, their hair brushed, their mouths and bottoms wiped. Thus there is a necessary everyday – 'good' – touching that is not without an erotic/sentimental thrill for the adult carer or for the child. For example, a familiar but actually rather disturbing experience involves the child having their face wiped by a tissue dampened with the parent's spit, an act that is simultaneously intimate, disgusting and ordinary.

Children are also obliged and expected to hold each others hands: to hold, on demand, an adult's hand and thereby to touch each other and to touch adults known and unknown. Like the bride, a child can have their hand taken by another – and since we understand that to take possession of the hand implies in the marriage contract the possession of the whole self, 'body and soul' and is therefore a metonymic gesture, this means that the action of holding another person's hand is both a simple and erotic act.

To touch a child, then, is riddled with ambivalence – whilst physical affection and a caring touch are seen as essential for the child to become properly socialised and emotionally secure, to touch a child is also a sensual, possessive act. The necessary, effective 'handling' of children relates to the child's status as an object, a not-yet-subject that must sometimes be physically constrained. This restraining touch may be as benign as holding on to a child as she balances precariously on a wall. Alternatively, we might remember that it has only recently become a crime to physically assault your child, and that smacking is yet another kind of (now) bad, violent and often uncomfortably sexualised kind of touch. Equally, children constantly touch things they shouldn't and poke fingers into places they ought not to go. Their 'little hands' get everywhere. The exuberant tactility of children provokes adult tenderness, irritation, excitement, anxiety and fear.

This myriad of conflicting emotions and potential surrounding touch in relation to the child is expressed clearly in tickling – a form of touching frequently done to children and rarely to adults. Adam Phillips, commenting on the tickling of children, observes:

> Helpless with pleasure, and usually inviting this helplessness, the child, in the ordinary, affectionate, perverse scenario of being tickled, is wholly exploitable...Through tickling, the child will be initiated in a distinctive way into the helplessness and disarray of a certain primitive kind of pleasure, dependent on the adult to hold and not to exploit the experience. And this means to stop at the blurred point, so acutely felt in tickling, at which pleasure becomes pain, and the child experiences an intensely anguished confusion; because the tickling narrative, unlike the sexual narrative, has no climax.[4]

There are certain assertions here I am not sure I agree with but which feed productively into the following discussion. For example, why is it that the pleasures experienced here by the child are 'primitive'? Presumably this implies that certain sexual pleasures, practices (those of the adult) are placed in opposition to such unruly delights and are therefore, in contrast to the child's pleasure, 'civilised'? Read in this way, the word 'primitive' is also exposed more directly as raced – does Phillips mean to imply that it is primitive as in 'savage'? Both these problematic assertions are played out in the films discussed in this chapter: that childish sexual pleasure is 'helpless' and uncivilised, and that the children's expression of sexuality, their erotic expansiveness, is easily, naturally aligned with the supposed excessive and unruly sexuality of the non-white other.

In addition, I am also concerned by the masculine ending of Phillip's version of the sexual narrative. I wonder, does the sexual narrative always have to end in a climax? Or, is it that he believes that there need only be one significant climax, which functions as an index, a visible eruption that says 'the end', that that is 'enough'? As Phillips goes on to note: 'It has to stop, or the real humiliation begins. The child, as the mother says, will get hysterical.'[5] The suggestion is that by not reaching a satisfactory climax, the child that is 'tickled for too long' is, in its erotic frenzy, in its hysteria, feminised – helpless but dangerous, humiliated and aggressive. To simply extend the middle of the pleasurable sexual narrative is not 'satisfactory' and is both dangerous and humiliating (for whom exactly?) The assumption is that the normal (appropriate) sexual narrative must be goal-driven, seeking a result: a satisfactory ending which implies (for adults) the possibility that conception might take place. The problem, as Phillips goes on to confirm, is that for the child this pleasure is not suitably directed or legitimated by a biological, presumably reproductive, impulse: rather it is a selfish, sterile activity. He notes; 'Certainly, there is no immediate pressing biological need in this intent, often frenetic contact that so quickly reinstates a distance, only equally quickly to create another invitation.'[6]

Being tickled, as Phillips observes, is not the same as masturbation; you cannot satisfactorily tickle yourself. It is a relationship, a contract of contact between (most often) an adult who tickles and the child who takes pleasure in this touch. If it is a relationship that, as Phillips points out, has 'no immediate pressing biological need', children's potentially sexualised encounters with others are therefore positioned as unnecessary and, as Phillips hints, perverse. Accordingly, children's sexuality, as other writers have increasingly suggested, may be aligned with a queer sexuality; a sexuality that is also often characterised as perverse, uncivilised, odd, sterile and excessive. It is therefore not surprising that some of the most compelling work on child sexuality and the erotic encounters between adults and children can be found in the expanding field of queer studies of literature and film.

The focus of this chapter, however, is on the playing out of a heterosexual romance between adult and child. This is also an area addressed by other scholars, most prominently by James Kincaid whose work I necessarily draw on.[7] My aim is to contribute by identifying the racial and frequently racist aspects of that narrative, to examine why and how the 'whiteness' of the little girl is so important and to suggest that her idealised purity is, as Lewis Carroll's little white girl, Alice, might put it, contrary-wise. Whilst the little girl's whiteness and all it signifies – including but not limited to purity and innocence – is determined and supposedly threatened by the darkness that surrounds it, at the same time her necessary but perverse childishness creates dissonance, a disturbance, expressing a sexuality that must be constantly, obsessively restrained, even enslaved.

Broken Blossoms (*Dir. D.W. Griffith, 1919*)

This classic of early North American cinema, directed by D.W. Griffith and starring Lillian Gish, is based on a short story: 'The Chink and the Child' by Thomas Burke. A melodramatic love story set in London's Limehouse slums, it follows the fate of a girl – Lucy. In the original story Lucy is 12, but in the film as played by a 26-year-old Gish, she is aged – at least by the inter-titles – at an apparently more mature 15. Nonetheless, Gish's performance emphasises the childish rather than the potentially adolescent qualities of the girl. Lucy, who has no mother, lives with her brute of a father, the boxer, 'Battling Burrows', for whom she effectively exists and works as a slave: she keeps house, mends clothes and prepares food for him. It is implicit that along with frequent beatings (two of which we see in the film) she has also been sexually assaulted by her father.

Nonetheless, her fledgling, alabaster beauty has not gone unnoticed, as we witness the 'Yellow Man', a Chinese storekeeper played by Richard Barthelmess (a white actor), admiring her through his shop window. One evening, after a particularly savage beating, Lucy coincidentally collapses through the open door of the Yellow Man's shop. (Although the inter-titles never call him anything but the Yellow Man, his name, Chen Huan is painted on the outside of his shop.) He takes her in, washes her cuts and bruises, dresses her in a fine robe and lets her sleep peacefully on his bed as he kneels worshipfully beside her. Indeed, as the inter-titles inform us, he gently holds her 'grubby little hand' all night long. The next day, Lucy's haven is discovered by one of her Father's cronies. Enraged by his belief that she must have had sexual relations with the Yellow Man (despite her protestations that it 'Weren't nothing wrong'), her father drags her back home – under the cover of a heavy fog – where he beats her to death on his bed. The Yellow Man, in despair at finding her gone, initially weeps hysterically into her abandoned robe and then takes a gun and confronts Burrows, ultimately shooting him dead. He then retrieves Lucy's body and carries it back to his shop. With Lucy laid peacefully on the altar of his bed, the Yellow Man takes his own life (stabbing himself) before the police can reach him.

There are several reasons for beginning with this film: a melodrama in which the 'pure love' of an adult male for a little girl allows for a brief interlude of joy but which then ends violently is a narrative arc which informs many of the films I will discuss. Equally, the confusion of sexual and romantic love and the path from possession to revenge will also feature again and again. Yet it is predominantly the presence and performance of Lillian Gish which provides an affective repertoire of feelings, gestures and above all 'whiteness', which resonates so particularly for my argument. Gish, who was born in 1893, had worked as a child performer (appearing on stage from the age of six) but by 1919 she was established as a star of numerous films and associated strongly with D.W. Griffith, appearing as one of the white heroines of Griffith's notorious earlier film, Birth of a Nation (1915), which had celebrated the Klu Klux Klan. Unlike her peer, Mary Pickford, Gish was not (as Pickford increasingly was) confined to 'child' roles, for though her characters were usually innocent maidens (child-women), they were not necessarily children. In fact, Gish herself has suggested in relation to Broken Blossoms that she was concerned about playing a child, indicating that she was 'too tall' for such a role. Apparently, she was convinced by Griffith who argued that the role must be played by an adult, as it demanded a far greater range of expression than a child would be able to demonstrate. Thus, like Pickford, Gish in this film was a child impersonator, but crucially, 'acting' in a way that it was felt would be impossible for a child. Gish therefore performs childishness, yet registers in her presence and in her performance something that is apparently only available to, or possible from, the adult. In the performance of actual child stars this dynamic would be inverted; as real children they would act with such professionalism, or register a sensibility (off screen and on) that made them seem like adults. This lurking maturity is attributed to Shirley Temple when she is likened to 'Ethel Barrymore at four', or when Dakota Fanning is described as 'nine going on 19'. Either as a woman masquerading as a child, or a child assuming the responsibilities and demonstrating the performance skills of an adult, the knowledge or fantasy of an adult persona attached to the child character performed on screen is significant. This is because it seemingly protects – from exploitation – either the absent child performer (for whom Gish substitutes) or the exceptional little actor (such as Temple or Fanning, who are deemed unusual in being 'mature beyond their years'). At the same time, as others have argued, this duality creates ambiguities in terms of the viewing audience's response to the child character portrayed on screen. Julia Lesage, in her famous essay on Broken Blossoms – 'Artful Racism, Artful Rape' – quotes Angela Carter, who is commenting directly on the figure of Lucy in the film.

> She could be as enticing in her vulnerability and ringletted prettiness as she was able but the audience knew all the time that the lovely child before them was a mature woman whom the fiction of her childishness made taboo. The taboo against acknowledging her sexuality created the convention that the child could not arouse desire; if she did so, it was denied. A sentimental transformation turned the denial of lust into a kitsch admiration of the 'cute'.[8]

The peculiar and unsettling qualities of the 'cute' as it applies to little white girls will be returned to – particularly in relation to Shirley Temple. Here, it is enough to confirm one aspect of the little white girl's appeal performed by Gish: that she 'cannot possibly', but all the same still *does*, produce an erotic frisson for her audience – both male (as Carter is arguing) and female (as Lesage goes on to elaborate). In this performance, Gish arguably embodies in a more tragic and less feisty manner the same liminal appeal of Mary Pickford, described here by Gaylyn Studlar:

> The multiple possibilities of how Mary Pickford was received by her historical audiences – male and female – suggest that Pickford's persona as the erotically attractive yet not quite marriageable young woman functioned culturally and psychologically for her audiences in potentially far more complex and contradictory ways than is generally acknowledged. Pickford's on- and off-screen masquerade of childishness and the slippage between eroticized adult femininity and her inscription of aesthetically perfected

> children were attached to some meanings that appear to be
> quite historically and culturally specific to the waning days of
> the 'age of the child'.[9]

Like Pickford, however, Gish is not actually cute, although aspects
of her look and expression – her smooth white face, large eyes,
mouth pursed in a moue, curls in her hair and a willingness to
please – do recur in the archetype of the 'cute little white girl' as
played by Shirley Temple. In fact, Gish (as Lucy) is more ethereally
pretty, graceful and pathetic than cute would ever allow. Lucy's
'beauty' is in part created via Gish's performance skills. In reality
her mouth was larger than the child-like moue she adopted
and her face was expressive rather than classically pretty. Yet in
the films she seems, and is deemed, beautiful. Named 'White
Blossom' by the Yellow Man, and with references to her alabaster
skin, it becomes evident that her beauty is – overwhelmingly –
determined or located in her glowing whiteness. It is therefore
all the more exciting and provocative to place her so intimately
with a man who is (here masquerading as) not white, as this
both reinforces her whiteness (through a contrast with his non-
whiteness) and sets up a deliberately racially inflected tension
around this non-white male's threatening position in relation
to her. This is a position that Gish had previously played out so
powerfully (and notoriously) in Birth of a Nation, where she rejects
the passionate advances of a male mulatto. In that film, Gish is
playing a young woman and thus the national rape is of an adult
white virgin by a black man. The essential differences in Broken
Blossoms are that Gish's character is quite clearly a child and – as
has been suggested – not actually a virgin.

This latter distinction is significant because it implies that,
while she is a child, Lucy is not without sexual knowledge. In fact
at the beginning of the film, it is made clear that Lucy is aware
of how sex – for women – functions in the Limehouse: either
as reproductive drudgery (she spends time with a harassed and
exhausted mother of a large family) or as a degrading economic
exchange (when she meets two prostitutes who urge her not
to join their profession). Implicitly, we also suspect that she
understands sex to be an equivalent experience to – indeed, a
substitute for – the regular beatings she has from her father. What

Lucy does not understand at the beginning of the film is that sexual relationships might be a source of pleasure.

The potential for Lucy to enjoy some kind of (primitive?) erotic encounter is nonetheless evident, since she is clearly a sensualist. At one point, when she is on her own in the house, we see her stroke the satin and ribbon left to her by her mother, and we later witness the way she yearns for the flowers she sees and touches tenderly when she is out shopping for food. Indeed, Gish's performance exhibits the exuberant tactility of children and is distinguished by the delicate fluttering touch of her hands and fingers (this was true of her performance style generally but is particularly marked in this role). Her fingers are everywhere the focus of our and her attention – as she strokes and fiddles nervously with her hair, touches her face to express fear, joy and surprise and finally as they scrabble at the walls in the closet as she tries to escape from her father. It is not until she meets the Yellow Man that she begins to relate her sensuality – her excitement and interest in different touches and smells – with her sexuality. We see the Yellow Man dress her in smooth silk and offer her incense to smell, and he then gives her a small doll which she pets and cuddles with pert fascination. On one level, her question to the Yellow Man, 'What makes you so good to me Chinky?', seems charmingly naïve since it appears that she fails to recognise such attention as part of the courtship of a heterosexual romance – an indirect buying of sexual favours. But perhaps, for Lucy, who is not naïve about sex (she clearly knows the facts of life), it comes as a surprise that this exchange might also involve an answer to her own desires, since until this relationship there is no reason why she should understand that sex could be pleasurable.

The one scene which indicates that the Yellow Man might be about to sexually assault Lucy is particularly interesting. This sequence, in which the Yellow Man advances menacingly towards Lucy (signalled by the fact that he is pictured in a looming close-up) is inter-cut with Battling Burrows's boxing match. As Burrows is clothed only in his boxing shorts, the editing makes it seem as if his near-naked white male body stands between, or stands 'in for' the sexual tension between the Yellow Man and Lucy (who both remain fully dressed). The erotic frisson of the 'impossible encounter' between Lucy and the Yellow Man – impossible since it would involve the taboo activities of both miscegenation and paedophilia – is conducted, or aligned, with the only near-naked body on display, which belongs to Burrows, making him, in turn, sexualised. Yet since Burrows is actually on display in an all-male, all-white environment, this re-routed erotic frisson emphasises the flamboyant, excessive aspects of his performance and the homoerotic quality of his aggressively butch masculinity. Ironically, at the very moment of his success (he wins the fight), Burrows's position as a supremely powerful heterosexual white man is undermined. For in the familiar terms of the narrative dynamic set up by the parallel editing (closely associated with Griffith's films) it is clear that Burrows cannot possibly 'get there in time' to save Lucy. The editing therefore reveals that he is unable to protect his daughter. Since he clearly does not really care for her as a person, this is perhaps legitimated by what we know of his character. What is perhaps unexpected is that his excessive display of virility and power is also simultaneously exposed or 'queered'.

Deciding, at the last moment, that he is unable or unwilling to assault Lucy, the Yellow Man simply kisses the hem of her sleeve and moves away. Yet significantly, this is not the end of the sexual narrative. Here, Lesage describes what happens next:

> After the Chinese man withdraws, we see Gish examining the sleeve that had been kissed and then stirring in bed. Both gestures indicate the child's emotional, indeed sexual, involvement with this gentle yet seductive man. The visual lushness of this sequence, the child's gestures of preening and of loving the doll, the advances of the Chinese man, and the child's awakening to both maternal and sexual emotion: all the visual details offer a clear erotic message, a message that is then ambiguously denied.[10]

Just because the sexual narrative between the Yellow Man and Lucy does not reach a climax, or remains ambiguous and unfinished, does not mean that their encounter is not erotic. In this sequence and elsewhere in the film, there are a host of ambiguous emotions are expressed. For my purposes, it is enough to note the confusion of illicit desires – of incest, miscegenation and paedophilia – in the context of an excessive display of white masculinity. Additionally, it seems that this white masculinity may be threatened, exposed and even queered by this confusion. I also want to remark on how the child's desire and pleasure is performed here via an excitable sensuality, expressed through touch and encountered in the smallest, most innocent of gestures, such as holding hands.

War Babies (*Dir. Charles Lamont, 1932*)

This short film is Shirley Temple's second starring role, one of *The Baby Burlesks* series she made for a small film company (Education Films) associated with Universal Studios, run by Jack Hays. The series was designed as a spoof of adult films: for example *Runt Page*, the first in the series, was a parody of *The Front Page*. *War Babies* was a pastiche of different war movie clichés. The action takes place in 'Pete's Buttermilk Bar' where some white soldiers (little boys with military caps and large nappies [diapers], who are otherwise naked) are being entertained by a French 'saloon gal' Charmaine (Temple). The plot involves her splitting her affections between two soldiers who attempt to bribe and seduce her by offering her 'money' – lollipops. As Charmaine, Temple performs a solo dance dressed in a flouncy top and a large nappy fastened with an outsize safety pin. In her autobiography, *Child Star*, Temple Black describes her performance in this way:

> 'Me, monsieur?' I said coyly, as one diaper-clad dough-boy yanked me to his side. A jealous Frenchman dropped a scoop of ice cream down my shirt making my dance solo a heartfelt cross between a shimmy and a samba. I rather enjoyed all the international flirtation, but my foot hurt to dance, right under the instep strap of my Mary Jane shoe.[11]

Inter-cut with Temple's dance, a little black boy (called only 'boy') initially fully dressed in dungarees and shirt, performs a striptease on a table by shimmying out of his clothes down to his boxer shorts. Other incidents include milk bottles spurting milk into different characters' faces, and a small white child on all fours sucking milk from the finger of a rubber glove, in tandem with a little dog sucking on another finger. The action concludes with Charmaine bidding farewell to her two 'clients'. Whilst hugging one, she manages, simultaneously, to kiss the other on the lips. As the two soldiers later compare notes, one of them proffers the rose from Charmaine's hair as proof of her affections; in response, and clearly trumping his rival's trophy, the other little soldier flaunts her nappy pin.

Simply describing the plot of the film in the context of contemporary sensitivity in relation to the sexuality of children, it seems shocking or at the very least dismaying, but passing moral judgement on Temple's parody of adult sexuality here is not my main concern. It is – along with the milk spurting incidents and the little black boy's striptease – clearly meant to be a joke. Children mimicking adults by dressing up and saying the 'darndest things' is still, in the 'appropriate context' (that is the home, or a carefully managed television sitcom) seen as funny today.

One of the peculiarities of the film is its use of the little black boy. There was a precedent for his appearance: the long-running film series, Hal Roach's Our Gang (1922–1944) (transmitted later on television it was called the Little Rascals) was clearly the inspiration for The Baby Burlesks and had always included black and white children in its comic short films. While the black characters in the Our Gang series sometimes took centre stage in the narrative, in many of the films they simply acted as a gawping audience (a mute chorus) to the antics of the white children. In War Babies the little black boy may seem to serve a similar purpose since he is not part of the plot. However, it is curious that his stripping routine is inter-cut with Temple's own supposedly provocative dance, and strangely he is the only other child, aside from Temple, who exhibits his body directly to both the 'soldiers' in the saloon and the film audience. This makes the film particularly uncomfortable viewing and confusing, as a faked, or parodic, adult sexual display is directly mapped on to either the little white girl's or the small black boy's body, suggesting that their relative positions and sexual availability – vis-à-vis the little white soldiers and the film audience – are the same.

Once again it would seem that, as with Gish, the little girl's whiteness is enhanced by her association and contrast with non-white others on screen. As other writers – notably Ann duCille – have noted, the presence of black performers in Temple's films (in later movies they appeared as pickaninnies, slaves, cooks, servants, butlers and doormen) function to shore up racial stereotypes. DuCille writes:

> This, then, is what pained me about the Shirley Temple films that filled my girlhood: her adorable perfection – her snow-whiteness – was constructed against my blackness, my racial difference made ridiculous by the stammering and shuffling of the 'little black rascals', 'darkies', and pickaninnies who populated her films.[12]

It is certainly difficult to watch Temple's later films without cringing at the characterisation of many of her black co-stars, particularly those characters played by Stepin Fetchit who re-creates the imbecilic 'coon' in several of her movies.

There is something interesting in thinking through the affective inheritance from Temple's early performance in the *The Baby Burlesks*. In the *Burlesks*, the children are not playing 'children', and what is prized, flaunted and controlled is not their childishness but their littleness and their ability to simulate white adult behaviour yet retain their similarities to (and the appeal of) other 'less than human' bodies (midgets, black bodies, dogs). By acting or dancing as adults (acting 'un-naturally'), the manipulation of the child actor's body is made particularly explicit. In these crude, exploitative films, the animation required of child actors and so noted in Temple's performance style appears to be the animation of a body without agency. As in the animation of objects in trick films, this process – the manipulation of the child's body – is fascinating and disturbing (freaky). Animation is uncanny because it gives life to something that we do not believe to be living. In these films, the child-as-object is doing something – acting, dancing, talking – in a manner that they are not meant to be able to do, thus disturbing the boundaries between child and adult and troubling the seemingly fixed distinction between animate and inanimate, object and subject. The status of the child and its body as 'a thing' rather than a subject is thus exposed. (Indeed, the child as 'thing' has a history in numerous stories and films where the child is, or becomes, a doll, puppet or robot.) In its explicit association between the body of the little white girl and the performance of the little black boy, *War Babies* establishes a connection between the little white girl who performs and the memory and history of enslaved black bodies which have also been categorised as 'things': objects controlled and owned by their white masters.

Lori Merish, in her article 'Cuteness and Commodity Aesthetics', makes this link between the other and freaks with performing children on stage and film, demonstrating how the appeal of the nineteenth-century 'freak show' (featuring midgets, African 'wild men' and medical curiosities) became entwined with the Victorian sentimental fascination with the child. She suggests:

> Tellingly, a popular term for 'freak show' was 'kid show'. Midgets – a term reserved, in general usage, for perfectly shaped and proportioned 'little people' – were especially popular in these shows, as well as in popular theatre and, later, vaudeville. In nineteenth century popular culture, there was a productive exchange between the cute child's performance and the midget's commercial display: part of the pleasure of watching a precocious child and 'little person' perform derived from how they unsettled, in a contained, but dramatic fashion, the conventional boundary between child and adult.[13]

Thus, *War Babies* and other films in *The Baby Burlesks* series act as a bridge between a freak show aesthetic and the cuteness of Temple as a child star.[14] What it confirms is that the little white girl's appeal has its origins in the uncanny manipulation and fascination with other bodies; that is, little bodies, raced bodies and animals. This inheritance, Merish suggests, continues to haunt the feature films in which Temple went on to star throughout the 1930s:

> Indeed, embedded within her song-and-tap dance numbers are historical traces of Jim Crow performances and resonances of Sambo-like obsequiousness in her always-ready smile and effort to please. This racial doubling of Shirley's body is rendered explicit in those scenes in which she is paired with Bill Robinson ('Bojangles') as dance partner. References to antebellum 'Jim Crow' and the history of slavery complicate the structure of feeling (of maternal cherishing) the cute works to construct, exposing the forms of power and coercion at its core.[15]

It might seem obscene to associate the performances of the highest paid little white girl in 1930s America with the exploitation of black performers. Yet, in reference to her experience filming *The Baby Burlesks*, Temple Black is at her most unambiguous in describing her dancing and acting as coercion, and discusses various methods through which Lamont used to control his child actors. In particular, she recalls the 'black box', an empty sound booth which had a block of ice inside. She comments:

> Several times I wound up banished inside Lamont's black box. It was really a devilish punishment. Take one small, obstreperous child. Heat it under bright Kleig lights until perspiration starts. Remove child directly to the chill of the black box until sufficiently cooled and chastened. Remove child, reheat under the glare of Kleig lights, and carry on with work. The box proved the ultimate enforcer. Increased obedience followed as night follows day.[16]

In this instance, Temple's treatment off screen demonstrates the hidden manipulation and coercion in all her performances. In my opinion, even her mother's reportedly benign direction to

Figure 6 'Dancers for money': Virginia (Shirley Temple) and Uncle Billy (Bill Robinson) dance in *Littlest Rebel* (Dir. David Butler, 1935)

'Sparkle, Shirley, Sparkle' seems a little menacing. I am reminded of Battling Burrows's admonishment to Lucy in *Broken Blossoms* to 'Put a smile on your face why don't ya?'

Interestingly, in *Littlest Rebel* (1935), in which she is partnered by a slave (Bill Robinson as 'Uncle Billy'), neither of their dance routines together are 'for fun' or strictly spontaneous. Their first dance is organised as a distraction for a Union Colonel who is looking for Temple's father (a Confederate scout), who is hiding in a loft. The second song-and-dance routine is a professional performance on a street corner through which they raise the train fare to Washington. For both Virgie (as Temple's character is called) and Uncle Billy, therefore, dancing is actually a ruse, or simply work, it only *seems* like fun. Merish again:

> The alignment of cute Shirley with the body of the African-American male evokes the history of slavery and its coercive appropriation of the body – a body forced to work, to reproduce, and, at times, to sing and dance, at the white master's will. By constructing an equivalence between female white child and black male slave, these scenes render ambiguous the fantasies of benevolent ownership and familial assimilation endemic to the cute, disrupting and denaturalizing the identificatory structures in which the cute child is enmeshed.[17]

So what, specifically, does Merish mean by 'cute'? It is partly established by Temple's physical dimensions – large head, rounded limbs, short stature (the allure of neoteny). It is also, as Merish suggests, underpinned by her whiteness. This whiteness not only defines her prettiness but also her value and thus her 'right' to protection. In *Littlest Rebel*, when Temple temporarily blacks up (with shoe polish), her feisty nature seems likely to get her into serious trouble. Yet as a little white girl she has been able to be naughty with impunity; earlier, when Temple sings 'Dixie' in an attempt to infuriate the friendly Union Colonel and uses her catapult to fire pebbles at him and his soldiers, she is arguably at her most 'cute' and is certainly interpreted in that way by the Colonel and other adults on screen. Her apparent aggression is so limited and ineffective that it actually exposes her vulnerability, whilst her size, white skin and golden curls remind the white Colonel of his own little daughter in the way that a black child would not. Cuteness, as Merish contends, is reliant on the stirring of a protective impulse, a motive generated unfailingly in Temple's later films as she is nearly always in need of adult care, despite her claims to the contrary. Here, cuteness is tied to whiteness not just because it signifies purity or innocence, but because cuteness 'makes respectable' the desire to own and control a little girl's unruly behaviour and, implicitly, her sexuality. The good 'white father' (or even the bad white father) wants the little girl he desires to be white, as only then does she have value for him in confirming his own racial identity and associated power. By expressing or reclaiming his ownership of her, he confirms his own whiteness and civility; furthermore, his control of her sexuality will determine the future whiteness of his descendents (providing she remains innocent, not 'dirty'). Significantly, for such a relationship to remain civilised, cuteness requires the disavowal of both the girl's and her adult protectors' sexual and sensual desires and interests.

> Staging the disavowal of child eroticism and the sublimation of adults' erotic feelings toward children, cuteness is the sign of a particular *relation* between adult and child, simultaneously establishing the 'innocence' of the child and the 'civility' of the adult spectator.[18]

In Merish's argument, cuteness is a way of positioning the little white girl so that her unruly qualities (precociousness, sexuality, exuberance) can be contained. Despite Temple's short skirts, her frilly pants, coy looks and frequent protestations of love for adult white males (including both actual and temporary father figures) as well as all the other ways in which she retained some of her adult sexual appeal exemplified by her appearance in *The Baby Burlesks* series, in her later films Temple had to be innocently cute. Her cuteness ensured that the desire to possess her was not illicit but safely, appropriately, paternal – even patriotic. Indeed, as Charles Eckert, in his seminal article on Temple argues, Temple's star persona and the narrative of the majority of her feature films were clearly aligned with an ideological project which established the apparent naturalness and central importance of a patriarchal national 'family' in an era in which this family seemed under attack from the economic and social effects of the Great Depression.[19] What is sometimes under-explored, however, is how important and how obvious it was that this family was, and should remain, white.

Even during the 1930s, Temple's façade of cuteness did not convince everybody. Graham Greene, writing as a film critic in the 1930s, wrote an infamous review of her 1938 film *Wee Willie Winkie*, which is quoted – almost in its entirety – by Temple Black in her autobiography. Greene had claimed:

> Infancy with her is a disguise, her appeal is more secret and more adult. Already two years ago she was a fancy little piece. (Real childhood, I think, went out after the *Littlest Rebel*.) In *Captain January* she wore trousers with the mature suggestiveness of a Dietrich; her neat well developed rump twisted in the tap dance: her eyes had a sidelong searching coquetry. Now in *Wee Willie Winkie* wearing short kilts, she is a complete totsy ... Her admirers, middle-aged men and clergymen, respond to her dubious coquetry, to the sight of her well-shaped and desirable little body, packed with enormous vitality, only because the safety curtain of the story and dialogue drops between their intelligence and their desire.[20]

Despite the fact that this was not the first time Greene had commented on the dubious or ambiguous appeal of Temple (evidently, his earlier review for *Captain January* in 1936 had already noted the peculiarly mature allure of Temple dancing in trousers), Mrs. Temple and the studio decided to sue for libel and effectively closed down the magazine which carried the review – a short-lived, relatively high-brow publication called *Night and Day*. However, it would seem that for most viewers, Temple's masquerade of cuteness made her expressions of desire and affection appropriate and comfortable, since she directed them only at adult white males and not at other children, or adult black males, even when dancing. As duCille notes:

> Restricted to dancing toe-to-toe, Temple and Robinson ... had to work at avoiding the almost organic sensuality of the male-female pas de deux. The same little girl who spent most of her film career in the arms and laps of white men never got closer to Robinson than a handshake.[21]

DuCille claims, plausibly, that the on-screen relationship between Temple and Robinson worked and remained uncontroversial because their characterisation as either cute (Temple) or as an emasculated 'Uncle Tom' figure ('Uncle Billy') contained or erased any sexual potential in their partnership. There is certainly no erotic frisson between the two of them as they dance. And Temple never caresses, kisses or cuddles Robinson as she does her adult white male co-stars. Yet, by following Merish's argument and acknowledging Temple's own implicit otherness as a 'thing' rather than a fully human subject with agency, we can see that there is still a glimmer of a close, hidden relationship between the little white girl and the adult black male. The smallest of gestures and most routine of practices – holding hands, the exchange of looks, the shared talent for mimicry, their choreographed mirroring and the off-screen and on-screen tutelage in tap (Robinson taught Temple to dance on and off screen and acted as choreographer for one of her other films) – all generate a rapport, a sensual accord between

Figure 7 'And so to bed': Lloyd Sherman (Shirley Temple) and Walker (Bill Robinson) as partners in the famous 'staircase dance' in *The Little Colonel* (Dir. David Butler, 1935)

Robinson and Temple that she did not achieve with any of her white co-stars. The Temple and Robinson song-and-dance routines confirm that the 'little white girl' and the (enslaved) black man share a history in which the existence of their unnecessary, uncivilised and potentially dangerous sexuality is equally impossible.

Robinson's and Temple's song-and-dance routines are diversions in two senses. First, as entertainment they are a spectacular diversion for the audience who find the little white girl's and civilised black man's exhibition of skill as fascinating and as unthreateningly titillating as a freak show. Second, they divert attention from the energies, excitements, interests and attractions that the little white girl and the black man possess but must work hard to obscure, less their agency, desires and erotic potential serve to openly disrupt the hierarchy and relations of the patriarchal white family (or indeed the patriarchal white nation) that Temple's films otherwise worked so hard to restore.

Lolita (*Dir. Stanley Kubrick, 1962*)

Lolita — based on the novel by Vladimir Nabokov — is as a film, and as a recurring and compelling motif, at the centre of this chapter. The narrative of the film details — with dedicated irony — the erotic obsession of a European, educated, urbane, white adult male, Humbert Humbert (played by James Mason), for an American 'little white girl', Dolores Haze. (The diminutive of Dolores is, of course, Lolita, although Humbert also frequently calls her 'Lo'.) In the novel Dolores is 12, while in the film, played by Sue Lyons, she is 14. After his abortive marriage to Dolores's widowed mother Charlotte (played by Shelley Winters), which ends when she is killed in a car accident, the film then follows Humbert as he takes Dolores on two extended 'road trips' and lives briefly with her as her 'father'. What is described in some detail in the novel, but remains implicit in the film, is the opportunity this intimacy presents Humbert for a series of persistent and frantic sexual violations of Dolores. The novel and the film's conceit is that the story is presented entirely from Humbert's obsessed, intellectualised and romantic point of view. He legitimates his actions, presenting events alternately as a tragic love story or an academic exercise. (In the novel, Humbert's prose is also presented as if it were an extended psychoanalytic case study.)

The content of the novel and the film is explicitly about a paedophile and his sexual abuse of a little white girl. Yet the narrative complexity of the novel and the detached playfulness of Kubrick's film reverberate in a manner which informs, confuses and contaminates the understanding of any and potentially all adult-child relationships in the twentieth century and beyond. The central confusion is often this: in many popular reports the understanding seems to be that the film presents Humbert as a tragic hero and that the narrative should be seen as a 'love story' (albeit of an unusual and dubious kind of love). Yet the film is not a love story, it is about the unrequited erotic obsession, sexual abuse and finally, perhaps, the love of an adult white male for a little girl. Dolores never loves Humbert, although she does fall in love with and have sex with other males – both those of her own age (while at her summer camp, 'Camp Climax') and other older men. In fact she finally escapes Humbert by running away with another white male paedophile whom she does claim to have been 'truly crazy about': Clare Quilty (played by Peter Sellers in Kubrick's film). The confusion is two-fold: first, that Humbert presents himself as a pitiful and broken-hearted lover when he is also a calculating rapist; and second, that Dolores is not innocent but sexually active, although this does not mean that she enjoys or wants sex with Humbert.

The story as it unfolds in the film is complicated, loaded with inter-textual references and, as one character says in the film (speaking of a play staged within the film), 'heavy-handed symbolism'. In the context of this chapter, one important motif – as other critics have noted – is the novel's (and less explicitly the film's) references to Hollywood and the phenomenon of the 'child star' epitomised by Shirley Temple. Charlotte makes reference to the fact that Dolores thinks she is a 'star' but is actually a 'brat', and both Quilty and Humbert, at different times, feed Dolores's fantasies of a studio contract and of becoming a Hollywood star. Another cinematic inter-textual reference occurs at the very start of the film as Quilty emerges from a chair, dragging a white dust sheet (which originally covered both him and the chair and is now draped over him like a toga). In response to Humbert's direct question, 'Are you Quilty?', he answers 'No, I'm Spartacus, have you come to free the slaves or something?', directly referring – as many critics have noted – to the film Kubrick completed before Lolita, the Oscar-winning 'Roman epic' Spartacus which tells the story of a slave rebellion led by the eponymous hero. In many ways, Quilty's conversation (apparently mostly improvised by Sellers) and his endless double entendres are the key to the film's attempt to transpose the irony, sophisticated word play and deliberate heavy-handed symbolism from the novel to the film. As the opening scene continues, Quilty forces Humbert to play a game of 'Roman' ping-pong with him, as if they were 'two Roman senators'. This suggests that they are two powerful, civilised white men of equal status, and that, implicitly, Dolores – as trophy and slave – has been (or will be) passed back and forth between them. After Humbert pulls out his gun, Quilty retreats, looking for a drink, muttering about sore losers. He then suggests that 'you [Humbert] are drunk and I [Quilty] am a sick man', when the opposite is in fact the case. Both the game (ping-pong) and the transposition of physical states directly refer to the mirror image that Quilty presents to Humbert, although Humbert Humbert is also, of course, a name which mirrors itself, signalling the character's narcissistic world view.

While this mirroring of Quilty and Humbert is a central conceit of the book and the film, it may also be that Quilty is not Humbert's double but his shadow. Aside from the fact that Quilty follows Humbert for most of the film, several of Quilty's encounters with Humbert create situations in which Quilty emerges 'out of the dark' to torment him. This most obvious instance is when Quilty waits, as 'Dr. Zempf', in the dark of Humbert's own living room (Quilty suggests, mischievously, that he is saving electricity). Later in the film, after he has taken Dolores from the hospital, Quilty telephones Humbert in the middle of the night, appearing once more as a voice in, and from, the dark. That Quilty is Humbert's shadow is even hinted at when their paths first cross at the summer high school prom (although they do not meet) – Humbert is in a white dinner jacket and Quilty in a black evening suit. Quilty's mysterious female companion, Vivian Darkbloom (an anagram of Vladamir

Nabokov), who has long dark hair and is always dressed in black, also imbues Quilty with the quality of a 'shadowy figure'. Yet by the end of the film, Humbert and Quilty's positions would seem to be reversed, since it is evident that it is Humbert who has 'been in the dark' all along, and it is he who must now run after Quilty. Quilty, initially draped in his toga, is no longer blackened but dressed in white.

Another reading – more plausible perhaps in the context of the novel – would be that Quilty is actually a 'side' or a projection of Humbert's own diseased imagination. The possibility that a father figure who is potentially a predatory and dangerous adult male is not a real person but the 'other side' to the personality of what would otherwise appear to be a little girl's 'good' father, was recently played out in the film Hide and Seek, starring Robert de Niro and Dakota Fanning. In this film, nine-year-old Emily (Fanning) is taken by her psychiatrist father David (de Niro) to live in the countryside to recover from the apparent suicide of her mother. Initially, it seems that Emily deals with her loss by creating an imaginary friend, Charlie. (Whilst Charlie's age is never established, he does not appear to be a child.) As the film progresses, events escalate and Charlie becomes increasingly violent, driving David to desperate measures in order to save Emily from a figure that seems to become even more 'real'. The climax of the film reveals that Charlie is not Emily's invention but a persona of David's, who was responsible for his wife's death. The association with Lolita is not simply that David/Charlie are doubled in a similar manner to Humbert/Quilty but that the presence of the 'other man' serves to legitimate the 'good father's' aberrant behaviour. When Charlie is initially identified as a product of Emily's unbalanced imagination, the narrative deliberately implies that Emily is mentally ill and thus his presence serves to distract us from the real danger that is actually posed by her father, David. Similarly, Quilty's existence as the 'preferred paedophile' diverts attention from Humbert's warped pathology, since Quilty's presence implies that Dolores would have, even without Humbert, sacrificed her innocence (and thus her right to protection) in a paedophilic relationship. Conveniently, this would suggest that Humbert was not entirely to blame for Dolores's fate.

An entire academic industry could be said to be devoted to Nabokov's work and *Lolita* in particular. The differing texts of *Lolita* (including the novel, Kubrick's film version, Nabokov's published screenplay, a musical and a later film adaptation) provide enough material for a book in themselves. My intention here, therefore, is to restrict my observations and analysis to the ways in which the film encroaches on the concerns of this chapter – that is, the ambiguity of touch and the significance of race.

First, the question of touch: as the film was made in 1962, contemporary censorship meant that in order to secure mainstream distribution the film would not be able to picture any real intimacy or sexual activity between Humbert and Dolores. Kubrick himself commented on the problems this caused for the film:

> The film was successful, but there's no question that people expected to see some of the things that they had read in the book – or hoped they might see those parts anyway. The film should have had as much erotic weight as the novel had. As it was, it had the psychology of the characters and the mood of the story…but it certainly didn't have as much of the erotic as you could put in to it now.[22]

Yet my argument would be that the limitations in terms of touching, or the restrictions placed on the physical expressions of the erotic, amplify the ambiguity of the 'innocent' touches that do feature in the film. In a film in which we know that two of the main characters are having a sexual relationship yet we never see them kiss on the mouth or in bed together, arguably every touch, every instance of proximity, has the potential to be eroticised instead. While the book is more explicit about what happens physically between Dolores and Humbert, much of Humbert's early obsession is based on his belief that she is unaware of the erotic pleasure he derives from her innocent physicality, proximity and casual touch. What *Lolita* as a book and as a film does, is to articulate what James Kincaid has identified as the 'erotic projection' instigated by the Freudian categorisation of child sexuality as 'latent'. This suggests that while the child may inspire, or in fact experience, sexual arousal, he or she does not understand this as sexual, since he or she is unable to 'separate out' the pleasurable feelings stimulated in themselves or in others as different from their ordinary, everyday experience. Their knowledge of and potential for sexual experience is therefore understood to be unconscious or 'latent'. What this means, Kincaid suggests, is:

> Latency is an erotic term, an erotic projection onto the body of the child that renders that child fully an object of sexual forces, forces that operate deeply in and through the child and manifest themselves in any and all directions: thus, while no activities are *really* sexual, there are no activities which are really *not* sexual either.[23]

The irony is that the child is not *less* sexual than the adult but is potentially sexualised by anything and everything he or she does. In relation to *Lolita*, there is an early comic sequence at a drive-in movie, in which Charlotte, Dolores and Humbert enact the confusion of 'who is holding whose hand'. Equally, the film's title sequence famously pictures an adult male hand carefully painting the toenails of what would appear to be a young girl, an image that is innocent yet simultaneously erotic. Later in the film Humbert does indeed paint Dolores's toenails, and while he is fully clothed she appears to be wearing a bath robe. Yet the sexual nature of the scene is ambiguous – Humbert kneels by the bed, and thus does not 'share' Dolores's bed. Coincidentally, Humbert's position here mirrors the Yellow Man's posture in relation to Lucy in *Broken Blossoms*, meaning that Humbert's position could also be read as an innocent, even worshipful position, placing him in a role as the little girl's male attendant and not her abuser.

The Abuser in the Dark: Race and *Lolita*

What is intriguing about *Lolita* is the way in which race informs or surrounds the narrative and impacts upon the formal qualities of the film, which would otherwise appear to be entirely 'white'. In some senses, the film is perhaps even 'whiter' than the novel, as one of the significant changes of colour from novel to screen is that Dolores, in the film, is a platinum blonde and not, as she

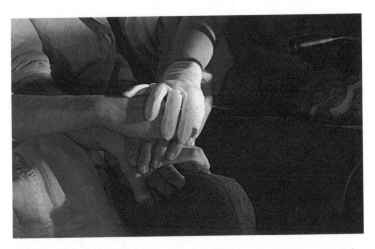

Figure 8   'Who is holding whose hand?': at the drive-in in *Lolita* (Dir. Stanley Kubrick, 1962)

is described in the novel, dark haired. In the following analysis of the film and its racial dynamics I am indebted to an essay by Steven Belletto – 'Of Pickaninnies and Nymphets: Race in *Lolita*'. In this essay he responds to a challenge laid down by Toni Morrison, who, in a series of lectures (later published as *Playing in the Dark*), identified the under-examined presence of an 'African persona' in American literature when it appears to be at its most 'white'. She argued: 'Even, and especially, when American texts are not "about" Africanist presences or characters or narrative or idiom, the shadow hovers in implication, in sign, in line of demarcation.'[24]

Exploring Kubrick's adaptation of *Lolita* from this perspective suggests, for instance, that if Quilty is Humbert's shadow, it is a suggestively *raced* conceit. I can therefore link *Lolita* back directly to my earlier discussions concerning the disavowed sexuality and the alliance of the black man and the little white girl. In their arguments, Morrison and Belletto seek out the 'hidden in plain sight' aspects of race – in characters, as metaphor and in symbolism – and the ways in which they inform the narrative and mood of (in Morrison's argument) some of the established classics of American literature, or (in Belletto's essay specifically) Nabokov's novel. In following this line of thought, I am not reading Lolita (or Nabokov, or Kubrick) as racist but, like these critics, trying to discern the ways in which the aesthetic of the film is imbued with certain affective motifs which draw the themes of child sexuality, child sexual abuse and race together. In his conclusion, Belletto claims:

> My point lies...in how the novel is concerned with racial undertones. Tropes that perpetuate racial categories are not as obvious as tap-dancing pickaninnies, but can rather come in the form of aesthetic affinities, can be inherent in the way one manages descriptions, and can thus stand as part of the very fabric of a culture's self-understanding.[25]

Once we become alert to race, certain aspects of the film become plausible or significant in ways that open up a host of different readings. Quilty's opening line – 'I'm Spartacus, have you come to free the slaves or something?' – now resonates not simply with an inter-textual reference to Kubrick but to the film's own themes of slavery, of ownership and control. Quilty's suggestion that he and Humbert are 'like two Roman senators' places them equally at the pinnacle of a white hierarchy in which Dolores – 'Lo' – is presumably at the bottom. (This implicit hierarchy is also alluded to, or reverberates with Humbert's initial query to Charlotte, during his tour of her house; he presumes, on first hearing her name, that 'Lolita' must be Charlotte's Hispanic live-in maid and not her daughter.) Yet the racial dynamics of the film are more complicated than this: as the conversation between Quilty and Humbert progresses (and Quilty slides in and out of a bewildering array of accents and poses), Quilty suggests that Humbert must be a European refugee or an Australian and tells him that he should 'run along now' because this is a 'Gentile house' – implying that Humbert's racial identity is not as secure as it appears. If Quilty is Humbert's shadow, or his double, the instability and ethnic ambiguity that Quilty enacts also reflects upon Humbert. Humbert's desire to possess Dolores may then be inspired by his anxiety to assert his own 'whiteness' rather than simply, or solely, his erotic fixation. In Belletto's analysis of the novel, he suggests: 'The possibility of Humbert having miscegenated blood haunts much of the novel and affects his description of Dolores's pollution, descriptions which…suggest that the racialized aesthetic informs the novel's larger ethical arc.'[26]

Kubrick's film cannot and does not incorporate all of the racial implications that Belletto identifies in the novel. Yet Kubrick does include one key black character, 'Tom' the bellhop at the Enchanted Hunters hotel. (In the novel this figure is identified as an 'Uncle Tom' figure and described as a 'hunchbacked and hoary negro'.) Though a minor character, the two instances in which Tom interacts with Dolores and Humbert in the film are, I think, significant. We first encounter Tom as he carries Humbert's and Dolores's bags to their room; Humbert is clearly flustered and awkward, Tom oblivious, patiently stacking the luggage on a bench at the foot of the bed when he is actually instructed by Humbert to leave them on the floor. As he leaves, Humbert tips him, but does so through an ungainly dance around Dolores. Tom's presence works in two ways: one obvious, the other less so. First, Humbert's awkwardness undermines his pose as Dolores's father and makes the ambivalence of her relationship to him more explicit. Second, the performative excess in this short sequence opens up a racially inflected interpretation that lurks underneath this otherwise innocuous scene, since it could be read as an incident in which we are seeing the exchange of money, involving a black man, in a room where a little white girl is about to be raped. (From this perspective, it is not coincidental that Dolores is the only other character in the film – aside from Tom – who Humbert pays off with money.)

The second time Humbert encounters Tom – in which they struggle to set up a cot bed together in the bedroom – is not in the book. Its presence has surprised and irritated several critics (including, apparently, Nabokov himself). Kubrick includes it, I think, for several reasons. As a 'screwball comedy' sequence it acts – like the song-and-dance routines of Temple and Robinson – as a diversion, since while we may be laughing at this routine, we are also waiting in anticipation for the first sexual contact between Humbert and Dolores. Ironically, in our sympathy for Humbert (who does not want to wake Dolores) we forget that we are actually sympathising with a potential rapist, since he is clearly hoping to attack her while she is sleeping (in the novel he has drugged her).

Figure 9 'Dancing around the subject': Humbert (James Mason), Dolores (Sue Lyon) and Tom (John Harrison) in *Lolita* (Dir. Stanley Kubrick, 1962)

The scene is quite prolonged and involves first Tom and then Humbert, leaping or falling into the cot to straighten it out. Such are their exertions that Tom even takes time to remove his jacket. It is probable that I am tempted to read 'too much' into this sequence, but it does feel uncomfortable and not simply because the viewer is anxious that Dolores should not wake up. The discomfort, I would suggest, is inspired by 'Africanist' associations. For instance, it is possible that Tom's presence as an (albeit emasculated) black man in a little white girl's bedroom creates an extra frisson for the viewer. Furthermore, the fact that Tom is constantly hushed by Humbert and once more paid off (with a considerably more generous tip than before) adds a specific, visible yet unacknowledged, racially imbued undercurrent to the scene. In visual terms, the 'film noir' qualities of the mise-en-scène in which barred shadows cross over Dolores's bed – a visual cue closely associated with the 'noir' thriller and in which, as here, the bars often suggest that the film's characters are imprisoned – encourage an atmosphere that foregrounds an association between darkness and illicit sexuality. In addition, the way in which Tom and Humbert face one another across the cot bed may also imply that Tom acts as yet another mirror, double or shadow for Humbert. Indeed, as Humbert and Tom enact a comic dance of 'give and take', they also replicate the game of ping-pong that Humbert will later play with another 'shadowy figure' (Quilty). Like Quilty, Tom acts as an (apparently unwitting) obstacle, as someone who gets 'in the way' of Humbert's desire to possess Dolores. As Belletto points out, in the novel Humbert briefly but specifically identifies himself as a 'hoary hunchback abusing himself in the dark', and while this is never referred to in the film, there is some trace of this alignment in this scene.

The other instance in which race informs the film's narrative is the scene in which Humbert reads to Dolores from Edgar Allen Poe's 'Ullalume'. Poe is a key figure for Humbert in the novel and it is clear that Humbert both identifies with, and models his own writing style on, Poe. (There is a brief suggestion of this connection in the film, as we hear the beginning of a clumsy, repetitive poem that Humbert has written, that he demands that Quilty read and which seems to be a pastiche of Poe's 'over-heated' rhetorical style.) The association between Poe and Humbert is hardly surprising; Poe, notoriously, had a 'child bride', Virginia Clemm, who was to die at a young age. It is no coincidence, then, that 'Ullalume' is often interpreted as a description of Poe's own mournful journey to worship at his child-bride's tomb. In addition, aside from this aspect of his biography, Poe's work is itself imbued with overt and covert expressions of paedophilic desires. As Peter Coviello observes: 'Among Lolita's many rewards is the riotous candour with which it realizes how very thoroughly we are haunted in our understanding of Poe by the many ghostly traces of paedophilia.'[27] Coviello also reminds us of the significance of the Gothic, the genre of literature Poe is most strongly associated with. He notes of Poe's work that it is characterised by a 'thematics of encroachment, doubling, and self-erosion.'[28]

Like many of Poe's characters, Humbert is similarly afflicted with fears of encroachment and self-erosion. He too is chased by shadows and, as I have suggested, is doubled by other characters. The doubling of characters can even be discerned between Charlotte and Dolores in a manner that functions over and above the obvious fact that they are mother and daughter. For while they are not physically similar, in their extraordinary blondeness and vulgarity, as well as the fact that they share or compete for the same men, they also function as rivals, or as distorted mirror images of one another. In relation to the Gothic qualities of the narrative, it is also worth remembering that Lolita is a film in which every major character dies (although in the film Dolores's fate is not revealed, in the novel we are told that she dies in childbirth).

In Coviello's argument, Poe is not only significant because his presence allows for a sly reference to paedophilia and confirms the Gothic character of the story, but because his writing is alive with racial thinking and racial tension. As Coviello points out, it is Morrison herself who suggests that there is '[n]o early American writer ... more important to the concept of American Africanism than Poe.'[29] Poe's inclusion and his retention by Kubrick in the transposition from novel to film thus relates to the film's sensitivity towards Humbert's racial anxieties and prejudices as well as his illicit sexual desires. The importance of Coviello's analysis is that he determines that these two aspects of Poe are not distinct from but mutually inform one another:

> the forms and figures of racial meaning that traverse Poe's writing are not exterior to its sexual peculiarities; they might be described more accurately, as the engine that sustains, through a range of permutation, the ongoing drama of sexual promise and sexual frustration in Poe's work.[30]

In Coviello's erudite and complex essay, he develops a range of associations and possibilities that indicate how Poe's work – populated by animate corpses, illicit desires, 'morbidly white' characters and incest – is charged with the anguished attempt to confirm, or keep intact, the hero's own whiteness and racial superiority. In relation to Lolita I want to focus on two aspects of his argument. First, he notes, as I have, the way in which the animation of the inhuman or, in Poe's work, the reanimated corpse, carries with it the association of other (raced) bodies and persons categorised not as human but, in the context of slavery, as things. He points out that Harriet Beecher Stowe's initial title for her abolitionist melodrama Uncle Tom's Cabin was 'The Man That Was a Thing'. Thus the fact that Poe's narrators and heroes are frequently alarmed by the likelihood of their own death, or by the suspicion that they are already dying, is an anxiety related to their fear of not being 'white' enough. Coviello suggests:

> Poe's signature style, in other words, produces almost as a rule, narrators who are forever discovering themselves to be only quasi-animate – narrators who are forever in danger, then, of succumbing to a state of deathliness or morbidity, through whose bodily symptoms they become alarmingly slave-like, alarmingly less white.[31]

Humbert may not appear at risk of seeming, or feeling himself to be 'quasi-animate', but he is someone who could be said to be rotting from within. His teeth are apparently bad (indicated by his – possibly faked – neuralgia which is mentioned in the film) and he has heart disease. In the film, another indication of Humbert's close association with morbidity is provided by the way in which the drive-in movie (the first 'date' involving Humbert, Dolores and Charlotte) is incorporated. The drive-in movie scene occurs directly after the first meeting between Humbert and Dolores. This meeting, which takes place in the garden, concludes with an exchange of close-up 'looks' between Dolores and Humbert. In an edit that is funny and scary, the final shot – which is of Dolores's face – does not return us, as we might expect, to Humbert, but to another close-up, this time of a monster's face inserted from the horror film that Dolores, Humbert and Charlotte are watching at the drive-in. The unexpected substitution of the monster's face for Humbert's face in this sequence resonates, and not just because it suggests that Humbert is actually a 'monster': rather that it is a particular kind of monster from the classic 1959 film The Mummy. Indeed, it is almost too apt because a 'mummy' is a reanimated corpse – a monster that is also a 'thing'.

More tellingly, as in Poe, the overt expression of morbidity in Lolita is forced, or as Coviello suggests 'sequestered', onto the figure of the adult woman, in this instance Charlotte. One of the most bizarre aspects of the film is that Charlotte has a shrine to her late husband in her bedroom and keeps his ashes in an urn, which she does not remove even when she has married Humbert. Charlotte's association with death is confirmed when she dies suddenly and horribly, and it is perhaps no coincidence that hers is the only corpse we actually see in the film. (Quilty, who we see being shot by Humbert, actually dies behind a painting so we do not see his dead body. The painting is a picture of a woman who looks like Charlotte in large broad-brimmed hat which looks like Charlotte; confusingly, the hat is also reminiscent of the straw hat Dolores wears in the garden scene.) Humbert's revulsion for Charlotte is therefore partly based on the sense in which she is 'close to death' and thus reminds him of his own mortality. In contrast, his passion for Dolores is tied to the fact that she represents – from Humbert's warped perspective – the only opportunity for a sexual relationship which does not carry associations of death. In this manner, the function of the 'nymphet' is equivalent to the figure of the child-bride in Poe. As Coviello argues;

> Within [Poe's Gothic fictive] world, only very young girls, who are not yet encumbered by the revulsions of adult femininity, seem capable of providing a site for stable heterosexual male desire...since only they do not appear liable at any moment to mutate into some quasi-animate monstrosity.[32]

Lolita – as a novel and in Kubrick's film – provides a diversity of uncomfortable and uncanny associations which reverberate within all the films discussed in this chapter. However, the novel and the film are slippery and seductive texts and my analysis should not be seen to provide a coherent critical template. Some aspects of the little white girl in Lolita actually contradict my interpretation of this figure and her sexuality in other films. As I suggested at the beginning of this chapter, I am interested in exploring how certain anxieties and associations are played out in all these films in ways that rub against each other as well as make connections. In Broken Blossoms and War Babies and now in Lolita, I have explored the qualities and the erotics of innocent touching, examined the significance of race and suggested that slavery emerges as a recurrent motif. In my following discussion of Taxi Driver and Man on Fire, Lolita's touch makes me sensitive to additional elements. First, the significance and recurrence of the Gothic aesthetic; second, Lolita provides a model of an adult male hero who uses a little white girl (and her sexuality) as part of a desperate attempt to shore up his own sense of decay and racial insecurity; finally it is important not to forget Dolores, who continually eludes and eventually escapes Humbert's framing of her as his 'Lolita'. Although she is orphaned, abused and exploited, Dolores does not see herself as a victim, and finally the film reveals that she has actively plotted, lied and cheated to get what she wants. The little white girl, in fact, may not be as passive or as innocent as she is made out to be.

Taxi Driver (*Dir. Martin Scorsese, 1976*)

Taxi Driver is a film about Travis Bickle (Robert de Niro), a Vietnam War veteran who, haunted by his inability to sleep and sense of alienation ('a person should become like other persons'), takes up work as a night-shift taxi driver in New York. In perhaps the film's most famous lines, Bickle's voiceover presents us with his view of the city:

> All the animals come out at night: whores, skunk pussies, buggers, queens, fairies, dopers, junkies, sick, venal. Someday a real rain will come and wash all the scum off the streets.

As I suggested at the beginning of this chapter, a great deal of my argument has been inspired by a reading of this particular film by Lesley Stern in her 1995 book, *The Scorsese Connection*. She persuasively reads *Taxi Driver* as a revision, or a re-description of John Ford's 1956 Western, *The Searchers*. As she states, the most obvious connection between the films may be that 'central to both films is an impulse to rescue – to "return home" – a woman who does not want to be saved.'[33] Actually, in both films – and incidentally in *Broken Blossoms* – it is a little white girl and not a woman who is rescued by an angry and potentially psychotic white man. Therefore, while I am indebted to Stern's interpretation of the film, my intention here is to adapt and adopt her critical strategies to demonstrate how *Taxi Driver* re-enacts the tactile, emotional and racial dynamic of films which feature little white girls and specifically, to illustrate this particular film's close relationship to Kubrick's *Lolita* (although it is evident that *Taxi Driver* repeats themes and motifs explored in *Broken Blossoms*). The connections between *Lolita* and *Taxi Driver* are notable: both films are about solipsistic white males who believe themselves to be set apart from general humanity; both protagonists write diaries and, ultimately, both men shoot and kill their rivals in an act of apparent revenge, and this killing is rooted in their desire to possess and control the sexuality of a little white girl. (In *Taxi Driver* this is a child prostitute, Iris, played by 12-year-old Jodie Foster.)

Aside from the narrative similarity of both films, the initial association between *Lolita* and *Taxi Driver* is predominantly one of tone. Both films present their audiences with a film in which the 'hero' does unspeakable things while demanding our appreciation and even our participation in his world view. Stern observes:

> Scorsese, learning from Ford, manages a brilliant manoeuvre: he renders Travis Bickle as a psychopath, weaving a complex imagery of glittering putrescence, invoking a delusional world structured according to a dynamic of filth and purity, sickness and health; he exhibits this, and yet he immerses us within it.[34]

Where *Lolita* is ambiguous and deceitful in its presentation of Humbert Humbert and his fantasy, *Taxi Driver* is compelling and, as Stern suggests, 'beguiling', prompting some critics to see it as a neo-fascist manifesto. Yet, as with *Lolita*, *Taxi Driver* may be nothing more than a hallucination, the ramblings of a madman: each film is presented almost entirely from the protagonist's warped point of view.

Less obviously, *Lolita* and *Taxi Driver* share some generic similarities. Whilst *Taxi Driver* is most often categorised as an urban Western (and Stern's analysis thickens and complicates this categorisation), both films are also imbued with Gothic affectations. More obviously Gothic in tone than *Lolita*, *Taxi Driver's* mise-en-scène is frequently dark, dangerous and full of shadows flickering on the screens of the porn cinemas and from lighted windows. Yet the Gothic influence can be seen as equally important in relation to the characterisation of both Bickle and Humbert; both men are suffering from a sense of personal decay and a fear of self-erosion. Bickle comments frequently on his disgust at the filth and degradation of the city ('Each time I return the cab to the garage I have to clean the cum off the back seat. Some nights I clean off the blood'). He, like Humbert, is 'rotting from within' – at one point Bickle believes that he must have stomach cancer. In terms of the other characters and their relation to the Gothic, both Humbert and Bickle encounter female figures which double one another – Charlotte/Dolores and Betsy/Iris. In their blondeness, doubling and ultimately unsatisfactory status as objects of desire, these female characters suggest an association that touches on another Gothic melodrama about obsession and possession in which another blonde woman is doubled – Alfred Hitchcock's Vertigo. Taxi Driver does seem to owe something, or pay homage, to Vertigo: both films employ green and red filters; enact a narrative which details the hero's obsessive voyeurism; follow his restless driving around city streets; and perhaps most distinctively, employ an original score by Bernard Herrmann. Scorsese even incorporates a brief nod to Hitchcock's trademark cameo appearances in his own films. Scorsese's first 'blink and you'll miss it' appearance is not his later and more famous performance as Bickle's psychotic passenger, but takes place in the earlier scene in which Bickle first sees Betsy, the adult woman with whom he is originally fixated. As the camera locates and follows Betsy out of the crowd of pedestrians on the pavement and into the campaign headquarters in which she works, Scorsese (who does not speak in this scene) can be seen sitting near the steps leading up to headquarters which Betsy walks past. Scorsese's referencing of Kubrick and Lolita is less evident, although Iris's colouring and costume recall the iconic image of Dolores as she is first seen by Humbert in her mother's garden, as well as the famous poster image by Bert Stern, which was used to promote the film.

The Gothic aspects of the film are also made clear when Bickle, like Humbert, is doubled both by himself (the famous 'you talking to me?' scene in which he addresses himself in a mirror) and by another male figure, in this instance Sport, Iris's pimp. During Bickle's first proper encounter with Sport, Sport is dressed in jeans, shirtless, wearing a leather waistcoat, with his long dark hair held back in a bandana. Although a slick street style, it is also reminiscent, as Stern (and others) have noted, of the costume of an American Indian in Hollywood films. In this scene, Bickle in his plaid shirt and cowboy boots is initially positioned as Sport's counterpart – a 'cowboy' to Sport's 'Indian'. In the final scenes, however, Bickle's choice of haircut – the Mohawk – suggests that he too is (or has become) an 'Indian'. As Stern notes, Sport confirms this by suggesting that Bickle should 'get back to your own fucking tribe'. Aside from these distinctive costumes, there is an aural as well as a visual link between Bickle and Sport. In a scene in which Sport mollifies and seduces Iris by dancing with her, we see him put on some slow jazz music on a record player. The music is significant (and anachronistic), because although it is now presented to us as a record and sourced within the film, the music we hear is music we have heard before – it is the theme that is associated with Bickle, 'Travis's theme', which is most often heard when we are seeing things (often the women he is attracted to) from his point of view – or generally when we see him seeing. David Butler notes that the 'official music timing notes for the film refer repeatedly to the jazz theme as the "melody in the head" '.[35] The fact that this music is not just associated with Bickle but is actually a 'melody in [his] head' and may form part of his increasingly delusional state suggests that although Bickle is not a participant in the scene (and cannot apparently see Iris and Sport), he is nonetheless 'there' – perhaps seeing it in his imagination. In this way it could be that Sport enacts a romantic encounter that Bickle seems unable to manage himself and 'stands in' for Bickle.

The uncomfortable power of the scene is established by the way in which it makes clear that Sport's control of Iris is not solely through violence (which might have been suggested by our first encounter with them, in which Sport hauls Iris out of Bickle's cab) but through expert seduction – the exact power over women that Bickle himself desires but cannot sustain. We can speculate that Sport, like Quilty, is the 'preferred paedophile' and observe that, like Dolores, Iris is similarly bemused and indifferent to the intensity of Bickle's obsessive interest in her. She says to Bickle: 'I think I understand. I tried to get into your cab one night. And now you want to come and take me away. Is that it?' suggesting that what is obvious to Bickle (and to the viewing audience who are seeing and hearing everything from his point of view) is not obvious to Iris, who (however naïvely or mistakenly) does not see herself as a victim ('Hey, haven't you heard of women's lib?').

Figure 10 Iris (Jodie Foster) and Sport (Harvey Keitel), dancing in *Taxi Driver* (Dir. Martin Scorsese, 1976)

The Gothic quality of the mise-en-scène and narrative obviously engenders and reinforces another undercurrent in the film to which I have repeatedly returned – that of race. As in other Gothic tales, *Taxi Driver*'s association of dirt and filth with blackness, or with the other, is plain. Yet *Taxi Driver*, far more explicitly than *Lolita*, is about racial tension, for Bickle is clearly a racist and his actions are driven by racist motivations. In the initial development of the script, Sport was black – the fact that it was ultimately played by Harvey Keitel (a white actor) was apparently because Keitel lobbied Scorsese for the part and that both the producers (and Scorsese) felt that to make Sport black would be irresponsibly inflammatory. Nonetheless, as Stern's summary makes clear, Bickle's psychosis remains primarily informed by his racism:

> Travis is driven by an abhorrence of all that is other…but there are a number of quite specific assaults on non-whites. There is the black youth Travis shoots in the hold-up in the supermarket; on television there are the black couples dancing on *Bandstand* whom he aims his gun at; but most of all there is the decisive encounter with the psychotic passenger who talks about taking a .44 Magnum to his wife's pussy because she is with a 'nigger'.[36]

There are less explicit instances in which Bickle's racial hostility becomes evident: in the café where he stares with barely veiled hatred at several black men who are clearly meant to be pimps; and on the street where he aggressively stares down a young black man who is fooling around. His relationship with the one black taxi driver in the film – Charlie T. – may not be entirely hostile but it is ambiguous.

Once more, however, this Gothic protagonist's status as a white man in and not of the darkness is not entirely secure. How confident can we or Bickle be about his identity as a white man? We know, for example, that he is unable to sleep and that he believes himself to be rotting from within. Bickle is therefore a zombie – a half-dead man. As a 'taxi driver' there is a sense in which his identity as a man is lost to his function, he is a 'cabbie', a thing. Scorsese, for example, observed that Bickle is 'a man who is a fucking vehicle on screen', and the taxi's relentless propulsion through the city streets repeats and reinforces Bickle's psychotic compulsion (he is both driving and being driven). Even his ultimate exercise regime and 'cleaning up' serves to make him less of a subject and more of an object – as the hardening of his body and the home-made prostheses which he uses to attach his guns to his arms make him into a killing *machine*. In fact, Bickle even occupies a similar status to a slave: once a tool of the government (as a marine) he is now enslaved by his own psychosis. From Bickle's delusional point of view, he projects this racially determined anxiety outwards and perceives that the city and, ultimately, Sport therefore embody a direct attack on his integrity, on his 'whiteness'. Once again, the rescue of and desire for a little white girl may be as much about the hero's anxiety in relation to power and race as it is about sex.

Finally, *Taxi Driver* is also significant in relation to the expression and repression of touch. Travis never touches anyone except with a gun. His fear of contagion is closely associated with his fear of, yet desire to, touch others. Betsy's whiteness and her desirability are of course first determined by Bickle's belief that 'they' cannot touch her, and whilst he seemingly desires this touch for himself, it becomes clear that he is only able or willing to point (his fingers like a gun) at others or to touch himself (after the slaughter at the flop house he puts his fingers to his head and 'pulls the trigger').

It would be tempting to suggest that Bickle's fear of touching and of being touched, in alliance with his aggressive homophobia (made clear in his reference to 'buggers and queens' and his demand that Sport – with his gun in his belly – should 'Suck on this') might suggest a repressed homosexuality. I think that like Humbert, Bickle's real orientation is masturbatory – entirely narcissistic. As with Humbert, his desire is actually channelled into an obsessive, delusional fantasy of his own making (in Bickle's case, a series of fantasies). The corrupting narcissism of both Humbert and Bickle is ultimately resolved (temporarily) through a relationship with a little white girl which allows them to act out their pathological fascination with purity and pollution. On one level their ambitions may seem entirely different: Humbert wants to have sex with Dolores, whilst Bickle wants to 'save' Iris from working the streets. Yet in their inability to grant agency or personhood to these little girls or to acknowledge that Dolores and Iris may have their own sexual desires and pleasures, both protagonists share a deep anxiety about the sexual potential, or unruliness, of the little white girl. As little girls, their desires, hopes and pleasures may seem trivial, facile and naïve but they nonetheless express a wanting for 'something else'; a 'wanting' which might otherwise elude or undermine the rigorously hetero-normative (and ultimately generative) white male hierarchy that both Humbert and Bickle are trying so desperately to access.

Elsewhere in *Taxi Driver*, hands and fingers and the association of touch they carry with them recur as motifs. Betsy and her co-worker Tom (Albert Brooks) have a conversation about a (black) newspaper seller who only has two fingers on his hand. This seemingly inane conversation is recalled, not coincidentally, when one of the first injuries that Bickle inflicts on Iris's time-keeper is to blow off three fingers from his hand – preventing him from touching anyone or from taking money easily. Sport's fingers also create an uncomfortable resonance in relation to touch – one peculiar detail of Sport's costume is the polished red nail on his little finger (an affectation associated with heavy coke users at this time), which is disturbingly visible in the scene in which he seduces Iris. Following Stern's interpretation, it is also possible to see that the way this fingernail catches our attention is linked to the scene's effect and its ability to touch us:

> We see him put on the record, his greasy hair, gaudy jewellery and garish coke fingernail, and we hear his guileful murmurings of love. But on another level, there is something 'touching' about the scene, a tenderness that survives the set-up. It functions, I feel, to touch us with ambivalence, to immerse us in a dynamic – around touching – that is central to the film.[37]

The casting of an actual 'little' girl (here, finally, the child character and actress are the same age) establishes a particular quality to the scene. On the one hand, Iris/Foster's 'littleness' is emphasised by the way in which Sport/Keitel almost swamps her, and this reinforces the sense of her manipulation and vulnerability in relation to this predatory adult male. On the other hand, certain qualities that Foster brings as a 'body' and as an actress – she is neither cute nor conventionally pretty, her hair is lank and her body is awkward and tomboyish, her manner adolescent and needy – confuse our preconceptions as to who the little white girl is and perhaps, what it is that she wants.

The fact that Foster starred as the sexually rapacious 'Tallulah' in the children-as-adults musical *Bugsy Malone* (released, like *Taxi Driver*, in 1976) and as the precocious tomboy Audrey in Scorsese's earlier film, *Alice Doesn't Live Here Anymore* (1975), adds a further ambiguity and instability to the figure of this particular 'little white girl'. The scene therefore hints at an uneasy suspicion that Iris may really prefer her life on the street to the life she had before (that is at home, where, she tells Bickle, 'they hated me'). That it is her father and not Iris herself who writes, at the end of the film, to thank Bickle for rescuing his daughter does suggest that perhaps she did not want to return home. In the undertone of menace in the letter itself ('we have taken steps to see that she does not have cause to run away again'), it is hinted that the violence apparently not inflicted by Sport (Iris claims, 'he didn't beat me up or anything like that once') is more prevalent at home. The tension here is that we – the film audience, and Bickle – do not really believe Iris, and we want, need (?) to believe that she is not seeing things as they really are. This is a strange position for the viewing audience to be in when it is remembered that we are watching a film and aligning our perspective with that of a madman. Indeed, as Iris herself points out, in relation to Bickle – 'I don't know who's weirder, you, or me?'

Man on Fire (*Dir. Tony Scott, 2004*)

Man on Fire is based on a best-selling thriller by A.J. Quinnell. Written in the 1970s, the action in the novel takes place in Italy. The first film version, released in 1987 (directed by Elie Chouraqui and starring Scott Glenn as the hero, John Creasy), remained true to the novel's location. The most recent version, now under Scott's direction, was relocated to Mexico and stars Denzel Washington as Creasy and Dakota Fanning as Pita, the little girl he is hired to protect.

This film has been described by its producer, Lucas Foster, as 'one-half love story, one-half revenge movie'. Its narrative arc rather uncannily touches on or revisits elements of most of the films I have discussed. Here again, a little white girl inspires a protective impulse and, ultimately, love in a displaced adult male. Temporarily, their relationship blossoms, bringing fleeting pleasure to both the man and (in this instance) the little girl. The girl is then lost (stolen) and must be retrieved, rescued and avenged by the man in a murderous rampage. The twist here is that in Man on Fire the hero is played by a black man. The conclusion of my argument is an attempt to work through how this revises or literally re-casts the previous history I have explored, following the relationships between adult males and little white girls in American film.

In the promotional documentary for the film, Tony Scott discusses his choice of casting. Intriguingly, Scott had apparently hoped to direct the initial adaptation of the film in the 1980s, but was apparently 'prevented' by the studio. At that time, he suggests, he had thought of Marlon Brando or Robert de Niro for the part of Creasy. Finally developing the project in 2001, he suggests that it wasn't until he met Washington 'by accident' that he thought of 'going that way' with the role. Scott is not entirely clear what he means by this, but the implication is that choosing a black male lead would be a surprising or even a perverse choice, despite the fact that Washington was and is one of the few black male actors who could, at the present time, be cast as a lead in a major Hollywood film. Whilst the choice of Washington, as Scott makes clear, was primarily based on his qualities as an actor, there is also an intriguing aside on his DVD commentary on the film which makes implicit reference to the provocative racial frisson in casting Washington against Dakota Fanning. Fanning (as the producer tells us), had clearly been the only choice for Pita and was evidently cast before the male lead was confirmed. What Scott suggests is that he was intrigued by the possibility of casting this 'big black man' as a complement to this 'tiny little porcelain white nine-year-old' and believed that it would make for a 'fantastic, really odd love story'. This remark, unnervingly, takes us back to a suggestion made over 70 years ago, by D.W. Griffith, apparently in relation to Shirley Temple. Temple Black recalls:

> The pre-eminent legendary giant of motion picture history is D.W. Griffith. By 1935 with his important career waning, he had written to Winfield Sheehan at Fox proposing a controversial idea. 'There is nothing, absolutely nothing, calculated to raise the gooseflesh on the back of an audience more than of a white girl in relation to Negroes' he said.[38]

Temple Black implies that this suggestion may have been behind the casting of Bill Robinson in their first film together, The Little Colonel. The casting of Washington in Man on Fire therefore brings the two threads of my argument together. It stirs up, once again, inconclusive elements and speculations involving race, miscegenation, violence, disavowed sexuality and the possibility of a strange alliance between a black adult male and a white little girl.

It might seem unfair, or stretching a point, to suggest that the film is about child sexuality or about the romantic, erotic love of an adult male for a little white girl. Scott insists that the relationship between Creasy and Pita be seen as if it were father to daughter. In the promotional documentary, Washington himself refers to the (unspoken) back story of his character who lost his wife and daughters, which would suggest that Pita acts as a substitute for this loss, and that he stands in loco parentis to her, especially since her parents are so frequently absent. Yet this version of the relationship is not quite coherent or sustained, either in relation to Scott's commentary or within the film itself. Scott's commentary suggests – over a scene in which Pita gives Creasy a present of a medallion (featuring St. Jude, the patron saint of lost causes) – that her present is 'like an engagement ring'. Over an earlier scene, in which Pita and Creasy say their goodnights to one another, and which concludes with Pita happily spinning and dancing with her teddy bear into her bed, Scott comments that that sequence is a pivotal moment because Pita senses that now, 'she's got him'. Her evident excitement and Scott's summary suggest that her pleasure, while not sexual, is certainly romantic in nature. Creasy's curious positioning as both the object and subject of Pita's affections is made clear by the later revelation that she has called her teddy bear 'Creasy' and that in her diary she has written, over and over, 'I love you Creasy bear', demonstrating that her love for Creasy (the man), both incorporates and reaches beyond the child's love for a 'transitional object' – the object which, in psychoanalyst Donald Winnicott's terms, creates the bridge between the child's inner world and the real (exterior) world, and which often takes the form of a favoured toy, or blanket. As both 'bear' and 'man', Creasy's status is akin to the wolf in 'Little Red Riding Hood', who both is and isn't an (inappropriate) male suitor for the little girl.

In the novel, the romantic and possibly sexual elements of their relationship are much more explicit. Relatively early on in the story, Creasy has a brief sexual encounter with Pita's mother, which acts as a kind of substitute for the impossible sexual relationship with the little girl. This is alluded to in the first film adaptation, but in Scott's film there is no sexual relationship between Creasy and Lisa (Pita's mother), although the physical similarity between mother and daughter does give some hint as to how, in the novel, the sexual desirability of the little girl is projected onto the mother. More explicitly, in the novel, during the little girl's kidnapping, she is repeatedly raped by her captors. This is not suggested in Scott's film adaptation; one of the ironies that Scott and his screen-writer Brian Helgeland add to the story is that the head of the kidnapping ring is a family man and makes the ransom calls with his own children playing or sleeping around him.

The sexual or romantic potential of the relationship between Creasy and Pita lies outwith Scott's version of the film, although the contradictions inherent in Scott's personal commentary do suggest that the erotic and romantic aspects of their relationship – as it is described in the novel – have informed his film in some way. Nonetheless, like Bill Robinson and Shirley Temple before them, Fanning's and Washington's physical contact is limited: to two brief embraces (after her successful swim meet and at the end of the film) and to holding hands. Yet, also like Temple and Robinson, Fanning's and Washington's characters share a particular intimacy based on physicality and mimicry. Like 'Uncle Billy's' relationship with Temple's characters, Creasy helps Pita to learn a physical skill – specifically, he helps her to react faster to the starter's gun and thus improve her swimming (thus, it is a skill, like tap dancing, that is about timing), and the increasing speed of her response (which ultimately leads to her winning a race) is a shared physical pleasure for both Pita and Creasy. In the novel, and in the first film adaptation, the sport Creasy teaches the little girl is to run track. Scott suggests that he made the change from running to swimming so that he could include a series of sequences in which we see Pita swimming from under the water, which allows him to create what he suggests is a foreshadowing of the darker story to come. Water thereby becomes a kind of motif in the film, a link between Creasy and Pita, and thus legitimates the 'baptisms' later undertaken by Creasy in different pools after each revenge killing. Each time, as Creasy pushes himself under the water, blood from his wounds is released, reminding us that he is critically injured. In these sequences – in which we are seeing, perhaps, Creasy's memory, fantasy or desire – the small (ghostly) figure of Pita can be seen swimming over Creasy and his blood as it disperses into the water. In these scenes' slickness, odd seductiveness and symbolic messiness, Scott's origins as an advertising director are evident. The sequences are manipulative, yet if they act as an advertisement, what it is exactly that is being sold to us remains uncomfortably unclear.

In an earlier scene, which consolidates the increasing intimacy between Pita and Creasy, the two have a conversation in which they discuss concubines – a conversational gambit which seems uncannily appropriate. More than the oddly apt content of this conversation, I am interested in their final exchange (which according to Scott's commentary was apparently improvised by Washington and Fanning). Having made Creasy smile, Pita notes this and teases and reprimands him, indicating that it is the first time she has seen him do so. Creasy, semi-flirtatiously, refutes this and they stage a brief contest as to who will smile first (which Pita promptly loses). In this familiar game there is no real erotic frisson, but it is intriguing that they mirror one another, highlighting an alliance between them that is based on a gesture (smiling) so often demanded of little girls and subservient black men but which otherwise is notably absent from both actors' performances. A further irony is that qualities shared by Washington and Fanning as actors are seriousness and self-possession. Their improvised game of (withholding) a smile is haunted by the sense in which 'little girls' and 'black men' are always obliged to be self-conscious as performers and that they therefore share an intuitive understanding that smiling is an expression which has a particularly ambivalent quality (or history) for them, as performers and as individuals. White men – unlike women, little girls and black men – do not expect to be told to smile by others, and would rarely employ smiling as protection, or as supplication in their everyday lives. From this perspective, the forced, mechanical smile of a little white girl – we can recall, for instance, Lucy's pathetic smile in Broken Blossoms – and the stereotypical 'minstrel' smile, are alike in their lack of spontaneity and conciliatory aspects. The fact that up until this moment Creasy has not smiled not only suggests that his apparently spontaneous expression is all the more valuable, but reveals quite how unusual he has been, as an unsmiling black man who is effectively working as a servant. At the very moment at which Fanning and Washington are being at their most 'natural and spontaneous' as performers (in improvisation), there is an allusion to how their characters' low status in the social hierarchy means that part of what they share is that their everyday presentation of self is often about maintaining an appropriate 'face' via which they must effectively mask their actual feelings and ambitions.

Figure 11   Creasy (Denzel Washington) teaches Pita (Dakota Fanning) to swim, in *Man on Fire* (Tony Scott, 2004)

In some ways, both Scott and the film avoid, or at least downplay, the fact of Washington's blackness. The first comment that Lisa (a white Texan) makes to Creasy, for example, while shaking his hand, is 'You're an American', indicating that in the context of Mexico (and as opposed to her husband and the Mexican kidnappers) Creasy (and by default, Washington) has become an honorary white man. (Morrison observes: 'American means white, and Africanist people struggle to make the term applicable to themselves with ethnicity and hyphen after hyphen after hyphen.'[39] It seems that it is geography which allows Washington/Creasy to possess 'American-ness'.) The fact that the only two white men who do feature in the film are played by actors who carry with them a particular history also allows Creasy/Washington to substitute for the absent white hero. The casting of Christopher Walken, known for his weird, comic and villainous roles, and Mickey Rourke – his boxer's face distorted by age, hard living and plastic surgery – as the only significant white male characters in the film, means that the actual white men within the film appear as eccentric, damaged and oddly alien figures.

Washington's actions (in which he kills only Mexican men, since it is Pita's father – a Mexican – who kills Rourke's character) might be read as a recasting of a familiar story of American imperialism, where the American acts as the lone gunman (another cowboy, or a Rambo-like figure) who cleans up the mess in Mexico City, and where, in this instance, it is Mexicans and damaged white men who serve as the alien others who must be punished. In this way, the film allows mainstream audiences to be sympathetic to a 'big black man' who claims ownership of a little white girl and legitimates the extraordinary violence and torture in a series of executions that are wincingly intimate and sexual in nature. In the first attack Creasy cuts off his victim's fingers, one by one, and in a later scene he sticks a bomb up the man's anus and uses the count-down time to question him, before leaving him to explode.

Despite the extraordinary violence that Creasy orchestrates, Pita is 'right' to love and trust her big black protector. Yet the film cannot allow Pita and Creasy a future together with Creasy as her father or lover. It seems inevitable, and we suspect from the very beginning, that Creasy must die. (In fact, we are even given a brief glimpse of what will be revealed as Creasy's death scene at the start of the film.) This is a reversal of the original story: in the book and in the first film adaptation, Creasy only appears to die and is instead rescued via a version of witness protection. In the novel, the little girl has actually been killed by her kidnappers and Creasy is returned to a safe haven and a relationship with an adult woman. More daringly, in the first film adaptation, an epilogue suggests that Creasy will establish a romantic and thus presumably a sexual relationship with the little girl who, in this version, has survived, but is clearly damaged by her ordeal. It is not surprising that neither of these outcomes is possible for Washington as Creasy. Rather, the accumulation of rather obvious religious symbolism throughout the film – the medallion, Creasy's conversation with the nun at Pita's school, his reading of the bible and his final, Christ-like endurance – establishes Creasy's actions and motivation as 'saintly', and implies that he is an 'Uncle Tom' figure, a noble slave who sacrifices himself for the greater good – to secure the little white girl's safety.

My point is that it matters that Washington is black. I am not insinuating that Scott, or his screen-writer, are racist. But I do claim that the racial dynamic of the film is important. In insisting upon the importance of race in the narrative, I am particularly struck by Morrison's comment on the avoidance of racial interpretations in literature and in media. She states that 'Pouring rhetorical acid on the fingers of a black hand may indeed destroy the prints, but not the hand.'[40] Here she is referring to what she sees as a liberal disinclination to play (what Linda Williams has called) 'the race card'. This has meant that race as an aspect of ideology and politics is avoided as too controversial or inappropriate in a supposedly post-Civil Rights, and politically correct United States. What she contends is that the 'black hands' which serve in so many stories, often acting as key points of contact and exchange, should not be underestimated or ignored. The fact that she uses the analogy of a 'black hand' is particularly apt, as it is Creasy's hands – damaged by previous torture, bearing witness to his use as a tool by government agencies – which serve to remind us of Creasy/Washington as a body, as having a specific skin that he is living in. Washington's hands are frequently focused on by the camera. The camera seems drawn to those moments in which he cradles his head in these hands, or when he slowly strokes his head, first in a drunken stupor and later in anguish. We also see his hands in close up, as he catches bullets in his palm, and we are conscious of the shape, size and colour of his hand again, as he reaches down, in slow motion, to help Pita from the pool, clasping her 'little white hand' in his. Once more, race and the significance of touch are brought together.

To acknowledge that race informs the sexual and political dynamic of the film is not to insist upon an entirely negative reading. The sensual excess of the film certainly encourages a mixture of responses – the viewer is shamelessly manipulated and provoked but not always in the same direction. The vibrancy and frenzied nature of the visual image, the strangeness of certain

Figure 12   Creasy's (Denzel Washington) damaged hands, in *Man on Fire*
(Dir. Tony Scott, 2004)

voices and music (a diegetic and non-diegetic world of sound which includes Linda Ronstadt, Lisa Gerrard, Kinky, Chopin and the Nine Inch Nails), the mixture of languages (subtitles dancing provocatively across the screen), the baroque setting, the confused symbolism of the scenes in which Creasy bathes in his own blood, as well as Fanning's strange and somehow wizened charm, all hint that 'something else', or something more, is happening than can be properly expressed. It is not always clear what it is that we are meant to feel, or believe, either in relation to Creasy and Pita, the representation of Mexico City or the 'idea' of the American family in the twenty-first century. Certain touches – instances where the bodies on screen appear ridiculous and material – tug at the fabric of the film, unravelling its edges. The fact that Creasy is wearing white rubber gloves in the scene just after he has just inserted a bomb up the corrupt police officer's anus, or that Creasy encourages Pita to burp deliberately throughout her hated piano lesson, as well as Creasy's gentle stroking of the pages of Pita's diary after her kidnapping; these moments that are legitimated by the story, but somehow, their presence is both excessive and oddly disturbing.

The depth and complexity of the impossible/possible relations on which the film touches – fathers and daughters, adult men and little girls, modern slavery, greed and grief – are all, unavoidably, relations affected by race, violence and sex. The fact that these relations coalesce in a film in which the 'wanting' of a little girl haunts the narrative creates an odd climate which the film cannot

Figure 13   Creasy's (Denzel Washington) white gloves, in *Man on Fire* (Dir. Tony Scott, 2004)

make coherent. There is a sense that the little girl's wanting – which is both more and less than a silly crush – is the real something that cannot be expressed yet remains a powerful, disruptive force. Somehow we forget that it is her love which has inspired the extreme violence which dominates the second half of the film. In the sense in which the film both demonstrates yet occludes the violent emotions that Pita feels and has provoked, the film takes on the register of melodrama. As Linda Williams suggests:

> Increasingly…it is within the irrational, fantasmic, and paranoid realm of the melodramatic 'text of muteness' that race takes on a heightened mode of expressivity as a dialectic of feelings – of sympathy and antipathy – that dare not speak its name.[41]

In conclusion, I want to remind the reader that, as I said at the beginning, this chapter has been marked and inspired by the absence of the little black girl. The casting of Fanning (white-blonde and translucently fair-skinned) as the daughter of a Mexican man, albeit with a white North American mother, makes this absence painfully obvious, even when, perhaps particularly when, her protector is black. That Pita is small, blonde and fragile-looking, re-creates an all too familiar scenario in which the little girl must always be white because for her to matter so much, or simply for her to matter enough, she must inherit the legacy – or carry the burden of the fantasy – that is sustained by all those other 'little white girls' loved and lost, stolen and avenged.

Figure 14   Creasy (Denzel Washington) and Pita (Dakota Fanning) embrace, in *Man on Fire* (Dir. Tony Scott, 2004)

Chapter Three

Mud and Fairytales: Children in Films about War

When I was about eight years old I remember going to see a screening of *Gone with the Wind* with my mother, aunt and younger cousin. The spectacle gripped us all; however, I remember being surprised when – at the point during the escape from Atlanta when the horses pulling Rhett and Scarlett's carriage collapse and have to be left behind to die – my cousin burst into inconsolable tears. I knew that my cousin was crying because she was very fond of horses. I'm not, particularly, and at this point I think, for the first time perhaps, I realised that film-makers manipulated their audiences, and that the death of horses for some people could seem worse than the loss of human lives. Thirty-five years later, I'm sitting in my office at work watching a Japanese animated film, *Grave of the Fireflies*. The story involves two young siblings (an older brother and his little sister) who try to fend for themselves in the aftermath of the firebombing of their village and the death of their mother. After about 30 minutes, when it becomes evident that both children will ultimately die and as the little girl, in particular, becomes weaker and weaker, I begin to cry, and cry all the way (for at least another 60 minutes) to the end of the film and beyond. I know that, in part, I'm crying because I have young children, including a little girl about the same age, shape and demeanour as Setsuko, the little girl in the film.

Tears and emotion erupt when the innocent – dumb animals, little children – are seen to suffer. It is not just that my cousin and I felt sorry for the horses, or children, but that their suffering was not their fault. Animals and children are 'perfect victims', since they are blameless, they make the wrongs of war seem all the more wrong, and the viewer's righteous and explosive response all the more satisfactory. Satisfactory because morally it seems uncomplicated (horses and children 'did not start' the war) and because it puts the viewer in a superior position. We are feeling sorry for those who cannot care for themselves and for those we believe should be cared for as some kind of universal right. The innocence ascribed to children and animals often makes them an object, if not the subject, of films about war, in a strategy designed to provoke emotion and moral satisfaction.

By aligning children and animals, I am following an argument made by John O.Thompson, who, in turn, is developing observations made by André Bazin, which suggests that our response to children on screen is a form of 'anthropomorphism'. In a critique of a film made just after the Second World War – It Happened in Europe (Geza Radvanyi, 1947) – Bazin suggests that this film and others like it 'treat childhood precisely as if it were open to our understanding and empathy: they are made in the name of anthropomorphism'.[1] Here, as Thompson confirms, Bazin is implying that the way in which we perceive the otherness of childhood is akin to the perceived difference between men and animals. In both instances, there are circumstances in which adults disavow this otherness and see animals and children as entirely open to interpretation rather than 'other' – that is, possessed by intentions or a consciousness we do not recognise. By using the term anthropomorphism, Bazin is suggesting that in many films about war adults use children as a blank screen on to which they can project adult emotions and fears in a manner that is similar to the way in which we often ascribe – anthropomorphise – human qualities and habits to animals. Bazin goes on to argue:

> We demand of them [children] signs of complicity, and the audience quickly becomes enraptured and teary when children show feelings that are usually associated with grown-ups. We are thus seeking to contemplate ourselves in them: ourselves plus the innocence, awkwardness and naivete we lost. This kind of cinema moves us, but aren't we in fact just feeling sorry for ourselves?[2]

In films involving war, children are often ciphers for adult anxieties, fantasies and fears. It remains necessary for children to be different from adults since this makes them blameless. Yet since adult viewers can not, or chose not to understand what the children on screen are really thinking or feeling (or what they even appear to be thinking and feeling), there is a contradictory belief that the child can be other (innocent and vulnerable) while at the same time acting as a screen for the projection of adult emotions and fears (making the child 'like' the adult and somehow 'other'). This legitimates feelings of anger and pity, perceptions of right and wrong, despite the moral complexity inherent in any representation of conflict.

In a similar move, one child's experience, or more accurately their presence as a small, emotive figure, can be used to 'stand in' for many deaths. In these instances, the child's narrative function is effectively to act as a metonym for wider suffering. Perhaps the most well-known example of this in contemporary cinema is Steven Spielberg's use of the 'little girl in the red coat' as the only spot of colour in the otherwise black-and-white cinematography of Schindler's List. The little girl's passage from ghetto to crematorium is tracked, as the red of her coat makes her progress visible even at a distance, although who she is, what she feels and the details of what actually happen to her are never fully realised. Her presence and function is akin to the obligatory shot of a child's doll, often captured in news footage or in fictive reconstructions of the aftermath of disasters such as aeroplane crashes or terrorist bombs. In these sequences, the doll's body is a substitute for the child's body, whereas the body of the little girl in Schindler's List is used to remind the audience of the individuality of all the bodies destroyed in the Holocaust. Yet since it is the coat that is as important as the girl herself – her significance is that we can see her because she wears a red coat – ironically it is the individuality of the little girl herself which is sacrificed.

The erasure of the individual child's subjectivity can also be seen in Denise Youngblood's commentary on Ivan's Childhood, in which she suggests:

> Ivan's Childhood is more than a film about one child's childhood; it is a film about the fate of all children during the Second World War. (Tarkovoskii's use of the generic Russian name 'Ivan', the name given protagonists in most folktales, is one important clue).[3]

The metonymic function of the child in war films can be identified across a range of movies and not only those that address world wars. For example, in her discussion of Guillermo del Toro's The Devil's Backbone, a film set in an orphanage during the Spanish Civil

War, Anne Hardcastle claims of the child-ghost, Santi, that he comes to represent 'all the victims of Spanish fascism':

> In the context of this traumatic haunting, Santi comes to represent not merely one unjustly murdered boy, but all the victims of Spanish fascism relegated to the dustbin of history yet still eerily present as ghostly echoes of a past not entirely forgotten in the modern, cosmopolitan image of democratic Spain.[4]

In relation to the Spanish Civil War, the Spanish child actor Ana Torrent was frequently interpreted in both popular and academic contexts as representative in this way. Whilst neither of the two most well-known films made when she was a child, El espíritu de la colmena (Spirit of the Beehive) and Cría Cuervos (Cry Ravens), were explicitly 'war' films (although they both reflect on the legacy of the Spanish Civil War and the long dictatorship of Franco under which they were both made), Torrent functioned as an apparently innocent and readily interpreted representative of 'Spain' in troubled times.

Marsha Kinder suggests of Torrent's performance in Spirit of the Beehive:

> This film marks the screen debut of Ana Torrent the child actress who most vividly represents the children of Franco. With a brooding sensitivity that captures every nuance of emotion and perception within their field of vision, her luminous dark eyes confront us with a bold knowing gaze, conveying a precocious intelligence, passion and intensity that seem almost ominous in their power. Yet her pale oval face and slender birdlike frame create a fragility that also marks her as a victim – a delicate instrument for the registering of pain.[5]

The artificial and unstable nature of this attribution, as Paul Julian Smith has argued, is revealed if we consider that the politics and history of Spain were and remain contested. This means that what could be 'seen' (or expressed) in relation to the Spanish public sphere and seemingly what, in turn, could be seen (or read) from Torrent's face and expression necessarily alters over time. Torrent, who was just five when she made Spirit of the Beehive, was noted (as Kinder observes above), for her pale, impassive face and large dark eyes. Yet, as Smith demonstrates, what this face meant or revealed to the audience changed over time. He writes:

> While in the late 1980s Dunia read the meaning of those eyes as being that 'there was still a place [in the late Francoist Spain] for a forbidden ideal of freedom', earlier interpretations are quite different. An extended interview in Ya praises not only the 'naturalness of her performance' but also the 'simplicity of her Hispanic face', claiming that there are many 'Anas' in Spain, many young girls of her generation, facing so many difficulties with such a great capacity for endurance. The 'magical face' invoked in Telva magazine (15 March 1976) is also quite specifically Spanish, held to embody both the spirit of the nation (there are frequent references to the dark eyes of Goya portraits) and the history of that nation at a particular moment.[6]

The unreadable face of the child is therefore often interpreted or anthropomorphised to fit the political and emotional agenda of the interested adult critic. And the child, as a vivid and emotive presence, is all too often a vehicle for adult concerns and fears, and fails to act or represent its own interests and desires.

Another way in which the child figure acts as a vehicle for an adult agenda is in relation to the autobiographical story: the child that is now the adult author or director who remembers and revisits his wartime experiences. Some of the most famous films about war which feature children are either directed by men remembering their own wartime experience (Au Revoir Les Enfants, Hope and Glory) or based on memoirs or semi-autobiographical stories (Empire of the Sun, Diamonds of the Night, Fateless, Mirror). In each case the child figure is double-voiced; the child's limited and often unconventional view of the world and war is framed by the adult's knowingness and retrospective understanding. In Au Revoir Les Enfants, the film's poignant ending, which presents us with the forced departure of the three Jewish boys hidden at the protagonist's Catholic boarding school, it is anchored by an adult voiceover confirming their fate: which is, as most adult viewers would have surmised, to die at Auschwitz. The protagonist's earlier 'look back' – where he unintentionally gives away his Jewish friend by turning round to look at him in the presence of a Gestapo officer – refers to the primary motivation for the film itself: for the director to look back, to relive the past with all the immanent intensity of the presentness of childhood but tempered with the knowledge of loss located in a future yet to come. In this film and others like it there is an explicit tension between the apparent immediacy and openness of childhood experience – it is vivid and mundane, it makes the general, abstract story of war personal, unique and accessible – and the requirements of the adult who remembers and who may feel the need to make sure the viewer is aware of the wider history of which their story is a part. Yet the qualities of childish experience, which is narcissistic, fragmented, temporally chaotic, often context-less, are counter to the demands of the conventional narratives of history, which construct an omniscient and chronological perspective, thereby producing comprehensible, coherent stories informed by cause and effect. As Carolyn Steedman suggests:

> History offers us the fantasy that it may be found; that out of all the bits and pieces left behind, the past may be reconstructed, conjured before the eyes: found. Childhood – the idea of childhood – on the other hand, may tell us that the search is futile (though it may be necessary and sometimes compulsive); tells us that the lost object is not to be found, for the very search for the past in each of us changes the past as we go along, so that the lost thing is not the same now, as it was before.[7]

Here Steedman is suggesting that childhood, in its innocence, intensity of experience and its personal veracity, offers a compulsive route back to the past, but that it simultaneously reveals that this past may be changed or challenged in the process. It is not just the content of the past – what was seen, what happened when – that is challenged by the nature of childhood, but also the framework within which these events are interpreted: conventions as to how 'history' should be told, or criteria which dictate what events will be important in the future and should therefore be included. Films such as *Pan's Labyrinth*, *Tin Drum*, *Les Jeux Interdits* (*Forbidden Games*) and *Spirit of the Beehive* demonstrate how the child figure allows for (or really demands) the side-lining or ignoring of what is normally considered important, whether this is the intrigues of the adult world or the facts of the war. In these films and others, the framework through which the story is told is marked by temporal abnormalities and informed by narrative forms which might seem odd or inappropriate, such as the fairytale: history is told differently, presented as magical and irrational.

By making the child the figure that witnesses or participates in events there is what amounts to a form of prosopopoeia: that is, a conversation between the living (the adult survivor) and the dead (the child self, who may or may not be alive at the end of the film). As a practice, prosopopoeia is continually open to the possibility, indeed the likelihood, that what is being projected on to the 'dead' (here the child) may not be true. This is because just as the dead cannot really speak to the living, the child cannot speak 'properly' to the adult they have since become. Whereas the dead are beyond or without speech, the child cannot speak because as a child they are (or were) yet to become fully articulate (sensible). Prosopopoeia is a form of projection; a form of ventriloquism in which the living speak for or through the dead, just as the adult revisits, reshapes and retells his childhood experiences as if he were (still) a child.

In some analyses this projection is complicated and understood to be more of an exchange, a dialogue of sorts, suggesting that neither the dead nor the living remain unchanged by their interaction with one another. Following Emmanuel Levinas, Colin Davis suggests:

> The dead may not speak in any literal sense but they do signify, since the survivor continues to be the uncomprehending addressee of signs which cannot be attributed to any living subject. Death is both non-sense and a breach which opens up sense to unsuspected possibilities.[8]

Whilst the dead do not literally 'speak' to the living, the living continue to be affected by the dead in ways they cannot quite comprehend. As I have suggested, the child (remembered or reproduced) cannot speak 'properly' to the adult: and this adult self, I would suggest, also becomes the 'uncomprehending addressee of signs which cannot be attributed to any living subject'. This is because childhood (which is now actually dead to the adult who survives) is other (unknown and incomprehensible) but still continues to inform the adult self. Following on from this, it is possible that the unavoidable (mis-) understanding produced by the child's presence (as memory, as representation) and the adult (as writer, director or viewer) could also provide opportunities for the signification of 'unsuspected possibilities'. This will be possible even if the adults who make the film – producers, directors and/ or writers – are not remembering their own childhoods, but are aiming to represent events 'as if' they are from a child's perspective. Many of the most intriguing examples of war films which feature children do seem to incorporate and negotiate nonsense, and offer up breaches that distort and distend their narrative structure and realist conventions. In doing so they make it possible to sense the unsuspected possibilities or surprises that Levinas suggests may emerge when the dead speak to the living.

'This Is a Story of a Man Marked by an Image from His Childhood'

This sentence opens Chris Marker's short film La Jetee (The Pier). Appropriately, it is a film about time-travel and the dialogue between the living and the dead. However, the central protagonist is not (or no longer) a child but an adult sent back in time from a post-apocalyptic future. The protagonist-as-child only features at the very beginning and end of the film (although children do, non-coincidentally, appear elsewhere within the film even if their presence is not remarked upon). In many ways, I think this film articulates the formal and thematic qualities of films which feature the child and war. It demonstrates how the child figure and childhood enable film-makers to radically and creatively re-tell the past and, in particular, inform us about the strangeness, the murky ambiguities and the real trauma of war. It does this primarily because it is a film about memory: the story involves a man from the future who is obliged to undergo a series of experiments which seemingly enable him to travel in time, initially to the past and then to the future. He is chosen as a subject for these experiments because he has a particularly strong connection to a specific moment in his past: 'he sees a man die on the pier at Orly a few days before the outbreak of World War Three. But it is the face of the woman that draws him back.' For the man who remembers, it is the woman who draws him back in time and not the child he was, nor the man he sees dying that day. Ultimately, this is a fatal misrecognition and a misunderstanding, for at the end of the film he (along with the viewer) realises that the man who dies that day is the protagonist himself. It is possible that had he looked differently at this image from his past he might have attempted to escape his fate. What the film plays out is the intensity and limitations of childhood memory and the way in which adult perspectives (here the woman as a mysterious object of desire) obscure, and thus allow for a fatal misconception of what may be most significant in those memories.

The film is also significant because it is refers directly to the impact of war on a child. This is not as straightforward as it seems, as the film is not actually 'about' war, and in fact what is seen happening in the film happens *before* and *after* World War Three. However, the film is absolutely infected and informed by the experience of war – and specifically the experience of a child during war. Yet it refuses to tell us or show us this story. Instead, the protagonist's experience as a child during war time is one of the many gaps in the film, a narrative gap which mirrors the formal gaps famously inherent in the film itself, which is made up almost entirely of a series of still photographs rather than moving film images. In a further temporal confusion, the devastation of World War Three is represented in the film by archive photos of the devastation of the Second World War.

Gaps, breaks and breaches recur in different ways in many of the films I will explore. Andre Tarkovsky's films – Mirror and Ivan's Childhood – both employ, to a greater or lesser extent, breaks and omissions as they tell their stories of the child's experience and memories of the Second World War. Even a relatively conventional film such as Empire of the Sun is distinguished by a significant break in the middle of the narrative (a temporal jump of four years) which results in the protagonist's story, as in La Jetee, focusing not on the war but on the beginning and the end of the boy's war-time experience. In Empire of the Sun, the repeated scene of the boy-protagonist (Jamie) cycling – at the beginning of the film through his abandoned suburban mansion and, then at the end of the film through the now abandoned prison camp – hints

113

that like *La Jetée* the child's experience of temporality is not linear but circular. At the beginning of the film, the cycling heralds the end (of Jamie's childhood) and at the end of the film when he cycles again, we are being prompted to recognise (another) beginning (Jamie's future after the war). In *La Jetée* this circularity is catastrophic: the beginning of the film is literally the end (for the protagonist).

In other films, such as *Cry Ravens, Diamonds of the Night, Pan's Labyrinth* and *Spirit of the Beehive*, interweaving temporalities and ellipses provide a framework riddled with gaps and inconsistencies which represent the child's experience and, in some instances, the interference of the adult's memory with that experience. In *Ivan's Childhood* the recurring visual motif of the cobweb, a fractured series of circles of which Ivan appears at the centre, implies the paradoxical strength, real fragility and incompleteness of the child's perception. The cobweb is seen in the very first image of the film, within Ivan's dream. Later in the film the structure of the web is recalled, most overtly when Ivan encounters a bewildered old man in the ruins of his house.(See figure 1.)

The formal structure of Marker's film (a photo-montage) recalls, as several critics have noted, the French form of 'comic strip', the *bande dessinée*. It is this narrative architecture, often closely associated with (but not necessarily exclusive to) stories for children which is explicitly or implicitly recalled in several films. Two significant films – *Grave of the Fireflies* and *Barefoot Gen* – are actually drawn animation and thus literally graphic narratives. *Barefoot Gen* was based on a pre-existing Manga – a Japanese form of comic strip, or a kind of graphic serial. The structure, colour and composition of the comic strip are also recalled in several of the live action films, most explicitly in Guillermo Del Toro's two Spanish Civil War films that feature children as protagonists, *The Devil's Backbone* and *Pan's Labyrinth*. The feel or sensibility of the comic strip is also implicit in other films, such as *Come and See* and *Empire of the Sun*, which employ an intensely graphic sensibility, a mode of story-telling and presentation that is reliant on symbolic composition, static poses and extremes of expression.

The space between the frames in Marker's film allows for another key effect, the separation of sound from image. The sounds in the film include the voice of the narrator, jet engines, the whispered sound of the experimenters. The heavy buzz of the underground bunkers, the sounds of birds and children playing. Although many of the sounds illustrate or apparently anchor the images, there is a perceptible dislocation of sound from image. The sound, detached or relieved of its normal function, achieves solidity and a symbolic complexity aside from, or over and above, its relation to the image. This creates a series of effects in relation to the experience and understanding of time. Susan Howe, for instance, suggests:

> La Jetee, composed almost completely of photo stills, begins abruptly with a violent out-of-field-movement-sound-image, the roar of revving and hovering jet engines...Immediately time could be going either way.[9]

The jet engines imply, by association, the idea and possibility of travel but there is a strange separation of sound from image (we hear a sound implying motion played over images which are immobile). The sound refers to our dislocation in time: we are at once in a putative real present (1962 at Paris airport) which is revealed by the voiceover to be the history of a possible future that has not taken place ('a few days before the outbreak of World War Three') and which, simultaneously, is also a memory from the future (since the man is remembering his past). The felt gap between sound and image allows for a play with, or a suspension of, linear historical temporality. The clarity of the sound, the close proximity of the voiceover and the careful selection of relatively few sounds exacerbate the silences and make even the most natural of sounds (bird song for instance) resonate oddly. We are obliged not just to hear the sounds but to listen to them, troubling the superficial associations they initially suggest.

Sound is important in many of the films under discussion: in the Tin Drum, the child-dwarf protagonist, Oskar, is often selectively mute, but his obsession with his toy tin drum creates a noise that serves, at different times, to orchestrate both his collaboration with and his subversion of the organised sounds and music of the Nazi Germany in which he lives. In one significant sequence, Oskar hides underneath a podium erected to stage a fascist parade. Hidden from sight but audible, he uses his drumming to transmute the strident sounds of the Nazi's militaristic music into a waltz, ultimately disrupting the parade. His other special talent – a piercing scream that can destroy glass – leads to the sound of windows smashing that is indelibly associated with Kristallnacht, and it also gives voice to Oskar's inarticulate rage and anxiety, acting as symptom and weapon.

At one stage in *Come and See*, the boy's temporary deafness (caused by the shelling of the partisan camp he has joined) reinforces his dislocation from the world he knew. The prolonged period in which he and the audience are unable to hear properly confirms his isolation and our increasing disorientation. It is an inversion of his (and our) earlier position, in which the boy hears, but is unable to listen to, concerned adults – an old man and his mother – who try to explain, through inference if not directly through their words, that war is terrible and not a game. Now his muffled hearing means that he (and we) can no longer really hear or comprehend what is being said. Instead, on his return to his home village which has been destroyed by the advancing Nazi army, we are now obliged simply to listen to the anxiety and fear manifest in the timbre and tone of the wailing and lamenting voices of the remaining villagers, not to what they actually say.

In Jan Nemec's film, *Diamonds of the Night*, adapted from a semi-autobiographical short story by Arnost Lustig, there is an entirely self-conscious use and dislocation of sound. From the beginning of the film, where we encounter two young boys running through a field and up a steep muddy hill, there is a deliberate mismatch between sound and image. The cinematography is in black and white, the camera hand-held and the sequence is shot almost entirely in close-up – close to the faces, hands and feet of the boys as they make their escape. We discover later that they are running from a train that is carrying them between two concentration camps. Some of the sounds we hear, a train, gun shots and yelling, seem initially appropriate, as they both tell the story and are in line with their apparent source within the context of the film. At the same time, the exhaled breaths and grunts of the boys as they run up the hill are too close and dry so that in terms of the auditory space being created, it is as if the boys are right beside the spectator rather than located within the environment of the scene. Our proximity in relation to the sound the boys' bodies make is sustained throughout the film and brings us necessarily close to and intimate with the boys and their plight. Significantly, the emphasis awarded to the small sounds their bodies make as they encounter the environment around them – breathing, sighs, feet sloshing in mud and the sound of rain falling on their skin – makes these sounds (unusually for film) as important as speech. It is some way into the film before either of the boys speaks at all, and it comes as a shock. The surprise is that our relationship with the boys has advanced so far and that we have become involved in their journey without needing them to speak. There are good reasons for the lack of speech: the boys do not need to speak to each other and they need to save energy. Later, we discover that their mouths are so parched and ulcerous that simply eating bread causes them to bleed. The absence of speech also relates to the boys' inability adequately to describe what has happened to them, and their silence, another kind of gap, powerfully evokes the unspeakable aspects of their experience.

Elsewhere in the film, sound effects are used in a modernist, playful manner to both disgust and confuse the viewer. In an extended sequence, we watch as a group of old men, the 'home guard' of the territory, celebrate their capture of the boys by eating and drinking. Not only does this activity remind us directly of the boys' hunger but the sounds of eating and drinking are loud and close, making the men appear all the more disgusting as they chew and slurp their way through their food. In a climactic sequence in which the boys appear to have been shot, the sound of gunfire is replaced by applause, this substitution seeming to suggest a bitter flourish, implying that this is now 'the end' of the boys' tale. Yet the sequence which follows apparently shows the boys walking (paradoxically) away, deeper and deeper into the forest. This implies that the use of the wrong (or a non-naturalistic) sound at the moment of the boys' death is designed to make the ending less 'real'. Lustig, who wrote the screenplay, says of this ending that he could not in good conscience let the boys die without ambiguity: it would have been like 'killing himself', as the story was based on his own experience, and thus was one which he survived.

Another film which deliberately uses sound and the tension between the absence and presence of speech to imply the impossibility of 'speaking' is *Spirit of the Beehive*. The film begins with a mobile cinema being set up in Ana's village. She, her sister Isabel, other children and many adults from the village then sit down to watch James Whale's version of *Frankenstein* (although the film itself is set in the mid-1940s, this version of *Frankenstein* was first released in 1931). As Xon de Ros suggests, the inclusion of this specific film – made during the early years of 'talkies' in Hollywood – is significant since the monster does not actually speak. This makes the monster, as a cinematic creation, perverse, since he is an iconic figure who does not speak at the very historical moment when synchronised sound and speech were becoming possible. This is an irony made all the more peculiar when it is recalled that in the original novel the monster does become fully articulate. De Ros suggests:

> The presence of Frankenstein's monster, together with the borrowing of features from the silent film, serve to reinstate speech in a visual, rhythmic, gestural and sensory totality where it is no longer the central and determining element.[10]

Highlighting key sequences in the film, notably when the two girls wait and listen for a train by railway tracks, de Ros goes on to argue that 'It is not as if in the film the visual and the aural are disconnected but their relationship has become more complex and autonomous.'[11] Certain sounds – bees buzzing, the sound of wind, a train whistle and the crackle of fire burning – recur at key points in the film, bridging image sequences and dominating the sound track. In this manner they acquire solidity and an ability to communicate that overwhelms their illustrative function in relation to the images they accompany. As in the other films, the importance of sound is emphasised by the way in which the protagonist does or does not speak. Ana barely speaks throughout the film, and when she does so it is often in a whispered conversation with Isobel. At the end of the film she is selectively mute and the final voiceover – in which she appears, alone in her bedroom, to be calling out to the spirit-monster she has become obsessed by – is actually in Isobel's voice.

The film is a complex meditation on emotional and political repression. Ana's parents do not speak to each other and the mother seems preoccupied by a lost love, possibly a Republican soldier who has apparently escaped to France. The harsh political reality of Franco's recent victory is made clear when a fugitive that Ana has befriended and who is probably another Republican soldier is summarily shot and killed. Yet the film is not a simple morality tale of innocence lost. What Ana actually believes or imagines about the real man and the imaginary monster she has seen on screen is never fully explained. Made when Franco was still in power in Spain, it seems probable that the ambiguity emerged, in part, as a response to possible censorship and in relation to what could and couldn't be said. The murky confusion between the fugitive, the monster and Ana's father (who may have had Republican sympathies) continues to disturb and seduce the little girl, and we see Ana twice submit willingly to her monster/fantasy. First by the river, where the monster appears, visually, to be the actor who plays her father, dressed as the movie monster, and second in the final sequence of the film, where the monster/spirit is directly invoked by Ana/Isobel. That Ana's silence paradoxically expresses what is unsaid or unsayable about the trauma of the Spanish Civil War seems evident. What lurks in the silence is her continuing desire for the incoherent figure or spirit that is the soldier, monster and father. As such, her desire is informed and haunted by the concept or fantasy of the father-as-monster associated with fascist dictators, including Franco himself, the 'father' of the Spanish nation.

A reflective play between speech, sound, music and voiceover is a significant aspect of Tarkovsky's semi-autobiographical film Mirror, in which memory and history are evoked in a series of inconclusive episodes through which a narrator seemingly leads the viewer into different 'rememberings': his own childhood; his mother's life; his disintegrating marriage; the Russian experience in the Second World War; the childhood of his own son. The film articulates the importance of gaps, breaches and inconsistencies in its evocation of memory and childhood. While the film could not be considered as primarily about the experience of the child in war, the effects of the Second World War – signalled through the use of archive and one significant sequence at a military training ground – are central to the film's exposition of the entanglement of private memory and public history. These two sequences are informed by the presence of a rebellious orphan boy, Afasyev, who, we are told, has lost his parents during the Leningrad blockade. Afasyev appears in the military training scene and acts as a silent anchor for the archive film which follows. In the archive film, young Soviet soldiers cross the muddy expanse of Lake Sivash. This passage is a prologue to one of the most famous advances of the Second World War and one which involved a huge loss of life. It is likely that most of the men pictured are about to die, as did the cameraman who shot the film. While the images were presumably originally silent, Tarkovsky uses the sounds of feet splashing and dragging through water, a distant sound of the specially composed electronic score and, ultimately, his father's voice reading one of his own poems, 'Life, Life'. Paradoxically, this simultaneously anchors us to and pulls us away from the content of images. Tollof Nelson describes the effect in this way:

> The disjunction of sounds has the remarkable quality of supporting the irregular rhythm of the men's feet even while it calls attention to, and holds onto, the historical distance between viewers and the bodies on the screen. It creates an aural daze in the viewing experience, one located in the disorientation of the ear to the reality of the image.[12]

While Afasyev does not speak to or over the images, his presence before and after the archive film, as well as his gaze into and later obliquely away from the camera, enfolds his unsaid but imagined personal experience into their material evidence. Nelson suggests that the fact that Afasyev is a child is a key element of the sequence's effect: 'This child is not merely an instance for the enunciation of a counterhistory or vision but a figure of the very dislocation and transformation of time itself.'[13] The child acts as a silent figure that articulates a confusion of temporalities – the times of story-telling, of memory and history.

Mirror begins with a seemingly anachronistic prologue, where in a television documentary an adolescent boy is miraculously cured of a pronounced stammer. As Nelson comments:

> The prologue is more than the metaphorical springboard for the rest of the film but that which metonymically imparts a

certain temporal tonality, tenor, and tremor to the various pieces of shattered experience of memory to follow.[14]

The presence of this stammering boy directly links to the concept of the child learning to speak and the struggle to express what is before speech — embodied personal experience, memory — into the 'after' of words. The relationship between the stutter or stammer and the struggles of the child who is learning to talk have been illuminated by Lindsay Smith in her work on Lewis Carroll, the author of the *Alice* books, who struggled with a pronounced stutter throughout his life. Smith suggests that this speech impediment may have formed a crucial element of Carroll's peculiar and some might argue pathological interest in children, expressed via his correspondence with them, his writing for them and, most notoriously, his photographing of young girls. Noting a particular sympathy that Carroll expressed for children who were fellow stammerers, she suggests:

> In Carroll's empathy for a child who stammers, stammering provides a kind of perpetual, if unwelcome, connection for the adult to his own child self, the self as frightened, disempowered, vulnerable. More emphatically, such a connection to the child through imperfect speech (in which the speech impediment comes to stand in for the speech of childhood) suggests a way of preserving, halting that imperfect speech, that state of disequilibrium prior to its translation into sense.[15]

In *Mirror* there is little in terms of sound that is nonsensical: the use of classical music; the speech of the narrator, his wife and mother; and his father's poetry indicate a musical, verbal and linguistic sophistication that would seem at odds with the difficulty in speaking, or the disequilibrium, that the stuttering boy represents. However, at the end of the film, in the final, impossible remembering of the narrator, the last sound heard is precisely without sense, an imitation of an animal cry. This sequence, which may or may not take place as the narrator is dying, portrays the narrator as a child walking through the fields surrounding his childhood home with his mother (who is, impossibly, the age she would be when he is an adult not a child). In this short passage nothing is said, although the music which accompanies this scene, the opening chorus of Bach's St. John's Passion, reaches a climax and then stops. It makes way for the final sound, the child's cry, a vocalisation or a crying out that communicates but that is not language. This sound substitutes for the narrator's last words, and although nothing is said it has meaning, suggesting a return to nature: his literal return to nature via his death and his return to the fantasy of the rural idyll he remembers as his childhood. It acts as a response to the stuttering boy at the start of the film, representing a communicative world that is possible without, or before, the struggle with language.

The tension between speaking and not speaking is central to debates concerning the performance and potential of testimony. Testimony, as evidence, witness, memory and history, is subject to a great deal of scrutiny in contemporary historical discourse. Much of this debate is informed by and circulates around the various written and visual records and accounts that make up the history and remembering of the Holocaust. Whilst the experiences of individual children in the Holocaust do feature in some of the films I discuss here, they are not all concerned with this specific event. However, in the way in which these debates have forced a questioning of how memory works and about the nature and articulation of trauma, they are relevant to many of the films I am investigating and to the way in which the child figure in these films does or does not speak or use his or her voice.

The central concern is this: is it possible to speak truthfully, or to speak at all, of an atrocity, such as the Holocaust, that is beyond comprehension? The terms in which we talk about the practice of language, such as the 'mastering' of narrative, indicate that events, feelings, violence itself, are tempered, tamed and contained by writing and speech. By writing and speaking of these events it becomes possible to normalise them, to comprehend them and potentially to dismiss them. The most famous encapsulation of this impasse, that to speak of the Holocaust would be to diminish its significance, was presented by Theodor Adorno. As Sara R. Horowitz has suggested:

> Following Theodor Adorno, critical discourse interprets his
> much cited statement about the barbarism of poetry after

Auschwitz to mean, variously, that one should not write lyric poetry, any poetry, any fiction, any 'literature', or anything at all in wake of the Holocaust, unless or even if one is a survivor of the Nazi genocide.[16]

Although later rescinded by Adorno, the impossibility of speaking as understood here and its further connection to psychoanalytic models of trauma, in which violence and horror are understood to be repressed and therefore what is unsaid or hidden is understood to be the origins of the patient's visible symptoms, has initiated a critical and philosophical investigation into the unsayable of trauma and how it might in fact be spoken. One contested but suggestive turn in the debate has centred on Giorgio Agamben's book *Remnants of Auschwitz*. In the book, Agamben concentrates on the famous memoirs of Primo Levi, specifically, *If This Is a Man*, *The Truce* and *The Drowned and the Saved*. Agamben's focus is primarily on the figure of the Muselmann, the animate corpse, the prisoner who has succumbed to the horror and deprivation of the camps to the extent that he barely exists. It is significant that his discussion also focuses specifically on a child figure from Levi's memoirs – Hurbinek. This is Levi's original description:

Hurbinek was a nobody, a child of death, a child of Auschwitz. He looked about three years old, no one knew anything of him, he could not speak and had no name; that curious name, Hurbinek, had been given to him by us, perhaps one of the women had interpreted with those syllables one of the inarticulate sounds that the baby let out now and again. He was paralyzed from the waist down, with atrophied legs, as thin as sticks; but his eyes, lost in his triangular and wasted face, flashed terribly alive, full of demand, assertion of the will to break loose, to shatter the tomb of his dumbness. The speech he lacked, which no one had bothered to teach him, the need of speech characterised his stare with explosive urgency: it was a stare both savage and human.[17]

In fact, Hurbinek does make one possible vocalisation, a possible word – which Levi transcribes as 'massklo', or 'matisklo' – but which is not understood by anyone, although there are many languages spoken in the camp. Hurbinek dies after the camp has been freed. Levi comments; 'Nothing remains of him: he bears witness through these words of mine.'[18] For Agamben this reveals the ethics or core of testimony. Hurbinek could not and can no longer speak. Levi can only imperfectly transcribe what he has heard, and what he has heard cannot be recalled or translated to any 'proper' or sensible language. Agamben determines that:

> This means that testimony is the disjunction between two impossibilities of bearing witness; it means that language, in order to bear witness, must give way to non-language in order to show the impossibility of bearing witness. The language of testimony is a language that no longer signifies and that, in not signifying, advances into what is without language, to the point of taking on a different insignificance – that of the complete witness, that of he who by definition cannot bear witness.[19]

This paradox is the way in which the unspeakable, the atrocity of Auschwitz, is vocalized. Hurbinek, who cannot speak but is nonetheless heard, makes sense but is not made 'sensible' in Levi's description. In this manner, Hurbinek is listened to in a way that recalls Jean-Luc Nancy's description of listening:

> What secret is at stake when one truly *listens*, that is when one tries to capture or surprise the sonority rather than the message? What secret is yielded – hence also made public – when we listen to a voice, an instrument, or a sound just for itself? [...] Which means: perhaps it is necessary that sense not be content to make sense (or to be *logos*), but that it wants also to resound.[20]

Resounding, reverberating, dislocation, sound and silence are used productively throughout the films I have discussed. The secrets and trauma of the child's experience are evoked by the gaps in the narration and in the carefully orchestrated soundtracks of the films. Agamben suggests that what the traumatised child demonstrates is the potential for a form of communication that is not corrupted by the constraints and compromises of language, a non-language that, as Nancy suggests, 'resounds'.

In the second part of this chapter, I take this concept further and explore how the child's experience of war is articulated in ways other than speech. It is the way in which film can portray the materiality of bodily experience that reveals how the presence of the child allows for a sensual impression and response that takes the viewer beyond meaningful/ meaningless silence to a more visceral or haptic confrontation with the violence of the war-time environment. I will address the representation of embodied encounters with elements of nature that are foregrounded as a consequence of war. That is, the child's experience of mud, rain and fire. A recurring context for these encounters is the child in the forest, and this is, of course, another archetypal relationship. The prevalence of these different aspects, relations of and with the body of the child, as well as the frequent appearance of literal and figurative monsters, also confirms that many of the films refer, implicitly and explicitly, to the fairytale. Initially, this might seem to imply that the presentation of the child's experience or the way in which it is remembered is determined by the constraints of narrative or via a sensible discourse. In fact, the fairytale is a far from sensible form of story-telling, situated historically somewhere between speech and writing, endlessly revised and retold, and it allows for a temporal dislocation, a validation of sensory experience and a promotion of the irrational to which the child has privileged access.

Into the Forest

> Inevitably they find their way into the forest. It is there that they lose and find themselves. It is there that they gain a sense of what is to be done. The forest is always large, immense, great, and mysterious. No one ever gains power over the forest, but the forest possesses the power to change lives and alter destinies. In many ways it is the supreme authority on earth and often the great provider.[21]

The forest features in nearly all the films I have been discussing. As a silvery birch forest in *Ivan's Childhood*, as the denser beech and pine forests of *Come and See*, *Mirror* and *Diamonds of the Night*, in the more varied forests of *Pan's Labyrinth* and *The Ogre*, as well as the sparse but evocative forest by the river that appears in what is probably Ana's fantasy in *Spirit of the Beehive*. Its presence in these films is twofold. First, as the citation from Jack Zipes suggests, the forest is the archetypal location of the fairytale, the site where children are abandoned, where monsters – witches, fairies, ogres and dwarves – live. Second, the forest is the densest and, for the European listener or viewer, the most familiar site of nature at its most benevolent and most terrible. The forest forces the child to encounter nature 'red in tooth and claw'. In these films nature is neither gentle nor unkind, it is indifferent. The forest offers the child somewhere to hide, but it is also where the child gets lost.

The films I am discussing are essentially different from another series of films that feature children in war. In the Italian neo-realist films such as *Germany Year Zero*, *Rome, Open City* as well as the British film, *Hue and Cry*, children are seen playing and surviving in the ruins of the city. In his discussion of the child figure in these films and others, Pierre Sorlin notes how much they have in common with 'Trummerfilm, ruin-films…films in which wounded or mutilated people roam amidst collapsed houses.'[22] As a historian, Sorlin is interested in these ruined-city films for the accidental information they reveal, for the information provided by the real mise-en-scène which the fictional characters inhabit. In contrast, my focus has been on films that have less evidential historical value, based as they are on memoirs and stories and made, in most instances, many years after the wars they depict. In calling on the fairytale, through motifs, locations, figures and as a mode of story-telling, the films are a-historical, or at least a-temporal. As Max Luthi explains, in relation to the beginning of the fairytale:

> *Es war einmal* ['Once upon a time'] by no means is intended to stress the fact that events in the tale took place in the past. The intent is to suggest the very opposite: what once occurred, has the tendency continually to recur.[23]

As in *La Jetee*, the fairytale is a story that is somehow of the past but is also about the future.

In relation to children and war time, the use of the fairytale is unsurprising. As Donald Haase has demonstrated, fairy and folk tales have a significant but ambiguous status in relation to the memories and stories told by child survivors of the Second World War.[24] Ambiguous, for as Haase notes, like the forest itself, the fairytale was used to promote conservative ideas of German nationalism, promoting the racist ideologies of the Nazis. Nonetheless, he points out:

> While the educational and cultural institutions of the National Socialists appropriated the fairy tale in order to shape and control responses to it, adults and children victimized by the Nazis reclaimed the genre to meet their own needs and purposes.[25]

This is evident in films such as The Ogre and Tin Drum in which fairytale figures and conceits are employed to actively critique the Nazi regime. This practice is evoked in a different context as a response to another fascist, Franco, in Pan's Labyrinth, in which the child heroine, Ofelia, uses fairy stories explicitly to construct another world away from the awful situation she finds herself in. The fairytale also features more obliquely in films such as Diamonds of the Night, Mirror and Come and See, where the mise-en-scène is dominated by the kinds of 'visible elements' which Luthi claims dominate the telling of the fairytale: that is, water and earth, fire and wind.

Fire as a powerful and spectacular force appears in several of the films. I am haunted by the way in which the burning barn in Mirror is re-presented as an event combining both awe and terror in Come and See. The 'barn on fire', which appears as a strangely beautiful memory in Mirror, becomes in Come and See a wooden church full of men, women and children being burned alive by the Nazis, which the young protagonist, Floryan, is forced to watch. As Gaston Bachelard has suggested in his book on the psychoanalysis of fire:

> Among all phenomena, it is really the only one to which there can be so definitely attributed the opposing values of good and evil.[26]

For the child protagonists in the films, fire is frequently mystical and/or enchanting. In The Ogre, as a child, Abel escapes from

Figure 15   'The burning barn', in Mirror (Dir. Andrei Tarkovsky, 1975)

his hated school, St. Christopher's, through the outbreak of fire, and is convinced that he is special since this accidental fire saves him from punishment, although it also kills his best friend. Later, in the military school in which Abel works, his favourite pupil is burned alive when he stands too close to the backfire from a bazooka being used in battle training. In *Spirit of the Beehive*, Ana is fascinated, hypnotised by a bonfire (over which her sister Isobel jumps three times) and later has to be pulled away from its embers which she is still feeding long after it has got dark and the other children have gone home. In *Pan's Labyrinth* one of the most disturbing scenes in the film is when Ofelia's mother throws the 'mandrake baby' that Ofelia's stepfather has discovered under her mother's bed into an open fire and we see, with Ofelia, the baby scream and squirm as the fire burns.

My concern here in listing, rather crudely, the different kinds of fire is not to uncover or determine its symbolism – its apparent or possible 'meaning' – but to demonstrate simply how often the child encounters fire as an elemental force. These encounters are not fully comprehensible. While superficially it is

Figure 16   Isobel leaps through the flames, in *Spirit of the Beehive* (Dir. Victor Erice, 1973)

possible to express what the child potentially experiences into words – Ana is perhaps mesmerised and Floryan is probably terrorised – the fire itself and the effect of the fire on the child and the environment take on a shape, have effects, consequences, a direction and power that function at a much more basic level, as a 'universal explanation'. Bachelard suggests of fire that:

> It is gentleness and torture. It is cookery and apocalypse. It is pleasure for the *good* child sitting prudently by the hearth; yet it punishes any disobedience when the child wishes to play too close to its flames. It is well-being and it is respect. It is tutelary and a terrible divinity, both good and bad. It can contradict itself; thus it is one of the principles of universal explanation.[27]

The relationship between fire and the child is irrational. It is not that it makes 'no sense', since the encounter often has a result – pleasing or awful consequences – rather, it is that the experience is significant yet escapes categorisation. An experience remembered not simply for what happened but for what it was, how it felt: warm or burning, fascinating or frightening, mundane and magical, sometimes all at the same time. The strangest or perhaps the least transparent scene in *Empire of the Sun* relates to fire. In a sequence which begins with Jamie and his fellow prisoners being forced into labour to construct a runway for the Japanese air force, the film does not focus on the danger or brutality of this experience, which as Jamie notes later would probably have ended in his and the others' death ('our bones would have been in the runway'). Instead, we follow Jamie as he approaches the Japanese planes under a shower of sparks (presumably the planes are still being welded). Lit by the flares and shadows of this fire, Jamie reaches up to a plane and caresses it and then turns to salute an approaching Japanese flight crew. It is an odd sequence, relating to Jamie's obsession with flight and planes, and linking to his admiration for the Japanese. It is a seductive and oddly disturbing sequence, playing upon the combination of seduction, power and violence in relation to modern machines of transport and flight that was to become such a feature of Ballard the writer (and thereby the adult that Jamie will one day become), and it is this which Spielberg is perhaps cautiously alluding to. Coming in the place of, or as a substitute for, a demonstration of the extraordinarily violent context in which the runway was built, it demonstrates the ambivalent quality of fire. The meaning of the sequence is not clear but it does seem to fit with Bachelard's summary of fire, with the animation that fire possesses and which Luthi identifies as the recurring trajectory of the fairytale: 'a significant recurring process…danger and redemption, paralysis and rejuvenation, death and resurrection.'[28]

Another significant elemental force the child encounters again and again is the earth – most commonly in the form of mud. In Pan's Labyrinth, Ofelia's first task involves her crawling into the bowels of an ancient tree where she faces a huge toad that explodes, an encounter that leaves her completely covered in slime and mud. In Come and See, after Floryan realises that his village has been decimated by the Nazis, he wades through a bog on the way to an island on which he (correctly) believes the remaining villagers will be hiding. In The Ogre, one of Abel's first significant memories as a small boy at St. Christopher's is when he licks mud and blood off the damaged knee of a fellow pupil. In Diamonds of the Night, the boys run up a steep muddy hill, dig in the earth for roots and drink water from swampy, muddy pools in the forest. In Empire of the Sun, Jamie's initiation – a task he undertakes so

Figure 17 Jamie (Christian Bale) and the fire, in *Empire of the Sun* (Dir. Steven Spielberg, 1987)

that he can enter the adult men's accommodation in the camp – involves him crawling in the mud into no-man's land to retrieve some captured game. Although Jamie barely escapes being shot by a suspicious Japanese officer, he is ultimately successful and makes a triumphant march to the men's housing covered from head to toe in drying mud. In *Ivan's Childhood*, Ivan negotiates his way through an elemental environment that is suspended between earth and water. The last sighting of Ivan alive is when we see him wading away through the muddy, swampy banks of the forest at the river's edge.

The mud in these films functions literally to impede the young protagonists, to manifest physically their struggles and their willingness to ignore one of the principle behaviours of civilisation – cleanliness. Like fire, however, mud has a contradictory status for children, since playing with mud and getting dirty are often recognised as one of the particular joys of childhood. Fire, mud and the earth are indifferent to the emotions and motivations of the child, and while it may seem like mud is an animate force (it seems to hold the child back, and has a fascinating and infuriating tendency to get everywhere; to apparently creep over the body – into the eyes and ears) it isn't actually alive, it simply is. Alphonso Lingis, in his intriguing article, 'Mirages in the Mud', recalls the experience of a mud puddle as one of his earliest memories and uses it to speculate on how these very earliest memories of infancy (before speech) may provide evidence of experiences that are pre-conceptual since they are pre-linguistic. His argument is concerned with whether it is possible to have fantasies 'without meaning', that is, without a 'layout of identities and categories and intelligible relationships'.[29] He is referring to an experience that is of the senses but which is not entirely or,

Figure 18 Ofelia (Ivana Baquero) in the bowels of the tree, in *Pan's Labyrinth* (Dir. Guillermo del Toro, 2006)

Figure 19 Jamie (Christian Bale) in the mud, in *Empire of the Sun* (Dir. Steven Spielberg, 1987)

satisfactorily, incorporated by the imposition of later symbolic meanings or categories, by 'meaningfulness'. He writes:

> I think it is far-fetched to try and assign meaning to the mud. Do we today have a concept of mud? Indeed, do we really have an intelligible concept of, for example, lemon? The word 'lemon' designates something we can know only through a sensuous experience, and later recall, of colour, sourness, juicy and fibrous texture. The mud puddle was something I as a speechless infant encountered through movement, movement of the toddling feet through it, feeling its warmth through contact, feeling it give way, gluey and sucking at my feet, but slippery as I slid through it, splashing its grey substance through the air but then it sticking onto my hands and clothes.[30]

While it may be tempting to ascribe symbolic meaning to the mud in the films, to read a civilised psychology into the child's experience of the wet earth, the prevalence and extreme nature of these encounters (the sliminess of the exploding toad, of licking mud, being up to your neck in stinking mud, getting covered from head to foot in mud) evoke this prior meaninglessness. Mud as both a terrifying and absorbing just-is-ness; demonstrating what is exposed, what is left, when the world is turned upside down, when the fragile civilisation that the child has barely understood has broken down. The contact with inanimate matter enhances the visceral, bodily sense in which the child has been 'thrown' into an encounter with the world. Nothing – no protective parent, no sense of civilisation – comes between the child and its experience of the earth. These recurring scenes recall the analysis of another traumatised child discussed by Emma Wilson in her analysis of Lukas Moodysson's film, *Lilya 4 Ever*. In an elegant argument foregrounding the way in which the film articulates a connection between the child figure and adult viewer, she suggests that:

> Through movement and the tactile, through the range of emotions summoned, Moodysson seeks to reattach us to child experience, to make its affect and range of sensation present for us. This strategy emphasizes film as a more than visual medium, its representation of children as more than pictorial.[31]

The central tenet of her argument is that it is not that we feel sorry for Lilya – she is first abandoned by her mother, then forced into prostitution – but that we feel with the child, in a way that touches us and moves us in a visceral and confusing way and which we might previously have dismissed as sentiment or pity. Wilson asks, 'Can viewing be open to an inbetween position, a position of alignment with a child, a sharing of her response, yet a refusal of infantilization, on the one hand, or parental responsibility and distancing on the other?'[32] In answer to this question, Wilson employs an argument advanced by Martha Nussbaum, who promotes emotions as part of a system for ethical reasoning:

> Her primary concern is with the adult subject's faltering in the face of a response to emotion which is in part unbidden, involuntary, and which draws its force from its mnemonic underpinning; she writes vividly about such experiences and the discomfort they provoke. Such experiences are not only disarming in themselves, however, and it is here that Nussbaum's second notion of lack of control becomes evident. Emotions felt, remembered by an adult temporarily dispossessed, also recall a child's (more extensive) lack of control over its circumstances, its environment, even at times over its own body.[33]

It is Wilson's focus on a key scene in the film that links her argument pertinently to the films I have been exploring. In this scene, Lilya at first pretends indifference to her mother's departure, but then, as Wilson describes, she suddenly rushes after her –

> 'Don't go, stay with me, I won't make it!' Her animal sounds of despair dominate the scene. The car drives off and Lilya runs after it. Unable to reach her mother, she falls in the mud and the film follows her complete regression: in the viscous substance of the mud, Lilya is infantilized, splattered, stained by the inextricable mess (of her emotions, of her visceral grief at her mother's departure).[34]

As Wilson goes on to suggest, this scene pulls at the viewer in a manner that recalls a bodily lack of control: an intensity that is also distinguished by Lilya's howling and babbling, suggesting that she has gone to the 'beyond' or retreated to the 'before' of language. As in this film, the encounters with mud in the films I have been exploring allow the child figure to provide evidence, to evoke sense memories of struggle and abandonment that characterises their experience of war, but do so in a way that is not mastered or directed by language, and which may thereby provoke a response that, like its manifest content, is both messy and meaningless.

As previously suggested, the encounter with mud for the child need not be traumatic. For Lingis, mud was pleasurable and remains so in different ways in his adult life. While in the films the encounters with mud are not necessarily pleasurable, other encounters with nature – mostly notably with rain – are initially welcomed and even enjoyed by the children. In both Come and See and in Diamonds of the Night, the two pairs of children experience heavy rain whilst in the forest. In both encounters the rain comes as a relief and respite. In Come and See, Floryan and his girl companion, Glasha, respond to the rain in a particularly idyllic scene in which they shake the birch trees in the sunshine after the rain to wash themselves and their clothes. Glasha later dances exuberantly in a rain-drenched clearing. Nature here, as in some fairytales, seems kind, although the scene is the only 'golden' interlude in the whole film – it is immediately after this scene that Floryan returns to his village to discover the Nazi massacre. Similarly, in Diamonds of the Night a heavy rain shower is welcomed by the parched fugitives who stand open mouthed, gulping in the rain, their heads hanging back and their arms open wide in an embrace. This scene too is short lived, and as the rain grows harder and harder (and the sound of the rain louder and louder) the encounter becomes implicitly more brutal and the rain seemingly less benevolent. As in fairytales, the forest and the natural world can appear animated or alive in the sense that they seem responsive to the child. Yet the revelation that nature and the elements are in fact indifferent to the child's fate enforces the sense in which an anthropocentric view of the world is proved redundant and irrelevant in an environment destroyed by war.

The framework which the fairytale provides emphasises key features of the child's world which are powerful yet ordinary elements of their environment (mud, earth, rain and fire). This form of narrative also ensures that the child is centre stage – since children (actual children, or sons and daughters) are frequently protagonists of fairytales. These stories present children not just as victims (abandoned in the forest, terrorised by witches and ogres) but as resourceful agents who often find their way home, richer and wiser than before. Yet it is in these endings that the link between fairytales and the films seemingly breaks down. In the writing on children's actual use of fairytales in war by scholars such as Bruno Bettleheim and Ernst Bloch, the utopian trajectory of the narrative – the happy ending – is seen as a key resource for the frightened or traumatised child. Yet the films I have been discussing do not seem to hold good to this promise. Only *Pan's Labyrinth* and *Empire of the Sun* offer the child a 'happy ending', and then in *Pan's Labyrinth* this is only *after* the child has apparently been killed in the 'real world'. In *Empire of the Sun*, Jamie's re-uniting with his parents comes, in relation to the rest of the film, almost as an afterthought and is not presented as such in the original novel. Two of the films, *The Ogre* and *Spirit of the Beehive*, finish before we know what will happen to the characters. (Will the adult Abel make it across the frozen lake carrying the small boy on his shoulders? What monster will Ana conjure up from her bedroom window?) In the other films, *Come and See*, *Mirror*, *Ivan's Childhood* and *Diamonds of the Night*, the child protagonists are either dead or retreat into the forest. The effect of these 'endings' is to refuse closure, to allow the child and viewer to remain suspended in the narrative, or to veer off back into the fairytale world, the fantastic world or real forest.

To refuse endings makes sense if we examine the actual practice and experience of listening, reading and looking at the fairytale. As performed stories, or as illustrated texts, fairytales always resist linear or narrowly focused investment by the reader/listener. Fairytale illustrations, such as the familiar images produced in numerous books by artists such as George Cruikshank, Gustave Dore, Edmund Dulac and Arthur Rackham, have always had an important part to play in the meaning and feel of the fairytale. For most children it is the images they can comprehend before they can fully understand the words. It is often these images that draw them back and which serve as a focus for their memory of, and investment in, the stories. As such, the relationship between image and text in the fairytale is not that the illustration simply supports the text or that it pushes it forward. Rather, the illustration may actually suspend the narrative, draw the child in and distract them from the ending, with details, shadows and potential meanings that are only hinted at in the economic prose of the tale itself.

In her analysis of the illustrations drawn by Maurice Sendak for the Grimm's fairytale *Dear Mili*, Hamida Bosmajian points out how his illustrations work in tension with the 'straight narrative line' of the story itself:

> His metaphoric overlays of romantic art and documentary photographs with the conventions of the picture book and his own characteristic ways of telling through pictures contribute to a synchronicity that abolishes linear time/narration.[35]

Dear Mili is an apt example, as it is a fairytale about the impact of a war on a young child. A mother and her young daughter Mili live at the edge of a village; they are poor but happy. War approaches the village; to keep her daughter safe, the mother urges Mili to go into the forest and hide for three days. Mili does as she is asked, and after an initial period of terror in the dark and gloomy forest she is welcomed and cared for by an old man who appears to be St. Joseph. After staying and working for him for three days, she is reluctant to return but is persuaded when St. Joseph gives her a rosebud and says that once it is in bloom they will be together again. Going back to her village she is surprised to see that a great deal has changed and when she reaches her mother, who is now a very old woman, it becomes clear that she has been away not for three days but for thirty years (although Mili herself has not aged and remains a young child). Her mother greets her joyfully and they spend a happy evening together. The next morning they are discovered dead, lying side by side, with the rose in full bloom between them. In a similar manner to the films under discussion, the forest is a key location within the story, and acts both as a place of fear and as a refuge for the child protagonist. As Bosmajian points out, the forest dominates the story not because it is returned to again and again in the written text, but because in Sendak's illustrations it occupies, or encroaches upon, every image. It is through the detail of his drawing, in the objects and figures present in the shadows and corners of the illustration, in the use of colour and texture, that attention is diverted from the progression of the story as plot (what happens next) to the depth and synchronicity (the all-at-once-ness) of the image. The traces of a real war, such as the silhouette of Auschwitz, the ruins of a Jewish cemetery and the figure of Anne Frank, appear within this fairytale forest, in the background or at the edge of the frame. Literally they are part of the picture, and they tell the reader/viewer something but are not directly referenced by the written text. The ambiguity of the images and the vitality of the forest (which may or may not be purgatory) allow Bosmajian to agree with Sendak, who claims that 'the ending is not sad'. Other critics have disagreed; however, it is possible to see how the reader of the images and the pictures would be able to hold the contradictory understanding that the characters are dead, yet simultaneously and paradoxically, living happily with St. Joseph in the forest.

In different ways, the visual aspects of the films under discussion offer a similar aesthetic pull on the viewer that disrupts the conventional chronology of the fairytale as a story which traditionally culminates in the 'happy ending'. Certain films, Pan's Labyrinth, Mirror, Ivan's Childhood and Spirit of the Beehive, offer a detailed and lavishly 'illustrated' image, using strong colours or affective contrasts of light and shadow to draw the viewer in. Of all the films, it is Pan's Labyrinth that is perhaps best known for its fantastic use of colour and detailed special effects, featuring gorgeously realised monsters and fairies as well as books which write themselves. Yet by using simpler, childishly executed and hand-drawn pictures in its title sequence (apparently drawn by Ana Torrent), Spirit of the Beehive demonstrates how the film emphasises that children see the world differently, that they often understand and interpret their environment and imagination through drawing and through visual rather than linguistic modes of expression. The film employs a mise-en-scène that pulls the viewer into images that are emptier than the richly detailed images of Pan's Labyrinth but which are equally alluring. The sequences in which we follow Ana running from room to room in the interconnecting apartments of her house create an effect that magically expands the space, so that doors open onto doors upon doors as if it were a Chinese puzzle box. In both films the child inhabits an environment that is animated, rich in colour and texture, and which hints that good and bad things may lurk ambiguously at the edge of the frame, or just around the corner.

In *Come and See* there is an unusual repetition in terms of a particular shot composition, which provides the viewer with a series of different, lingering close-ups of the characters, foregrounding the children's faces in a way that confronts the viewer. *Come and See* acts as the title and as an injunction to the viewer: it asks that we share the traumatic events the characters experience, but it also demands that the audience observe, in intimate detail, the impact of the war as it is etched onto the faces of the children. Floryan's face is originally glowing with excitement; by the end of the film, his eyes are blurred and staring, his skin prematurely aged and his mouth fixed in a grimace of terror and loss. A similar change, not coincidentally, is presented by the final photograph we see of Ivan, presumably taken just before his execution, which is found by his older comrade, Lieutenant Galtsev, in the ruins of the Nazi bureaucracy after the fall of Berlin.

All the films employ images that are full, images that tell more than the story, which hint at possibilities that are not quite spoken or written elsewhere in the film. *Diamonds of the Night* does this most self-consciously in its employment of a definite surrealist touch in its visual aesthetic. In a series of succeeding sequences, as the boys lie down to rest, or collapse during their escape, certain shots reveal a developing hallucination or vision in which one of the boy's bare feet, his hand, and finally, his face, are covered with crawling ants. Deliberately referencing the surrealist landmark film *Un Chien Andalou*, it is evident that the images are not meant to be realistic but, as in fairytale illustrations, they are confusing and disturbing, implicitly violent and strangely cool in their expression and delivery. The fascination many surrealists had with fairytales is well known; it would seem that the apparently arbitrary qualities of the fairytale narrative, as well as the alignment of a cool or flat prose style with the violent events such stories frequently depict, is very much in accord with the dream world so central to the surrealist aesthetic.

Many critics and historians of the fairytale note the characteristic flatness of its prose style yet confirm the curious and tremendous affective power of the stories. This suggests an aesthetic contradiction which is mirrored by the way in which the fairytale requires a move between the mundane (the everyday world) into the miraculous (the fantasy or potential of the fairytale narrative). In the films, this is sometimes managed by a literal transition which the child manages from one world to another (as in *Pan's Labyrinth* and *Spirit of the Beehive*). In the other films, it is as if the formal register of the film becomes increasingly uncanny, as the world familiar to the child is made strange by the disruption of war. In *Come and See*, the sequence in which Floryan returns to his wooden house in his village but finds it abandoned resonates in this way; things seem the same but they are not. At one point, Floryan sees the two dolls owned by his little sisters lying side by side on the bedroom floor. On one level this demonstrates that the family must have left in a hurry, but on another level it is almost as if his sisters have been magically transformed into the dolls themselves. The dolls' position, side by side, facing the open door of the bedroom, as well as Floryan's horrified reaction suggest that an uncanny transmutation may have taken place. From this perspective, the dolls are no longer the clichéd substitute for the bodies of the real little girls: they *are* the real little girls. In *Empire of the Sun*, the incongruity of certain objects (such as an adult man's shoes) and their passage within the film is not dissimilar to the way in which ordinary or previously mundane objects gain particular totemic qualities or magical properties in the fairytale world. The distinctive brown and white leather golf shoes with spikes are first seen in the film when they are carried by Mr. Lockwood, who ties them around his neck when he is transported to the prison camp (they are here an incongruous symbol of his previous suburban lifestyle). The shoes then appear tantalisingly (at least, to Jamie who has discovered the importance of shoes) by Lockwood's bedside as he dies in the camp hospital (now serving as a sign of redundant extravagance in the context of war). Next, the shoes are passed by Dr. Rawlins to Jamie, for whom they function as a reward. Jamie finally wears them on his passage from the family quarters to the men's accommodation, although they remain several sizes too big. They are finally useful but still ridiculous – as a key element of Jamie's journey they are now akin to the fairytale's magical 'seven league boots'. Jamie's ultimate separation from his previous benefactor and hero, Basie, culminates in an exchange, in which Basie demands of Jamie: 'Haven't I taught you anything?' Jamie's retort – presented completely without irony – is, 'Yes, you've taught me that people will do anything for a potato', demonstrating how ordinary, common-place foodstuffs accumulate different meanings, and are thereby magically transformed in a context dominated by war and starvation. This transformation is similar to the way that in fairytales, ordinary objects such as shoes, breadcrumbs, apples, salt mills, pepper pots and spinning wheels accrue a particular significance for the protagonist or become imbued with magical properties.

In the films, as in the illustrated fairytale, the distraction and information provided by richly detailed and symbolically loaded images present uncanny changes and familiar objects in ways that are both mundane and magical. These images, transformations and objects are encountered by the child as part of the natural and economic trajectory or movement of the plot, which is frequently episodic and constrained in terms of context. In fairytales and in the films, the context of the story is limited in relation to what is available to the child and expands or develops only when the child needs it to do so; in the same way, we have no idea how big or how dense a fairytale forest is, or who lives there, until the child goes into it. It is this narcissistic and idiosyncratic worldview which makes children compelling but, for the historian, frustrating as witnesses to historic events. The child protagonist acts as one example of the traditional 'story-teller' eulogised by Walter Benjamin:

> The most extraordinary things, marvellous things, are related with the greatest accuracy, but the psychological connection of events is not forced on the reader. It is left up to him to interpret things the way he understands them, and thus the narrative achieves an amplitude that information lacks.[36]

The films allow the viewer, via the child, access to 'extraordinary things, marvellous things' (whether they want to or not) and they do so in a manner whereby these things are realised in exquisite, even laboured, detail, yet the events are not interpreted by the child for the viewer. As in real recollections, the extraordinary devastation of war may only be (perhaps mistakenly) interpreted or contextualised by the adult that the child becomes *after* the event. In his book on childhood memories during the Second World War, *Witnesses of War: Children's Lives under the Nazis*, in which he explores the diaries and drawings of children (Jewish children and children of Nazi families), the historian Nicholas Stargardt illustrates the curious tension between the child witness and the adult who remembers. Citing an interview with Hans Medick, who as an adult had become a 'left-wing, strongly Anglophile social historian', but who had been a five-year-old child in Nazi Germany, Stargardt demonstrates how Medick had significant memories of his experiences, which he wished to contain and contextualise for the interviewer. As Stargardt explains, as the memories existed only as fragments and, additionally, had an extraordinary visual power and strangeness, despite his attempt to rationalise what he saw, what Medick's memories might actually mean, or refer to, remained ambiguous.

> What he remembered from childhood was no more than a single image, 'the green faces, their skin tightened into a permanent grin.' In the next breath he went on to say, 'But it was deserved'...Filling the gulf between the two thoughts, the memory and the moral conclusion, lay the passive construction 'it was deserved'. The 'it' could only apply to Nazi Germany in the abstract, never to the actual people he had seen in the square. Behind these two thoughts lay half a lifetime of strenuous moral engagement with the legacies of Nazism.[37]

Significantly, Stargardt concludes:

> The outcome had been to resist the allure of giving primacy to his own early and powerful memory, for which he may have had no words at the time; and the memory had remained an isolated fragment whose meaning stayed stubbornly unclear.[38]

The films express this contradiction or tension: they pull the viewer in different directions. On the one hand, the films present us with a children's story within a fairytale framework, apparently simplifying the narrative and reducing the need for context or explanation. Yet the seductive, nightmarish, fairytale world (realised through the images) complicates our response to the events. The child provides access to incidents that are banal and traumatic, events and scenes that we may recognise as symbolically dense and significant – historically, emotionally and politically – but which cannot satisfactorily be 'made sense of' by the child. The child does not represent innocence but rather challenges the conventions of a certain kind of history-telling which demands a chronological narrative determined by cause and effect, populated by the recognisably 'deserving and the undeserving' and which, by default, presents events as fate rather than as chance.

The fairytale, as A.S. Byatt has observed, presents a particular challenge to the seeming distinction between fate and chance: 'Everything in the tales appears to happen by chance and this has the strange effect of making it appear that nothing happens by chance, that everything is fated.'[39] Chance and fate are equivalent in the fairytale; an effect that is both potentially liberating and terrifying. On the one hand, this simply expresses the child's limited perspective (their failure to see the 'bigger picture'). On the other hand, it reveals that traditional historical narratives find fate in a succession, or collision, of events, lives and acts of violence, and that this is, as Steedman suggests, always already a work of fantasy:

> We have always, then, written in the mode of magical realism.
> In strictly formal and stylistic terms, a text of social history
> is very closely connected to those novels in which a girl flies,
> a mountain moves, the clocks run backwards, and where
> (this is our particular contribution) the dead walk among the
> living. If the Archive is a place of dreams, it permits this one,
> above all others…of making the dead walk and talk.[40]

The context of war is experienced by the child as irrational but remains one in which they must act decisively (as do fairytale protagonists) in order to survive (though they may not do so). For as Stargardt observes, children caught up in war are not simply witnesses but agents.

> Children were neither just the mute and traumatised witnesses to this war, nor merely its innocent victims. They also lived in the war, played and fell in love during the war; the war invaded their imaginations and the war raged inside them.[41]

Chapter Four

The Impropriety of Performance: Children (and Animals) First

An older female actor, 'Granny', addresses a four-year-old boy, Dong Bowen, the actor with whom she shares a key scene in the Chinese film, *Little Red Flowers*. The following speech is taken from the 'making of' documentary available as an extra on the DVD release.[1]

> 'We are working for a film. They hand over you to us. That means you have to listen to us. You just don't study the lesson. What a good chance. If you can't do it I will tell them to change your part; that's the way. Change to some other kid. Do you agree with me?'
>
> The little boy/actor starts to cry, his eyes visibly welling up with tears.
>
> 'Hurry up, roll the camera.'
>
> Off screen, a male voice says: 'Action!'
>
> Dong Bowen: 'I want to go home.'
>
> This could relate both to his role within the film, a little boy who is left at a kindergarten, or to the actor's actual desire.
>
> Granny: 'Was it OK?'
>
> Male voice: 'Fine, OK.'
>
> Granny: 'How's the focus? All done: great.'
>
> She turns to the little boy.
>
> 'Come on, don't cry.'
>
> He continues to cry as she picks him up.
>
> 'Hurry Up! Take a picture of us. Don't cry. Don't cry!'
>
> At this point it is unclear whether she is addressing him in her role as the head teacher of the kindergarten, or comforting the child actor.

I want to contextualise the discussion of children acting in film in reference to the concept of risk. Risk can be understood in relation to the real and potential exploitation of the child actor who may be particularly vulnerable to the demands and expectations of directors and fellow actors. In the description of the scene from the documentary on the making of Little Red Flowers there is an uneasy fascination with what, at its most benign, may be the manipulation necessary to make the little actor cry convincingly and, at worst, the emotional bullying of a small child who is separated from his parents for the duration of the shoot. All actors – adult actors, children and 'performing' animals – are vulnerable in this way. As Nicholas Ridout suggests, any actor is in danger of being exploited yet this is not generally recognised unless the adult actors are performing actions of a sexual nature. What the apparently more immediate or greater concern for children and animals demonstrates is 'the reality of theatrical employment itself, irrespective of the status or ability of the employee, as involving a particular form of exploitation.'[2]

There is also a risk in production terms: most child actors are non-professionals and/or very young, and even when the children acting are established professionals they are more likely to produce unpredictable performances. In both instances the director and other actors may be unsure that they understand how to behave on set or know how to perform for the camera. It is usually in this sense that the much quoted aphorism attributed to W.C. Fields that one should 'never work with children or animals' is often understood. Child actors increase the possibility that in relation to their performance they will do something unexpected and things will go 'wrong'.

As child actors are unlike adult human actors, there is frequently an uncertainty as to the value of qualitative judgements made about their performance. In the majority of contemporary films, a good performance may be recognised as naturalistic, one that is integrated into the fictional narrative, and in tune with the other actors' performances. Ridout suggests that this kind of assimilation is akin to the domestication of animals as household pets. In theatre and film, the child's acting is judged in relation, and as a response to, the performance of the other actors – usually adults – they are working with. The perceived experience and skills of these adult actors and their associated acting style will reflect on the child's performance. For instance, it is important to recognise Shirley Temple's acting as a response to, and in relation with, film actors from the 1930s. It should be remembered that what might now seem the overly stagey acting style of Lionel Barrymore in the 1935 film The Little Colonel was then regarded as skilful and entertaining, suggesting that Temple's acting, now seen as too cute, mannered and ostensive, may have had a different effect on the audience at the time, and should be considered within its particular historical context. Similarly, Dakota Fanning's more measured, introspective and naturalistic performance in I am Sam (2001) needs to be understood in relation to the excessive, 'Method' – oriented style of the adult actor, Sean Penn, who plays her mentally retarded father.

Whilst the child actor's skill and acting style need to be contextualised within the film text and the historical period of production, it does seem to be evident that success is based on possession of an idiosyncratic quality that makes the child, perhaps, 'abnormally interesting'. In using this term, I am borrowing directly from the way in which Joseph Roach has defined the quality of having 'It'. 'It' originates, as Roach outlines, in relation to the 'It Girl', the 1920s film star Clara Bow. As a quality, It has since been associated with later stars (in the 1950s Marilyn Monroe and Marlon Brando) and by Roach himself, retrospectively, on to earlier figures such as the character of 'Renee' in George Meredith's 1876 novel Beauchamp's Career, in which she inspires this description:

> There are touches of bliss in anguish that superhumanize bliss, touches of mystery in simplicity, of the eternal in the variable. These two chords of poignant antiphony she struck through the range of the hearts of men, and strangely intervolved them in vibrating unison. Only to look at her face, without hearing her voice, without the charm of her speech, was to feel it.[3]

Later, I want to examine more closely the affective power of this 'poignant antiphony' – the paradoxical embodiment or the enactment of conflicting emotions and meanings – and how it relates to the peculiar resonance of the child performer on screen. For now, I want to emphasise the inhuman status of the term It and underline how being or having It – like Fields's dictum – connects children to animals and as other to the adult human. As Roach suggests:

> There is a kind of freakishness to having it; and despite the allure, a potential for monstrosity, which haunts the meaning of it as the proper neuter pronoun of the third person singular, used to refer to things without life, of animals when sex is not specified, and sometimes of infants (OED).[4]

If the successful child actor is often blessed (or cursed) with It, then another risk accrues to their presence beside adult actors – that they will upstage these actors and draw the audience's attention and admiration towards them unfairly. I remember, during the televised interviews which took place 'back stage' immediately after the 1993 Oscar ceremony, the actor Jeremy Irons suggesting that the 11-year-old winner of the Best Supporting Actress award, Anna Paquin (for her role as Flora in *The Piano*), should not have won. The reasons for this were not clear but it is worth disentangling the various motivations for Irons's apparently churlish remarks. It may have been that he was concerned that someone so young had been thrust into the role of celebrity. Especially as another young winner, Tatum O'Neal, 10 years old when she won the same award for her role in *Paper Moon*, did not fare well professionally or, for a time, emotionally. It also seemed that he was implying that Paquin was not as 'good' as her adult rivals, notably perhaps the British actor Emma Thompson, who was nominated twice that year for both Best Actress and Best Supporting Actress but who, in the end, won neither. There was also a sense that somehow, Paquin was not being awarded for her acting ability but for successfully or merely being 'a child' on screen. The performance of a child actor who is playing 'a child' might be understood as having an unfair advantage and present a threat to the hard-earned skills of the trained adult actor because child actors, albeit in a rather circuitous manner, seemingly naturally possess (an unskilled) advantage over adult actors. As real children they inevitably and unconsciously express child-like attributes that allow them to seem believable as children. Another way of understanding this threat would be to suggest that a truly disabled actor has an unfair advantage over an able-bodied actor if the character they are playing is similarly disabled. Notoriously, of course, able-bodied actors frequently win Oscars for their performances of disabled characters and thus, in part, for their performance of a disability they don't possess. In contrast, adult actors rarely get to play children. Whilst there are a small number of films that allow them to perform as children – generally the character is a child transposed into an adult body, as in *Big*, *Freaky Friday* or *Vice Versa* – the effect is usually intended to be comic and is less likely to attract the attention of the Academy. This may be seen as doubly unfortunate for adult actors since childish attributes and characters who are children frequently allow for the expression of a 'poignant antiphony' that is particularly attractive on screen. Or, to employ Roach's term once again, the exhibition of characteristics which make them 'abnormally interesting'. Rather uncomfortably, and not particularly successfully (at least in terms of acting awards), Sean Penn's performance as an adult with a 'mental age of seven', the actual age of Fanning's character, was interpreted as an Oscar bid. Penn's character and performance are interesting in that he was attempting to co-opt both aspects of a potentially Oscar-winning performance: a virtuoso mimicry of a disability that he did not possess and the creation of a sympathetic character with attractive yet contradictory qualities – a child-like mixture of simplicity, naïveté and unconscious wisdom.

These paradoxical qualities are exhibited again and again by many child characters in film; indeed, they are inherent in nearly all the characters played by Shirley Temple in the 1930s. Temple herself won an Oscar in 1934 (at six years of age she remains the youngest actor to do so) but the Oscar was a 'juvenile' award, a category that was subsequently entered and awarded only sporadically. This peculiar categorisation and its relative lack of status within the Academy hints at the difficulties of making a satisfactory link between the success of different child actors, in terms of their appeal and box office significance, with a satisfactory evaluation of their acting abilities in relation to their adult peers. It seems difficult to distinguish the performance skills of a child actor who may – or may not – 'naturally' possess certain child-like abilities, qualities and expressions from these attributes as they are apparently actively performed by the 'child' they are playing on screen. Child actors may be more valued for who or what they *are* – inevitably or inherently – than what they can *do*.

Another risk that children bring to the screen is related to the fact that the majority of child characters are included in films to be attractive and sympathetic figures. The response to the child figure on screen needs to be managed carefully or audiences and critics may react negatively. As audiences are less likely to feel manipulated if they believe that the child actor is genuine or (a) natural – which implies somehow that the audience is not being duped – child actors often work very hard to hide their learned acting skills. In short, they must not be seen to be acting. Of course, a similar effect may be achieved if the child can remain apparently unaware that they are acting, and it is this version of the successful child performance (which may be more or less true) which often dominates the histories, biographies and publicity relating to children acting in film.

Child actors who present an unnatural appearance – too trained, too precocious, or what is often termed as too 'stage school' – are not only seen as 'bad' actors but are actively disliked. The appeal of the child actor Abigail Breslin in the film *Little Miss Sunshine* is based in large part on the fact that her different performances in the film – the performance by Breslin as her character, Olive Hoover and the ultimate dance performance of Breslin-as-Olive at the children's beauty pageant – are completely at odds with the stereotype of the unnatural and precocious child performer. (Ironically, this is actually what Olive aspires to be.) In the film, Breslin-as-Olive's exuberance and apparent lack of self-consciousness is contrasted with the mannered staginess of the other little girls who take part in the beauty pageant. All of the children we see on screen are acting, but the success and appeal of Breslin's naturalistic performance as Olive is reinforced by the way in which her character is presented as the subversive antithesis of the simpering mini-beauty queens she finally joins on stage. Yet these other child actors are also playing their parts to the best of their ability, although they are not encouraged or required to act 'naturally'. Instead, they are deliberately producing a particular kind of performance – one that is characterised by a precocious and extraordinary masquerade of femininity. For the majority of the audience for the film (who are likely to be bourgeois and educated, since Little Miss Sunshine is clearly an independent, 'art-house' movie) the precocity and exaggerated femininity of the little girls playing beauty queens is probably alarming and distasteful. While all the child actors may be 'good' actors (they all seem convincing in their allotted roles), the audience's sympathy is aligned with Olive and by default with Breslin, as she – as the character and the child actor – is presented and perceived as natural – more 'like a child'.

This tension, between the poise and maturity of a professional child performer and the necessity that the child actor should also be child-like, is expressed in slightly different terms by Vincente Minnelli in his discussion of the child actor, Margaret O'Brien. O'Brien was cast as the youngest daughter of the family – 'Tootie' – in Minnelli's 1944 film, the musical Meet Me in St. Louis:

> She did Journey for Margaret in which she played a disturbed child from the war zone. She became celebrated as a child star who could cry, get hysterical, etc. Well, by the time I got her, George Sidney's wife, Lillian Burns, a coach at the studio, had been working with her. Well, Margaret was like a Shakespearean actress. I went out of my mind getting her to be a child again... to act natural and be like a kid.[5]

O'Brien's professionalism and training are seen to undermine the precise qualities that should make her appealing and convincing as a performer. As Minnelli indicates, this is that she should be able – paradoxically – to 'act natural and be like a kid'. Within this assertion there is a contradiction that requires a child actor to 'act' and 'be' at the same time. This brings me to the final and perhaps greatest uncertainty or risk that child actors present to the viewing audience, which is that they confuse or threaten the understanding of what acting or performing is, and how it can be distinguished from not-acting or from 'being'. (That is, being for 'real'.) Child actors balance precariously on the divide between seeming and being, and they continually undermine the belief that while performing as an actor (playing a character) this performance is held – not necessarily securely but importantly – as distinct from the actor's individual, everyday, off-screen performance of self.

However, as the child is a being that is understood to be characterised by an unconsciousness of self (even a lack of self) and by naturalness and spontaneity, the distinction between what is actually the 'performance of character' by the child and its inevitable presentation as a 'child' is particularly hard to discern. It might be that the child actor shares the same predicament or an apparently similar lack of intent or agency as the non-human or animal performer, of whom Richard Schechner has suggested: 'There is no irony, no pliable back-and-forth play between the role and the performer, no trilogical interaction linking performer to performer, to spectator.'[6]

Yet children are not animals (or at least not quite), and it may be after all that the child performer is simply very successful at appearing to be like the child character they are playing. Acting 'naturally' is a skill – it is work. The child actor cannot be childish – that is, irresponsible and unprofessional – about appearing to be child-like. Nonetheless, the demand from directors and seemingly from audiences that child actors 'be' implies that these performers can and must unselfconsciously 'be' kids and that this insistence upon actuality will ensure that their performances as children are believable. The successful child actor negotiates this contradiction, and arguably, their naturalistic behaviour is not 'all an act' while, at the same time, their acting is probably not all 'naturalistic behaviour'. In her examination of the child actor on the Victorian stage, Anne Varty identifies how this overlap or negotiation between seeming (the mask) and being (the 'real' face) was then recognised as troubling but compelling : 'The child actor has neither a mask nor a face, but unsettles by possessing both in equal measure.'[7] A similar tension is also expressed in the closing paragraph from an article in *Photoplay* magazine published in 1943, after Margaret O'Brien's appearance in *Journey for Margaret*, in which the reporter suggests that the children at O'Brien's kindergarten must not realise that they have a movie star in their midst:

> They mustn't know, for just a little while longer so she can
> stay in their world of little children who recite sing-song
> rhymes and play with hand looms and wear brown shoes
> and don't cry out a heartbreak when a director says softly. 'All

right Margaret, cry now, dear'. Little children, who might not accept a movie actress as one of them, though the world will see her as Hollywood's Junior Miss Miracle.[8]

O'Brien must remain or be a kid, but she is actually a freak or 'miracle' who is likely to be ostracised if her abilities to recite professionally (not in a 'sing-song' voice) or to dissemble on cue (to cry when directed) are discovered by her peers. Yet she cannot isolate herself from her peers, as this will mean that she will no longer understand what it is to be a real child and she is of no use to directors if she produces a skilled but unnatural (Shakespearean) performance that is, essentially, too adult.

The unsettling and contradictory demands made of child actors suggest why so many of them are not, at least initially, professionals. Instead, they are often apparently selected from thousands of other ordinary children. There is a recurrent romantic narrative told in biographies and in publicity material which determines that particular child actors only emerged when the director identified them as the 'one' from many others. Here is the director Alexander Mackendrick discussing the casting of the child actor Mandy Miller for the role of Mandy Garland in his 1952 film, Mandy.

> On the studio floor there are silences of different kinds: there are silences when people aren't talking, just whispering, but the microphone can't pick it up; or there's the moment when people are standing absolutely still; but then there's the third kind of silence when they're holding their breath. Mandy's performance was so astonishing that the unit was struck rigid, with this electrifying silence on the floor. And I was in tears. Dougie Slocombe was in tears: and afterwards, both of us said, 'Cancel the rest, she's it'.[9]

In the selection of this child actor, the two aspects of Roach's interpretation of It meet and confuse one another. Mandy clearly has 'It' but she also is It with all the freakish, inhuman associations that implies.[10] This confusion reiterates the uncertainty identified previously, that is, are children in films really acting at all? This uncertainty is exacerbated in film-making more than other kinds of performance since acting for film is clearly embedded in so many creative and determining practices. This means that what it is, exactly, that the actor does, or what he or she can genuinely claim to have intended by their performance would seem to be limited. In *Reframing Screen Performance*, Cynthia Baron and Sharon Marie Carnicke reveal how this was interpreted by the very earliest film-makers and critics:

> In the early years of cinema, film director Vsevelod Pudovkin, playwright Luigi Pirandello, and cultural theorist Rudolf Arnheim all argued that film actors should be seen as stage props and film performances as constructed by others. Echoing their positions, Walter Benjamin shared his alarm that a filmic reaction of being 'startled by a knock at the door' could be created by a director firing a shot behind the actor without warning; responding to that possibility, Benjamin lamented, 'Nothing more strikingly shows that art has left the realm of the "beautiful semblance"'.[11]

Film actors perform within an over-determined, representational context where they have little control over setting, costume, lighting, editing choices, sound dubbing and music. Most films are shot out of sequence and scenes may be broken up into very brief sections, so that only minutes or seconds of performance are required from the actors involved. The necessary fragmentation of the shooting schedule will therefore disrupt the attempt to establish any controlled development by actors of their character over the duration of the film. Many different takes of the same scene may be filmed (and thus a variety of different performances are recorded) so actors will have little or no control over the final version of their performance. As it is generally the director and editor and not the actor who make choices as to which elements of each scene ultimately reach the screen, it is arguably their version of the character, rather than the actor's, which appears in the finished film. In other words, while actors may well have intended aspects of their performance, they have little control over the final or cumulative impression of the characters they play.

Two tactical ways in which adult actors have attempted to gain some authorship over their performance in film, or to reclaim some control over how the character they are playing is perceived, are through the acquisition and maintenance of 'star' status or (and sometimes additionally) through the adoption and advertisement of their use of the 'Method' style of acting.

A star is an individual who apparently possesses unique qualities and attributes: in fact, stars are very close to the kind of individual that Roach associates with those who have It. These qualities and attributes are then reproduced in different roles and may be more or less emphasised in the particular characters they choose to play. The limitations of stardom for the actor are related to the way in which aspects of the performer's body, voice and associated mannerisms are fixed and thus dictate what roles the actor may appropriately play. As the star ages or experiences physical changes (in hair colour, weight, and so on), perceived attributes such as beauty, vulnerability or strength may wither or become unsustainable, leaving the actor vulnerable in the first instance to type-casting and consequently to an inevitable diminishment of their star appeal. For the child actor all of these limitations exist in an exaggerated form, since the child actor's acquisition of stardom is sometimes entirely dependent on the apparently natural or essential attributes associated with 'being' a child: their littleness, cuteness, prettiness and precocity. When the child actor ages, the apparently inherent qualities which made them a star will no longer be manifest. Therefore, as a tactic, the child actor's acquisition of stardom may (literally) be short-lived. While this is not actually true for all successful child actors, the career of Shirley Temple, whose box office success did seem to diminish with her increasing age, is the best known example of this phenomenon.

The Method, as it is generally understood, is a training and a style of film acting originating from the work of the Russian director Constantin Stanislavski, as adapted and professionalized through the acting school of the American teacher and director, Lee Strasberg. As Baron and Carnicke indicate, the Method offers actors the opportunity for agency in relation to their performance. As a style it is concerned to promote the appearance of a naturalistic, authentic-seeming performance. The inspiration and direction for the performance is located in the unique personality of the individual actors who draw on their own inner personal experience, and requires the public expression of memories determined by private emotions. Actors train themselves to produce a conscious recollection of their unconscious actions in response to particular emotional states, which in turn can be used as material for their performance of different characters. Controversially, the Method, as espoused by Strasberg and his followers, does not necessarily require the performer to draw on memorable events that are appropriate to the situation of their character. It is the authenticity of the emotion (its 'truthfulness') independent of its psychological and emotional trigger that is important. This means that while the actor can lay claim to the authenticity of their performance, they are not necessarily creating or authoring the character, and some direction and selection is still required from directors and editors who necessarily create the character piece by piece from the actor's performance, achieved by asking for re-takes and via editing decisions. As Baron and Carnicke point out, in using or promoting the Method, the actor's agency is therefore still limited or negotiated.

> Film actors appeared to emerge as agents of their performances insofar as they drew on their personal experiences to create natural behaviour and emotion that could be selected by directors and recorded by cameras and microphones.[12]

In relation to child actors, even the circumscribed agency afforded by the Method is problematic and likely to be further limited. First, child actors are frequently untrained and there would seem to be an explicit sense in which professional training is seen as 'bad' for children. Second, the Method relies upon the concept of a developed subjectivity; an inner, mature or complicated self, a resource that provides memories of, and the inspiration for, actual (and thus natural) responses to different emotional experiences. The actor must be able effectively and consciously to recall those experiences and related behaviour. The belief that the child is defined precisely by his or her lack of self-consciousness and innocence (a relative lack of complex emotional experience) would suggest that the Method is not really available to child actors as a tactic that would allow them to control or claim authorship of their performance. Indeed, when they do attempt to do so, it can seem 'cute'. Whilst this effectively enhances the innocence of their child-like state (their essential characteristics and not their learned abilities), it simultaneously undermines the Method technique itself. For example, when asked in an interview how she is able to cry for the camera, Dakota Fanning has said that she thinks about the death of her goldfish.[13] As a trivial event (though perhaps important to the child), it coincides with shared fantasies as to the benign environment of the child's world and ordinary experience and thus reinforces Fanning's status as a real, if sensitive, child. We would feel much more uncomfortable if she spoke – as adult actors might have done – about the death of a close relative as the inspiration for her tears. At the same time, it also infers that the clichéd angst of the Method actor is somehow ridiculous. Shirley Temple Black in her autobiography makes an observation which similarly refuses the significance of recalled emotion or affective memory for her performance:

> Crying on cue had to be an acquired skill. Jackie Coogan's father reportedly took him aside and told him his dog had died. Mother had tried all sorts of tricks, even conjuring up sad thoughts until, theoretically, my eyes should have brimmed over. Perhaps I had nothing really to be sad about. Instead of being in anguish, we usually wound up in frustrated hilarity, mirth often so intense, it produced the tears that were proving so elusive.[14]

In some instances, in the descriptions or recollections of a variety of child actors' performances, emotional expression seems uncannily to come from nowhere. Here is the biographer Philip Kemp's account of how the director Alexander Mackendrick viewed Mandy Miller's ability to 'switch mood without having to work herself into it':

> One scene in particular stayed in his memory: when Mandy, miserable as a boarder at the school, is reunited with her mother. 'Having rehearsed Phyllis Calvert, playing the mother, and Dorothy Alison as the teacher who escorts Mandy into the hall, I knelt down and talked to Mandy very quietly and said, "See, Mandy, here it is – I want you to walk down the stairs, there I want you to see your mother and I want you to burst into floods of tears and run down to her." That's all I said. Well, while we were lining up the scene and Dougie

was lighting it, she's holding Dot Alison's hand, and Dot – she tells me this afterwards – is going through effective memory bits or whatever. And she's interrupted by Mandy, who turns to her brightly and says, "Why am I crying?" Dot is totally thrown and asked, "Didn't Mr. Mackendrick tell you?" and Mandy says, "No." So Dot, panicking, says, "Well, you know how it is – if you've been longing to see someone for a long time, but they're not here, and then suddenly you see them, you just want to burst into tears. You know what I mean, Mandy?" And Mandy says, "No." At that point, I called "Action." And Mandy walked down four steps, burst into floods of tears and ran to her mother. Which tells you a lot on that score.'[15]

In this description, Mackendrick makes several assumptions and assertions. First, that Miller needed no specific rehearsal or opportunity for emotional recall (he does not tell her why she is crying or how she might begin to cry) and that even when she is given some direction by an adult actor she doesn't understand it. Second, he is satisfyingly proved right, since Miller nevertheless does what she is required to do – that is, 'burst into tears'. What Mackendrick presumes, and what this incident tells, us is that not only is training ('effective memory bits or whatever') inappropriate for child actors, it is also, implicitly, a waste of time for any actor. He also appears to be suggesting that if the director is experienced and intuitive, it will be their ability to select the right child actor – the child who has It – which will be enough to generate a successful child performance on screen. In turn, this may also imply that the child performer – who exhibits or manifests It yet has no understanding of what their performance is 'about' and who can produce actions and expressive gestures from out of nowhere – needs no professional skills at all.

This belief is articulated similarly by another director, Luchino Visconti, discussing the child actor Tina Apicella, who plays a central role in his film Bellissima:

> Especially the child: one of a kind, she is. She demonstrates that having a sophisticated or adult intelligence has nothing to do with acting instinct. After fifteen days on the set, Miss Apicella knew all there was to know about the acting trade – so much

so that sometimes she left even the crew baffled. In one scene, for instance, she had to cry. She was quite calm, even tranquil, up to the moment that I gave the signal for action, upon which she immediately began to cry; and when I yelled 'Cut!' she immediately stopped crying. And she did this more than ten times in a row. All this from a child of five-and-a-half![16]

Once again, the freakish ability of the child actor to transform his or her apparent emotional state from one extreme to another is celebrated. On the one hand, this denies the child actor any real agency (since it is not necessary to possess a 'sophisticated or adult intelligence') and on the other hand, it conveniently implies that if the child can make such transformations so effortlessly, adult actors are misguided in their own sense of importance and in their acquisition of unnecessary skills or experience. However, in relation to Bellissima it is possible that Visconti is deliberately contrasting Apicella's simplicity with the complex performance and celebrated artistry of the much-lauded Italian actor, Anna Magnani, who plays Apicella's mother in the film. It is also the case that Bellissima, made in Italy in 1951, has been identified as Italian 'neo-realism' and that Visconti is speaking in relation to this specific context.

As a category of films and film-making practices, Italian neo-realism refers to a series of films produced in Italy during the latter part of the Second World War and for a short period afterwards. In these films, directors famously used real locations and non-professional actors. This was both expedient, since the infrastructure of the Italian film industry was seriously affected by the War, and a politically inspired move in which film-makers strove to re-create, on screen, events, experiences and people that were 'real', to present stories in which these people-as-characters were seen to have experiences, to dress and look (physically) as they would in 'everyday life'. As an auteur-led genre, in which the director was celebrated as the leading visionary and creator of a believable 'slice of life', the submissive obedience of child actors who do (only) what they are told to do, and possess no agency of their own, would allow the director to claim a creative ownership over what might otherwise be understood as 'captured reality'.

Many of these films featured children as central or significant characters. In addition to Roberto Rossellini's films, Rome, Open City (1945) and Germany Year Zero (1948), Vittorio de Sica's 1948 film Bicycle Thieves is perhaps the best known. Two of De Sica's other films also frequently identified as neo-realist, The Children are Watching Us (1944) and Shoeshine (1946), also feature children, played by non-professional actors as central characters. While employing children in these and other related films generates a heightened sense of melodrama within films that otherwise are concerned to emphasise their naturalistic effects, the particular relevance to my argument is that once more it is the child's apparent spontaneity and lack of self-consciousness which is being sought out and seemingly captured on film. In championing the non-professional and instinctive qualities of his child actor, Visconti is confirming the belief that non-professional child actors are superior to child performers (and perhaps even to adult actors) who have been trained to 'act'. This preference for the untrained child seems to be consistent, regardless of the film's genre or its production context. O'Brien, as we have seen, was required to act or be natural – to hide her professionalism – even when performing in the highly artificial context of the Hollywood musical. Yet Visconti's comments are not as straightforward as they seem. Bellissima's plot is directly concerned with a paradoxical critique and celebration of the use of non-professional actors, and particularly non-professional child actors in film.

On Acting and Not-acting: A Definition

It might seem that the uncertainty over whether or not the child is acting in film may be less complicated than I have so far suggested. In these descriptions of child actors on set, it seems clear that the child does not 'act' in the sense that they either intend or 'author' meaning from behaviour they deliberately choose to express. Instead it – the performance, the tears on cue – just happens, and the most effective performances can be captured from child actors who are akin to puppets (or animals) who do as they are told without individual guile, intention or agency. This evidence would seem to coincide neatly with the opinion of the film theorist, Béla Balázs, who suggests (in *The Theory of Film*, and under a sub-heading titled 'Children and Savages') that

> The acting of children is always natural, for make-believe is a natural thing to them. They do not want to 'register' this or that, like an actor; they just pretend that they are not what they are but something else and that they are not in the situation in which they are but in some other. This is not acting – it is a natural manifestation of youthful consciousness and it can be observed not only in the human young but in the young of other species as well.[17]

And further, that 'All those who have worked with children on the stage or in films will know that children should not be "directed", they must be played with. It is not their acting which is natural – their nature is play-acting.'[18] Balázs's assertions are provocative but at the same time entirely familiar in the association of children, animals and savages (or 'primitives'). As I have suggested in this chapter and elsewhere in the book, the conceptual alignment of the child, the savage and the animal recurs frequently and in many guises. In contrast, a more subtle assessment as to whether or not the child is acting might be drawn from Michael Kirby's explication of a continuum of not-acting to 'true' acting. In his 1972 essay, 'On Acting and Not-Acting', he proposes to

> examine acting by tracing the acting/not-acting continuum from one extreme to another. We will begin at the not-acting end of the scale where the performer does nothing to feign, simulate, impersonate and so forth, and move to the opposite position, where behaviour of the type that defines acting appears in abundance.[19]

In contrast to Balázs, Kirby would not say that children do not act or even that they 'play-act'. Instead, since child actors who appear in films have evidently been selected and operate within a highly symbolic set of representational codes – they are presented in costume, made subject to specific kinds of lighting, perform on sets, and their actions may be juxtaposed with musical and other sound effects – they cannot be understood to be 'not-acting'. What Kirby suggests is that while child performers may not apparently be 'doing' anything, they are, by their very presence in the film, 'done to'. For example, the adult actor Ana Torrent, recalling her acting as a five-year-old child playing 'Ana' in *Spirit of the Beehive*, has said that what she primarily remembers from the experience is that she was simply asked by the director Victor Erice 'not to smile'. At this end of his continuum, Kirby identifies how meaning and significance are attributed to a performer simply because they exist within a highly intended or symbolic context – what he calls a 'non-matrixed representation'. The creative choices made by the director, the set designer, the costume designer, the cinematographer, other actors and the composer create a meaningful context in which the child simply appears and in doing so apparently expresses meaning for the viewer whatever the child's actual intention may be. In effect, we are returned to the notion of actors as equivalent to props. Kirby writes: 'In "non-matrixed" representation the referential elements are applied to the performer and are not acted by him.'[20] In an earlier chapter, I described how Torrent's expressionless (not-smiling) face was awarded a host of meaningful associations by a variety of critics and viewers of Erice's film. In this sense, the child actor could be placed on Kirby's continuum in the position of 'received acting': the acting is not something done by the child, instead the child's behaviour is read as a performance because it is situated in a particular, meaningful context.

Yet, this is not true for all child performances, even those involving very young children: for if we press a little further into the limited material available which refers to specific child actors' performances, there are instances in which it is clear that the child is aware that they are being asked to perform and that they will require specific prompts in order to do so. For example, in the sleeve notes to the VHS release of Jacques Doillon's film *Ponette*, a film which focuses on a four-year-old girl coming to terms with the death of her mother, there is a short essay by the psychologist Marie-Helen Encreve. Encreve was employed by Doillon to observe and support the mental well-being of his child actors for the duration of the shoot. Her particular charge was the four-year-old child actor, Victoire Thivisol, who played the title character. Of Thivisol she observed:

> I can say that she rarely talked about the film, the character she portrayed, the difficulties of learning the text or even about the exhausting process of repeating a scene many times a day. One time she did casually tell me of 'a technique she used when playing Ponette' (in her words) 'crying for the camera'. She would ask Jacques Doillon to tell her off as long as it was not severely enough to frighten her.[21]

Evidently, Thivisol is here fully conscious that a specific emotional expression is required and seeks out a technique or a strategy to generate this expression 'for the camera', although at the same time, and to a degree, her tears are also a genuine response to an exterior prompt.

Another example of this kind of prompt can be located in the documentary on the 'Making of' the *Little Red Flowers*. In one sequence, the assistant director can be seen discussing with Dong Bowen how he is to cry as he runs down one of the kindergarten's corridors. During an energetic exchange, Bowen continually insists that the assistant director tell him that he 'will not see his mother and father for months'. Bowen is clearly attempting to recreate (or anticipate) the conditions of the scene and exchange with 'Granny' that I described earlier. In this instance, however, Bowen is not (apparently) being tricked into displaying genuine emotion, instead he is *asking* to be tricked, just as Thivisol made similar demands of Doillon. Fascinatingly, in this particular scene, the assistant director tries to suggest that Bowen does not need to produce tears in that way, and it is Bowen that remains adamant. Indeed, seemingly he raises the odds by increasing the number of months that the director should suggest that he will be parted from his parents. In both these instances, the child actor is not a passive recipient or a passenger within a heavily coded, representational context. Instead, they would seem to be expressing a level of self-consciousness, a degree of intentionality, agency and a subjectivity that is not generally associated with very young children. It would seem that some child actors do not adhere to category of 'received acting', instead, they may, in Kirby's terms, be expressing 'simple acting':

> it does not matter whether an emotion is created to fit an acting situation or whether it is simply amplified. One principle of 'method' acting…is the use of whatever real feelings and emotions the actor has while playing the role…It may be merely the 'use' and projection of emotion that distinguishes acting from not-acting.[22]

Simple acting, although it may be 'true' acting, is not akin to the skilled adult actor's performance which may more often adhere to the category of complex acting. For this latter category, Kirby suggests: 'Acting becomes complex as more and more elements are incorporated into the pretense.'[23] By this he means that, for example, when carrying out a specific act (such as the mime of putting on a jacket), if the actor implies more than one thing – not just that he is putting on a jacket, but that he is cold, that he is old or that he is angry – then their acting is complex. It is this complexity and not acting itself which is perhaps less evident in child actors. Yet older child actors have produced performances in which a complexity of emotions is on display. One might think, for example, of Jodie Foster's performance as Iris in *Taxi Driver*, and in particular of the breakfast diner scene which she shares with Robert de Niro. In her adult reflection on that scene, made during an interview for a much later DVD release of the film, Foster details how de Niro spent a great deal of time coaching and working with her in a variety of different diners, until she became entirely comfortable and confident in her ability to improvise and play against him in the scene. This recollection makes clear that she was fully aware of a fellow actor's generosity in 'training' her. In the same interview, however, she makes it clear that another acting prompt – her interaction with a former 'real' street child, Garth Avery, who appeared in some scenes as Iris's companion, did not work. Foster notes, wondering at Scorsese's intention in bringing her together with a real life model for her role: 'I don't know what he thought would happen…but we were just kids.'[24]

Kirby's model is non-judgemental: he is not concerned to suggest that one category of acting is 'better' than another. His continuum from not-acting to acting functions quantitatively and is therefore organised in relation to the 'amount' of acting that may be said to be taking place in an actor's performance. His explication of what acting is becomes useful in the context of my arguments in two ways: first, it confirms that the child performer is, in many instances, acting. Second, it suggests that the response of the audience to the child actor is not dependent on how complex or not the acting appears to be. Despite the title of his essay, his interest is also manifestly in 'performance' rather than a more conventional understanding of 'acting' and this is significant because he confirms that the non-vocal elements of the actor's performance – that is, their presence and appearance, their body and their physical expression – may be just as important as their ability to speak, to project, to remember and express a written script, aspects of a performance, that we commonly associate more closely with 'proper' acting. As children may be less effective as speakers, as they may not physically be able to produce long periods of uninterrupted speech and they may not be able to remember long speeches, Kirby's focus on performance allows for an understanding of how children may still be affecting and effective performers, even though they may actually 'say' very little in terms of dialogue.

Kirby's continuum is also independent of belief; that is, whether or not the actor 'really believes' in the performance or, whether or not the audience 'believes' in the actor-as-character.

> Many times the actor, when faced with a certain lack of 'belief' by his audience, protests that he 'really believed'. The important point, however, is that when belief is present or is attained by a performer, acting itself does not disappear. The acting/not-acting scale measures pretense, impersonation, feigning and so forth; it is independent of either the spectator's or the performer's belief.[25]

To that extent, the intention or not of the child actor becomes irrelevant: the child is acting and the audience responds.

Writing in 1972, Kirby's conclusion discusses the influence within contemporary theatre productions of the 'Happening' and highlights, specifically, the way in which Happenings used untrained performers and found locations. He relates this influence to an increased interest in and production of simple or received acting. In reflecting on his model, Kirby is aware that there is a fascination for certain kinds of acting and performance that actively or deliberately confuse the relationship between not-acting and acting, or which complicate the distinctions of being and seeming. Joe Kelleher has suggested that this may be particularly true of child actors, and claims: 'The presence of the child – as, perhaps, a peculiar case of actuality – inflects the drama's frame of representation.'[26] The child's presence reflects and informs an underlying uncertainty, risk and interest attached to the activity of performance itself. The anxiety is not whether the actor is acting; rather, it circulates around what it is that acting or performance reveals about what it is to be 'human'. In our horror or amusement at the uncomfortable suggestion that film actors are equivalent to props (or animals or puppets) we are responding to the fact that one aspect of the performance contract, which is to show what it is to be human, is being broken, or at the very least, undermined. This is, perhaps, why children and animals are deemed incapable of giving a 'proper' performance in the first place. This is what I think Alan Read is responding to in his recent book, Theatre, Intimacy and Engagement, where he elaborates on his concern and interest in what he has termed performance 'as such'.[27]

Whilst Read is concerned with live performance, in his focus on the theatrical exhibition and performances of children and animals (and their frequent alliance) his arguments offer a way to conceptualise and investigate the particular fascination of child actors' performances even when they are mediated by the operations of film-making. And it is his desire to champion 'those beings who dissemble the propriety of performance: infants and animals first' that inspire the following argument. As I have suggested, it is the 'impropriety' of children as actors, the risk that they present and risks that they expose, which dominate the discourse around their performances.

> Man is the animal that recognizes itself 'as such', man is the animal that must recognize itself to be human, and humans perform particular things to ascertain the limits of just such a conception within the general category marked Human.[28]

Here Read suggests that performance negotiates or marks out the boundary of what is to be human, and I interpret this as establishing what it is to be human and not something else, since the alliance or substitution of the child with the (or a) 'thing' (such as an inanimate or enslaved body) has preoccupied me elsewhere in this book. Additionally, I argue that children, particularly young children, do not satisfactorily fit that 'general category marked Human'. As should be clear from the descriptions of their uncanny ability to produce extremes of emotion on cue, in their association with animals, in the disavowal of their agency, in the alluring, fascinating sense in which they have It and in the belief that they are not, or could not be, capable of complex acting, children are perceived as not quite, or not yet, human. To reconfirm this, serendipitously, just as I was redrafting this chapter, I came across this recent description of a child actor in the 2009 film adaptation of Cormac McCarthy's novel, The Road:

> Kodi is Kodi Smitt-McPhee, an 11 year old Australian who plays the son and bowled everyone over when he tested for the part, greatly reducing the anxiety filmmakers feel when casting a child. Some of the crew privately referred to him as the Alien because of the uncanny, almost freakish way that on a moment's notice he switched accents and turned himself from a child into a movie star. Days after the filming of a climactic, emotional scene, people on the set were still marveling at Kodi's performance. A couple said they had puddled up just from watching the monitor and needed to sneak a tear-dabbing finger behind their sunglasses.[29]

Children and Animals

Some of the most interesting and provocative performances from children in films address or explore how the child is able to 'pass' between the (inhuman) animal and the human. In the Italian film, Padre Padrone, the central character is a 'young, barely literate shepherd boy'. In an early sequence of the film, this boy Gavino Leda (aged here at about five or six years old) is milking a sheep. He is entirely alone on a remote fold in the harsh Sardinian landscape, left by his father to care for the flock, and he lives, eats and sleeps with the sheep in the open.

In this sequence, the sheep repeatedly shits in the bucket of milk. Frustrated, Gavino jams his head against the sheep's anus in an attempt to keep the bucket clean. In voiceover we hear his thoughts performed by the young actor (Fabrizo Forte) playing Gavino, 'Shitty animal, I know that you are going to try that again ...' In response and over a shot of the sheep turning her head to 'look' at Gavino, we hear the sheep's thoughts, voiced by an unseen woman actor: 'I will play tricks on you as soon as you turn around. You hit me so I am going to shit in your milk so then your father will hit you'. The parity between the sheep and Gavino is explicit and both are, in effect, anthropomorphised, since they are assigned – through a voiceover – a subjectivity that presumably would not have been recognised or secured from their image alone. Within the sequence, Forte and the sheep are awarded equal screen time in terms of close-ups: we linger on the sheep's neck and head as Gavino kicks it into the mud, we move in closely to the sheep's head and eye as it looks round; Gavino's face and the evident damage done to his eye from an earlier beating is shown in close-up. Neither the child's or the sheep's face is particularly expressive, there appears to be mutual antagonism but, shot by shot, it is not possible to identify how or at which moment this apparent antagonism 'appears' – in that sense both Forte and the sheep are, in Kirby's terms, 'receiving' as actors. That is, the way in which I interpret what their 'performances' mean is not primarily because of what they seem to be doing, but because of the way in which the scene is edited and what is added to the soundtrack. Indeed, it is the sheep that might be said to be more expressive: her ears move back and forwards whilst her 'glance back' as if towards Gavino – edited to fit with her vengeful inner speech – involves more activity and thus offers more information than the child actor's expression which does not seem to change. In fact, his face is partly blocked from view, first, by the fact that he has his head jammed tightly up against the sheep's bottom and second, because he wears a large woolly hat pulled down closely over his forehead. The similarity between sheep and Forte as 'received' actors is reinforced by their position (both heads lowered, shot in close-up, from the side) and this association is further amplified as the sheep continues: 'I will succeed because you are stupid. You shiver, sweat and stink. You don't even know how to milk me with your little hands. You are hurting my udders Gavino Leda, so I am going to shit in your milk'.

Figure 20   'The sheep', in *Padre Padrone* (Dirs. Paolo and Vittorio Taviani, 1977)

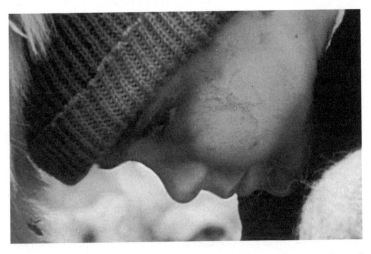

Figure 21   Gavino (Fabrizio Forte), in *Padre Padrone* (Dirs. Paolo and Vittorio Taviani, 1977)

By reinforcing the fact that the human animal also shivers, sweats and stinks, the sheep draws attention to the way in which Gavino's position in relation to the flock has to be earned; he is not guaranteed his assumed place at the top of the hierarchy (as human), he has to establish his authority through violence (just as his father establishes dominance over him). In terms of their framing in this scene and in their performance 'as such', the child actor and sheep are alarmingly (but naturally) aligned and the sheep is not necessarily 'something else' from the (human) child actor. However, having established this ontological parity between sheep and child, the film goes on to establish the humanity of the human animal and does this through the performance of personhood by Forte. After Gavino has flung the second bucket of spoiled milk away, there is a cut to two sheep mating. After this cut away we come back to the child who now stands upright, we hear music on the soundtrack, and for the first time, there is a flicker of expression, a suggestion, a performance of 'intent' which plays over the actor's face. Forte-as-Gavino moves up and around behind the sheep, apparently still breathing deeply from his previous frustration and exertion; as Gavino appears to be thinking we move to a close-up of his face as he closes his eyes and his lips move – suggesting that he is gritting his teeth. As the camera pulls away, we see Gavino bend down over the sheep and he apparently caresses its back and side. So, while we do not see Gavino fuck the sheep, it is evident that he is considering doing so or is about to do so. What is significant about this for my purposes is that the humanity of the character is signalled or established in two ways: first, that in his specific performance (in the passage of expressions that appear to be intended) the child actor moves from a performative positioning in which he seems to be the same as the sheep (they are the same, unreadable, anthropormorphised, 'stinky animals') and instead becomes a separated 'figure' (a simple or complex actor) who performs – literally acts – against what is now the 'ground', the something else or what Read would call the performance 'as such' of the sheep. Second, to confirm this, at the end of the scene the sheep is relegated compositionally to its (her?) lower position in the frame and becomes ultimately, anonymous – pushed back into the flock, it is no longer one sheep or *that* sheep, but any or many sheep. It is no coincidence that the way in which Gavino asserts his authority is through sex: it is evident that we are to understand that having sex with the sheep does not make him more of an animal, but more of a man; it confirms the established and naturalised hierarchies associated with species and gender. Additionally, in his performance of a 'sexual awakening' (in which Forte expresses both self-consciousness and an emergent sexuality) the child actor establishes his 'human-ness', a personhood distinct from the 'something else' of the sheep: the sheep, of course, can't do this. What is alarming and fascinating is that the child actor can, in this short sequence, be both like and not like the animal: indeed it is precisely because this sequence refers directly to the child's subjective experience as being liminal or in transition – since in his performance we can recognise the boy as 'something else' to the human – that we may be able to overlook, or at least understand Gavino's sexual transgression. The commonly employed excuse that 'he was only a child' identifies not just our belief that the child lacks (moral responsibility, understanding) but also that the child is somehow a separate order of 'being' from the adult human.

The relationship between a boy and the animal is replayed in a different manner in the second short film that makes up Bill Douglas's autobiographical trilogy – *My Ain Folk*. It begins, surprisingly, since all the films in the trilogy are otherwise shot in black and white, with a colour sequence; a climactic moment from the 1943 film *Lassie Come Home*. On one level the contrast is simple: the bleak black and white world of a small Scottish mining village in the 1940s is contrasted with the lush green and romantic landscape of a classic Hollywood family melodrama. Yet it is more than this: as Erica Fudge, writing in her book *Pets*, suggests of the original novel on which the *Lassie* films were based:

> *Lassie Come-Home* is, I think, the most explicit rendition of a story that humans have been telling themselves since the emergence of modernity about who it is that they are, but it is also a story about how this self-construction work shields a terrible insecurity.[30]

The story of Lassie is about civilisation, about the making and establishing of a home in which pets help confirm boundaries and reinforce the control that humans have – or must anxiously maintain – over their environment. In My Ain Folk, there is a cut from the cinema screening of Lassie to the close up of a boy's face and we can recognise Tommy, the older of the two brothers we met in the first film, My Childhood. Tommy is staring at the screen, his face wet with tears. This shot could suggest two things: first, that he is simply moved by the film; second, that on some level he understands (since the Granny who cared for him and his younger brother Jamie, has now died) that he, unlike Lassie, has no home to come home to, and that without a home he has no stable context on which to stage his own destiny or his own subjectivity, and indeed the suggestion of tears indicates that he has lost control.

In My Childhood, the boys' home is desperately poor but it acts or functions as a home, since it has, at least, established boundaries that define an inside from an outside. There is a door, Granny's chair, a table and beds. Their home therefore produces an inside space, a shared hearth that is distinct from the outside of street, school and pit. The home is also defined by the fact that the boys (for a time) both have pets: Jamie has a black cat and Tommy is given a caged canary by his absentee father. As Fudge writes, pets are key participants in the organisation and delineation of many homes. Whilst their status as both insider and outsider (as domesticated pet and as inhuman other, as non-human animal) may be ambivalent, the fact that most humans establish dominance (through violence or through affection) over their pets generates a sense of ontological security. As Fudge suggests:

> It is because they [pets] are animals in the home – because they are simultaneously outside and inside – that they are so valuable both to live with and to think with. They are a constant reminder of the fragility of our status and at the same time they show us how our status might be and can be secured.[31]

In My Childhood, the inevitable consequence of the forced and close association of a cat and canary takes place: during an air raid the boys and Granny leave their home for a communal shelter and the cat kills and eats the canary. In retribution Tommy kills the cat, and the destruction of the pets foreshadows Granny's death and the end of the boys' home and fragile security.

What interests me most, however, is at the level of performance, and specifically, the interaction between the child actors and the animals in the films, a relationship that is played out disturbingly in My Ain Folk between Jamie (played by Steven Archibald) and his other grandmother's pet – a whippet. At the beginning of this second film, the audience are now aware that Jamie and Tommy's mother has had some kind of mental breakdown and exists, heavily sedated, in an asylum. The brothers have different fathers; we have seen Tommy's father only briefly, when he appears and gives him the caged bird. Confronted and insulted by Granny, he takes flight, cycling away from the village. Jamie's father actually lives nearby; a silent, possibly simple-minded figure, he is at first embalmed in a suffocatingly close relationship with his mother. Whilst we see him tentatively acknowledge Jamie's existence, neither he nor his mother take any responsibility for Jamie until they are seemingly obliged to do so by Granny's death. Jamie is never formally welcomed or introduced into this, his second home; instead he stands silent, dishevelled and dirty in the corner of the spotless living room, ignored by his father and his grandmother. Tommy, we know, has been taken to a children's home. At first, Jamie returns, stubbornly, to the empty flat he shared with Tommy and Granny, but once the door has been locked against him (by his grandmother) he is forced to take shelter in his new home, first outside, then inside his grandmother's house, cowering and glowering in the corners. In a series of short scenes, a close association between the pet whippet and Jamie is established. The dog is a small, lean creature, with large dark eyes, frequently pictured with its tail curled tightly between its back legs. Read anthropomorphically, the dog seems sad, pathetic, nervous and needy. It barely makes a sound – we never hear it whine and it never appears to bark. It is well cared for, clean and frequently coddled by the grandmother, who often holds it in her lap, kissing it and speaking to it in caressing terms. The child and dog are therefore positioned and can be read as the same, since both are pathetic and needy, entirely dependent on the adult humans they live with. Both dog and boy are frequently framed with the camera looking down on them, isolated in the frame. Yet the conventional hierarchy between the dog and the boy in the home is subverted: the dog is the animal that is loved, cared for and caressed, and the boy-as-animal is neglected and ignored. Like the dog, Jamie rarely makes a sound in the house, frequently curling himself up tightly in corners, under tables, to take up as little space as possible. The sense in which Jamie seems like an animal is underpinned by Archibald's performance. Like the adult actors, but to an even more extraordinary degree, his performance as Jamie is marked, as John Caughie has observed, by the 'absence of "acted" emotion'.[32] In this sense, the dog and the child actor function as 'received actors' and the emotions and sensibility of their characters are established from other cues – through costume, composition and editing.

One particularly significant scene begins as the grandmother returns home with the dog. The camera frames her entrance into the living room at the dog's eye level (which is also Jamie's eye level) and the dog is centre frame, on a lead, close to her legs. As

Figure 22   Jamie (Stephen Archibald) cowers in a corner, in *My Ain Folk* (Dir. Bill Douglas, 1973)

she comes into the room and builds up the fire, we know that Jamie is curled up, knees to his face, under a table in the corner of the room. His grandmother does not, at first, acknowledge him. We also know something that the grandmother does not: Jamie has recently and deliberately pissed on the blanket in the dog's basket, an action that could be read as a covert act of revenge against the dog and the grandmother. This means that the dog, understandably, is reluctant to take to its bed. Noticing the stains, the grandmother assumes that it is the dog that has made the mess but does not punish it, and takes it onto her lap, and kisses it ('My darling'). Released from its lead, the dog then gets off her lap. This allows the grandmother to drink from the bottle she has been carrying in her coat pocket. It is only now, that without looking round, she throws her arm back toward Jamie, gesturing to him to come forward. There is then a cut to a shot of Jamie (seen from the back) sitting on his grandmother's lap. She drunkenly caresses him, calling him 'the best boy in the world'. There is then a cut to the dog, standing and staring into the camera, the clear implication being that it is looking at Jamie and his grandmother. It is not possible to read an emotion here, as it would be ridiculous to suggest that the dog is acting 'jealous' or 'confused'. What makes the scene unnerving is that it is obvious that Jamie is at this moment a substitute for the dog, who is, in turn, a substitute for the grandmother's two adult sons, both of whom are disappointing to her. As we cut back from the dog we still do not see Jamie's face, only the back of his head, but we witness the grandmother allow him to drink from her bottle and hug him tightly ('Ma wee putz'). The scene concludes with a shot of the dog curled up in its basket, which is then followed by a shot of Jamie in his bed. In voiceover, Jamie is heard asking Jesus to 'make ma Granny drunk every night'.

It is only the adult human actor – playing the drunken grandmother – who is allowed the opportunity for any expression at all, since we never see Jamie's face whilst he sits on the grandmother's lap, and in the bed, his face remains impassive and heavily shadowed. All that has happened is that, temporarily, the dog has been relegated to Jamie's ordinary position in the household, that of the ignored observer, and despite the grandmother's caresses, Jamie has not been granted personhood and is still being treated like a non-human animal – a pet – although he is, temporarily, preferred to the actual pet dog. Archibald's performance is here and elsewhere no more or less expressive than the dog's – in this sense Archibald does not perform as a human (he does not perform human-ness but as if he were a 'dumb' animal), and he is therefore akin to the 'something else' that is also embodied by the dog: the effect is both depressing and unsettling. Our pity for Jamie is also tinged with suspicion, for like the animal Jamie seems unreadable – is he scared or malevolent (or both), is he looking for a pat on the head or will he bite? In terms of Archibald's performance it is difficult to disentangle the emotive evidence we gather from closely observing his presence (the thick texture of his hair, the pale luminescence of his skin, his unsmiling gaze) from how we are encouraged to interpret his situation and emotions from the way in which he is being framed by Douglas's camera. Unlike *Padre Padrone*, the film offers no immediate opportunity for the child to pass performatively between the inhuman and human. At the end of this film, Jamie is removed to a care home in Edinburgh, and we last see him head down, being helped into a black van, his final journey reminiscent of a dog being taken to a pound.

> A child of four years who happens to be my daughter walks from somewhere off to somewhere on and accustoms herself to being watched. This acclimatisation has already begun between the off and the on and first manifests itself in her eyes. They are averted from the habitual assimilation of childhood that links foreground and distance, a visual dexterity that can give the youth-full that magical air of insouciance just beyond and out of the reach of the adult in a zone of myriad pleasures and fears.[33]

The last film of the Bill Douglas trilogy *My Way Home* (shot five years after the first two films) begins with a photograph of the Royal family and we can see Princess Elizabeth holding the baby Prince Charles on her lap, surrounded by her nearest relatives. We then cut to a stage with a young girl dressed as Mary holding the infant Jesus on her lap. Evidently, we are being reminded of the national and religious symbolic weight of family, since in this film, it is family (if not, now, a home) that Jamie lacks. Jamie, dressed in a white shirt and a kilt, is holding a small bunch of flowers and is 'waiting in the wings', off stage. Immediately, we are conscious that Archibald is no longer the young child of the first two films and indeed during the course of this final film, Jamie grows up, ultimately undergoing National Service in the Army. Whilst he does not take part in the awkward child performances of the nativity play (in which the one of the Kings recites in a dull 'sing-song' voice that 'We have come on a long journey') he does wait to make his entrance on to the stage. Ushered on by the head of the home, Jamie opens a door and begins to walk across the stage towards another symbolic family, the mayor, his wife and their daughter. He has been chosen to present flowers to the civic family. As he walks across the empty stage, his trouser legs slide down, revealing the (grown up) real boy underneath the ceremonial costume. This sequence effectively reproduces the scene described above, as witnessed by Read discussing the experience of watching his own daughter, Florence, in her first nativity play. What the nativity scene in My Way Home does is make explicit the parallel changes in the child actor and the character he plays. Jamie's entrance onto the stage therefore has a dual purpose – in terms of the fiction it reveals that Jamie has grown up (he looks different, he acts differently) and second, in a self-reflexive move, it literally re-frames and insists upon the artifice of Archibald's performance, thereby calling attention to the fact that Archibald is not Jamie, insisting that he is now (and in fact has always been) playing a part. Archibald is no longer a young child. He remains interesting but not fascinating, and our interest is inspired by the way in which the adolescent is and isn't the young child, that uncanny inhuman being we once observed so intimately. Archibald is no longer that being whose apparent lack of personhood and self-consciousness allows us to confuse the real boy with the fictional character. There is no longer an alliance between the unreadable, inhuman quality of the child with the otherness of the animal.

Archibald now performs as someone aware that they are being watched, as *someone* who is deliberately, overtly, expressing awkwardness, self-consciousness, as *someone else*. This reading of the performer's behaviour or belief that we know from this what the character is feeling is not simply based on Archibald's presence as framed by the film, but is made manifest by Archibald's performance as someone who is acting, evident in his stilted gait and his hesitant handling of the flowers. In the five years that have passed – both from the shooting of the second film, (and within the fictional story of Jamie), Archibald, and Archibald-as-Jamie, have both gained self-consciousness: a trait inherent to the 'performing human animal' that did not seem to be in evidence in the first two films. In a subsequent scene in which all the boys from the home are eating Christmas pudding together in the dining room, the head of the home, a kindly but detached figure, moves around the tables correcting the boys' table manners and asking them about the pudding. The boys, dressed in dark jumpers and shirts, all seem to have short dark hair and therefore look much alike. The head notices one boy who seems too unhappy to eat: he brings him over to his own table, encourages him to eat and even begins to play the mouth organ for him. For the latter part of this sequence we don't watch the head and this un-named boy but instead observe Jamie, who previously we had seen eating his pudding but who is now sitting silently, not eating, his head resting in his hand. Suddenly, he leaps up and pushes his plate onto the floor and runs upstairs to the dormitory. All the boys and the head then look up as a huge crashing and banging can be heard from above. Jamie, it appears, is no longer willing to be ignored: his rage is expressed openly, deliberately. In this sequence, Archibald-as-Jamie and Jamie-the-character self-consciously perform anger. The register of the performance is therefore distinct from the first two films – the confusion for the informed viewer of this film has been qualified: it is no longer whether Archibald is Jamie (that is, is Jamie really just Archibald inhabiting a fictional context?) but becomes exclusively, the curiosity as to how close Jamie's story is the actual biography of the film-maker Bill Douglas. Acting retrospectively, the third film clarifies the poetic opaqueness of the first two films and the story moves from the mythic to the specific as the presence of the disturbing child disappears from view.

This is not to say that Archibald's acting style differs greatly from the earlier films, since his acting is still deliberate, full of silences and averted gazes. Nonetheless, it is an uncanny coincidence that Douglas engineers Jamie's entrance into adulthood, and definitively distinguishes the character of Jamie from the 'real boy' that is Archibald, through the mechanism of the nativity play, the exact rite of passage Read employs in his meditation on the difference between the performance 'as such' of the child, and the performance of a child who is beginning to become self-conscious, or to understand what it might mean to perform 'as if' someone, not as something else. Read frames this beginning, this passing, into a question:

> If the entrance of the child's performance is simultaneously an exit, from where does the child believe that they might have come in order to leave, and where might they be intending to go?[34]

Jamie's entrance and exit here, in the context of the film, is an escape, since there is little of his childhood that we can believe that he would not like to leave behind. In Read's evaluation of his daughter's passing there is a greater expectation or anticipation of loss, and this is, presumably because her childhood is 'full' in comparison to the emotional and material poverty we have seen of Jamie's experience. Yet, even though this is what the narrative of the film is asking us to invest in, there is still, I would argue, a loss of sorts, still something 'less' about this older Jamie. This is because Archibald's parallel passing from a seemingly unconscious performer (alarmingly and compellingly akin to the animal) to a self-conscious actor (who no longer creates any ontological confusion or anxiety) means that the older Jamie as played by Archibald is less appealing to the viewer. As if anticipating our loss of interest, the camera remains, for the most part, further away from Archibald-as-Jamie, since we are no longer able to engage in his littleness, or in the texture and grain of his skin and hair, as the performer's body is no longer that of a child's. In a way, I am suggesting that the older Archibald no longer really has 'It', or as Read suggests, that 'magical air of insouciance just beyond and out of the reach of the adult'. Archibald is now acting or performing as someone playing someone else and this makes Jamie legible and less interesting. The audience recognises that Archibald is now 'properly' playing a character that he is both like and unlike. The trilogical interaction between actor, character and audience that Schechner describes is now in place. Thus the self-conscious boy playing the boy-who-becomes-a-man no longer embodies the something else that – in the first two films – made Archibald's presence and Jamie as a character so disturbing and fascinating.

'It Will All End in Tears...'

I now want to return to the other child actors that have featured in this chapter and draw attention to a similarity between them that deserves further exploration and which also relates to the question posed by Read in his exploration of performance 'as such'. In the descriptions of Bowen, Temple, Miller, O'Brien, Fanning, Thivisol and Apicella, the focus and fascination in their acting abilities, in their performances, is centred on the production of tears.

In the majority of the accounts describing child film actors, it is the ability of the child to cry on cue, for the camera, that is focused upon again and again. Why tears? As I have implied, the production of tears is often the specific aspect of the child's performance which inspires the most anxiety for adult viewers. Simply, the question may be, is it fair to make a child cry? Is it fair to ask a child to make themselves cry? The extraordinary response to a series of pictures made by the photographer Jill Greenberg in which she made a number of small children cry, by first giving them a lollipop and then abruptly taking it away, would suggest that many people are uncomfortable about children crying in the pursuit of art. An article on Greenberg reported:

> Rather than seeing the metaphor, people accused her of abusing the children, one of whom is her own daughter. A furious campaign was launched against Greenberg, spearheaded by an internet blogger, Andrew Peterson, a San Francisco investment adviser who has four young children. His initial blog read: 'Jill Greenberg is a sick woman who should be arrested and charged with child abuse'.[35]

The furore over the pictures was amplified by the fact that the children were particularly young and that they were (framed from the chest up) apparently naked. In addition, Greenberg attached overtly political titles (such as, 'Misinformation', 'Four more years',

'Faith?') to the pictures. My interest is not whether the furore was justified but in the fact that there was such concern about the children's tears, since, as I have indicated, the production of tears on cue is, less controversially, a fundamental and celebrated part of the successful child's performance on film. The second reason relates to the fact that children crying are such emotive figures, whether read unproblematically as metaphors, or prompting adult recall of their own childhood fears and pains. The response to children crying, I think, is part sympathy (poor kid) and part empathy (I sometimes feel, I felt, just like that). We might recall Andre Bazin's dismissal of the audience's response to sorrowful children in films about war as adults 'just feeling sorry for ourselves'.

The significance of the child's tears is that crying 'real tears' is not something that animals do. Equally, animals do not perform tears. As Read notes, the 'simple divide along the lines of lachrymosity is just one of the fault lines that separates humans from other animals.'[36] While animals 'cry out' they are not understood to cry to produce tears for whatever reasons the human animal has: in pain and in fear, or as a response to loss and excitement, or deliberately, on cue within a performative context. In witnessing children cry we are being reassured of their (and our own) humanity, whether this is in everyday life or as a performance: as a sign, tears are doubly potent – they are both essentially and performatively evidence of the humanness of the animal. As Jack Katz, in his book How Emotions Work, suggests, it is important to remember that crying can and does involve snivelling, weeping, wailing, sobbing and whining. Crying is therefore not a simple activity; it is nuanced, complex behaviour, one that may be self-consciously performed in everyday life as well as on stage and screen.

> Crying is not just a 'feeling' nor just a series of effects; it is a subtle range of corporeal doings, such as balking at speaking, resonant markings of pauses between utterances, and a manner of depicting the body as too light or too heavy a vehicle to bear or to hold on to language.[37]

The function of crying and tears as they are manifest in the performance of the child actor are various in terms of their effects, but on one level they encourage the audience to recognise the humanity of the character being played by the child. Yet on another level, the appearance of tears is confusing and emotive because the child's tears are potentially not representation and we may never be entirely certain that the tears we witness are 'all an act'.

Crying is messy behaviour: it is supposedly instinctive, yet it is often self-conscious; it may be apparently spontaneous and incontinent; or it may also be strategic; and it may be all of these things at different times in different contexts. The contradictory origins and motivation for tears may surface consecutively, or they may all be present at the same time. In relation to Kirby's model of acting (which distinguishes being 'done to' and 'doing' as an essential step from the performer who is not-acting to acting), crying – as actual behaviour and as performance activity – inhabits a grey area, or a margin of indeterminacy. This is perhaps particularly true in relation to children, who may cry or produce tears easily without necessarily distinguishing their reasons and motivations, or understanding their tears as appropriate or inappropriate behaviour. Despite this confusion there remains something stubbornly compelling about the physical manifestation of tears. We continue to see them as irrefutable evidence of inner anguish, even when we are sure they are not. When we witness a child crying, we cannot avoid confronting the element of exploitation inherent to (screen) performance itself. This is because either we are viewing a situation in which the child has been asked to exploit its own emotional resources or we are implicitly consenting to its direct exploitation by others (directors, mothers or other actors). No wonder that the child actor who can claim (or for whom it is claimed) the ability to cry naturally and for no apparent (or significant) reason is so celebrated. In this context, no one is guilty and we can sit back, relax and 'enjoy the show'. Yet the evidence, the fascination or obsession with tears in the biographies of child performers and the publicity material surrounding their performances on screen suggests that we are not entirely convinced by these stories.

One of the most fascinating and most complex scenes in which a child cries on film is from Visconti's Bellissima. The plot of the film concerns Maddalena Cecconi (Anna Magnani), a poor, working-class woman who is desperate to get her child into films. We see her take her daughter Maria (played by Tina Apicella) through a series of different auditions and ultimately to a screen test. In the latter part of the film, Maddalena and Maria manage to gain entrance to the studio as the director and his associates are viewing the screen tests, and Maddalena further negotiates their way into the projection room just as Maria's test is to be screened. Neither we nor Maddalena have actually seen Maria's performance for the test. Maddalena positions herself just by the projector and lifts Maria up so that they can both see out of the small projectionist's window onto the large screen in the darkened screening room below. Their faces are framed by this window and pressed tightly against each other. In the screening room, the director (played by the actual Italian film director, Alessandro Blasetti) and his associates sit in the dark, looking up at the screen. A dramatic triangle is set up: Maddalena and Maria at the projectionist's window; Maria on the cinema screen; the men (all men – except the one female secretary at the back of the

Figure 23   Maddalena (Anna Magnani) and Maria (Tina Apicella) in the projection booth, in Bellissima (Dir. Luchino Visconti, 1951)

room – and a dog) sit in a line across the room with some of the men sitting off to one side.

As the test begins, Maddalena's face is hopeful, eager, she speaks quietly to her daughter whose face is without emotion. We then cut to the test in which Maria, dressed ridiculously in a short tutu, heavily made up and with her hair dressed in tight, artificial curls, walks down to a birthday cake lit with candles. She tries and fails to blow them out. At this there is a cut to the men, who begin to mimic her, blowing and puffing saying: 'Blow! Blow! Poor thing!' As Maddalena witnesses Maria's difficulty she comments: 'Couldn't you manage? You have so much breath at home, but not there?' Maria remains impassive and does not speak though she appears to be watching intently. After the director asks for quiet the Maria on screen begins to recite a poem that we have heard her perform twice before. At first we see her in mid-long shot and she appears alarmingly, grotesquely huge, since our perspective places us, uncomfortably, with the men in the screening room and we are looking up at her crotch. The framing of the test image then moves to a closer mid-shot, and as Maria speaks we become aware that her eyes are brimming with tears. As she reaches the line 'Bread lacks, the cholera deadlier grows' she begins to cry in earnest, and tears spill down her cheeks. Indeed, she begins to wail; although intermittently she tries to carry on with the poem (demonstrating, as Katz points out, that crying is often a struggle with speech). We then cut to Maria and her mother in the projection booth and Maddalena asks 'Did you cry? Why did you start crying?', whilst Maria remains silent and impassive. There is then a close cut to the director, Blassetti, who is sitting forward, concentrating hard on the screen, in stark contrast to most of his associates, who are sitting back and laughing. At first, even as the laughter increases, Maddalena suggests that the men's laughter is, at least, expressing an interest in Maria. As if to finally undermine this last hope, Maddalena's comments are followed by a shot of Alberto Annovazzi (Walter Chiari), the conman charmer and lowly member of the film crew who has cost Maddalena so much in her attempts to make Maria a star. In a close-up, it appears as if he is laughing the loudest and, as we watch him guffaw, head back and mouth wide open, gasping for breath, we can hear Maria's wail from the test. We then cut back to the test itself, this time in close-up as Maria also struggles for breath, still wailing, to complete the poem. By this time the screening room is in disarray, with most of the men practically 'crying with laughter', as for instance, when one of the men is holding a handkerchief to his face as if to mop away tears. As Maria's tears begin to fall down her cheeks, her mother finally covers the little girl's face and puts her down so that she can no longer see herself on screen. By this point it is evident that Maddalena, eyes already glistening with imminent tears, will also begin to cry. The final straw comes when she hears one of the men snigger: 'She's a dwarf, look!' After commenting 'Bastard' Maddalena turns from the window to confront the men below.

It is difficult to describe quite how shocking this sequence is. In terms of the narrative, it is the climactic scene in which Maddalena finally realises that the dream of cinema stardom she had projected on to her daughter may not be the glamorous opportunity she believed it to be. It is an alarming scene in its revelation of the extraordinary arrogance and violence of the men and their explicit positioning of the girl child as other, as

Figure 24 'Crying with laughter', in *Bellissima* (Dir. Luchino Visconti, 1951)

a funny, incapable dwarf – as a 'freak'. In terms of performance, Magnani as Maddalena has the opportunity to express a range of complex emotions, from hope and anticipation to bewilderment, from sorrow to righteous indignation, all in close-up, her face beautifully illuminated by the apparent reflection of the projected image below. It is a bravura performance: sensitive, credible and compelling. Yet it is Tina Apicella's performance that interests me. The scene offers two kinds of performance from Apicella: the screen test and her response to the test itself. In watching the test, Apicella as Maria appears to offer nothing to read, her face is blank, after her initial excitement at seeing a rival being screened in the test immediately before, Apicella remains entirely silent, her lips pressed firmly together, she never looks at Magnani and appears only to watch her own image on the screen. She does nothing, but she is kissed, stroked and finally shielded by Magnani who covers Apicella's eyes with her hand. In this part of the scene, Apicella-as-Maria is therefore acting as a ground for the figural performance of Magnani as Maddalena. As she shares the frame with Magnani, Apicella is the prop that the adult actor uses to motivate and contextualise her captivating performance as a mother who is moved (finally) to protect her child. Yet in the test, Apicella-as-Maria is acting, as she struggles and fails to blow out the candles and she cries, producing tears and wailing loudly. We do not really know how the tears have been inspired; however, it is not just their presence but how they are managed by the actor (associated with the wailing, her struggles for breath and her punctuated attempts to finish the poem) which confirms that Apicella is doing something more than 'received' acting. Through her performance of tears she is expressing what it is to be human (to feel that one is uniquely exposed, ashamed and frightened). At the same time, in the context of the film within the film, Maria's performance appears to be a disaster because she is crying, and she generates a response from her audience in which they view her as that 'poor thing', that 'something else' that is so alarming and peculiar in children since it does not seem (as their comments suggest) quite human. That is why, after all, the men are laughing. Maria is performing improperly; or in other words, and as one of the men says, 'She can't do it', that is, 'act' rather than cry. Underpinning this apparent impropriety however, is the 'proper' performance of the actual child actor, Apicella. What is confusing is that the effect of the scene is amplified by the sense in which we are uncertain how the child actor (Apicella) is managing to cry for the camera. Despite Visconti's assurances that she is instinctive, that she can cry on cue because she is exceptional, the tears seem authentic and to be authentic there must have been some form of exploitation of the child actor. Can we believe that a young child could be that good at being a *bad* actor?

The final twist in the story of the film relates to what might, in the context of my arguments, seem to be the logical consequence of Maria's test. Maria's apparently improper performance reveals (to the experienced and talented eye of the director) that, in fact, she has, or is, It – she manifests the peculiar and fascinating appeal so often associated with children and animals. The part for the little girl in the film within the film (entitled 'Today, tomorrow and never') is therefore offered to Maria. The ending reveals, of course, that Maddalena, now wise to the exploitation inherent to the film industry, will refuse to sign her daughter's contract. After a long and tiring journey home from the studios to her flat, she is

Figure 25   Maria's (Tina Apicella) screen test – bad acting or good crying?, in *Bellissima* (Dir. Luchino Visconti, 1951)

reunited with her husband whom she tearfully embraces, as Maria sleeps quietly in the bed beside them. The final shot of the film is a close-up of Apicella-as-Maria, her hair brushed back from her face, and she does appear to be sleeping (really sleeping? We can't be certain). In terms of the narrative, the viewer is relieved that the family home has been restored, that Maddalena has come to her senses and that she has made the right choice. It is a relief to see that Maria is safe, sleeping in her own bed. Yet, as the music swells, and the camera moves in closer to frame this clichéd image of a child sleeping, I find myself distracted by a drop of water trickling down the side of Maria's face. She is not crying; the trickle probably originates in water used to wash her face and smooth back her fringe away from her forehead (erasing the least flattering aspect of the dreadful haircut Maddalena spent so much money on). In my fascination with this trickle of water, which emphasises the smoothness and whiteness of the child's skin, and in the simple sense that the child actor looks so beautiful and so graceful (despite, or *because* of, the fact that she is not actually doing anything), I realise that I am doing it again, I am reading into the child's presence something that is not necessarily there at all. Whilst Maria may not be exploited by the on-screen director Blasetti, Apicella continues to be objectified and depersonalised by Visconti for my pleasure.

As an exploration of the child-star phenomenon, *Bellissima* is wonderfully complex: on the one hand it articulates a satisfyingly moral dénouement: 'Don't put your daughter on the stage...', and it details with sharp, yet affectionate detachment the machinations and sacrifices of the 'star-struck' mother and her (apparently) hapless child. On the other hand, in its part reliance on Magnani's own stardom and the use of real settings (the Cinecittà studios) and real personnel (the well-known director, Blassetti, as himself), it inevitably celebrates the glamour, skill and professionalism of the industry (however corrupt some aspects are revealed to be). And while the film details the exploitation and vulnerability of the child performer, it must necessarily use child performers to do so. As Geoffrey Nowell-Smith argues:

> The morality of the artistic process is not that of life, and the cinema is an extreme case of this...Visconti points this out,

but to do so, in a film, he has himself been guilty of the same charge that he makes against the cinema in general because of the use he makes of the little girl Maria. There is then a second degree moral attached to the main theme of the film. One the one hand he wishes to denounce; on the other he must himself carry through the very process he condemns.[38]

For me, Bellissima, and in particular the scene between the screening room and the projection room encapsulates the risks, the excitement and the discomfort made manifest in many of the different child performances on screen that I have explored in this chapter and elsewhere in the book. It also unglues all the elements that, together, make up film performance itself: the scene plays with and reorganizes the relations between image and sound, real and fake, figure and ground, impersonation and 'captured reality'. In its separation and presentation of two different kinds of performance from the same child actor (Apicella as Maria in the test and as Maria in the projection room) it opens up the contradictory and competing understandings of what it is, exactly, the child does when it appears, or performs, in film.

Notes

Introduction

1. Steedman, Carolyn, *Dust* (Manchester University Press: Manchester, 2002) p.150.
2. Kathy Merlock Jackson's *The Image of the Child in American Film* (Scarecrow Press: New York, 1986) and Vicky Lebeau's *Cinema and Childhood* (Reaktion Books: London, 2008) offer a more coherent and chronological model than the present book. Lebeau's first chapter on the very early history of the child in cinema is an important background to some of my arguments.
3. Jones, Owain, ' "True geography [ ] quickly forgotten, giving away to an adult-imagined universe". Approaching the otherness of childhood' in *Children's Geographies* Vol. 6, No. 2 (May 2008) (pp.195–212) p.197.
4. Davis, Colin, *Haunted Subjects: deconstruction, psychoanalysis and the return of the dead* (Palgrave Macmillan: Hampshire, 2007).
5. Honeyman, Susan, *Elusive Childhood: impossible representations in modern fiction* (Ohio State University Press: Columbus, 2005).
6. Honeyman, *Elusive Childhood*, p.VIII.
7. Bond Stockton, Kathryn, 'Growing Sideways, or Versions of the Queer Child: the ghost, the homosexual, the Freudian, the innocent and the interval of animal' in Steve Bruhm and Natasha Hurley (eds.) *Curiouser: on the queerness of children* (University of Minnesota Press: Minneapolis and London, 2004) (pp.277–317) p.279.
8. Perec, Georges, *W*, trans. David Bellos (David R. Goodine: Boston, 1988), preface.
9. Nandrea, Lorri, 'Objectless Curiosity: *Frankenstein, The Station Agent*, and other strange narratives' in *Narrative* Vol. 15, No. 3 (October 2007) (pp.335–356) p.336.
10. Nandrea, 'Objectless Curiosity', p.336.
11. Nandrea, 'Objectless Curiosity', p.341.
12. Hoban, Russell, *Riddley Walker* (Bloomsbury: London 2002, first pub. 1980) p.7.

Chapter 1

1. Yoda, Tomiko, 'A Roadmap to Millennial Japan' in *The South Atlantic Quarterly*, Vol. 99, No. 4, (2002) (pp.629–668) p.661.
2. Davis, Colin, *Haunted Subjects: deconstruction, psychoanalysis and the return of the dead* (Palgrave Macmillan: Hampshire, 2007) p.13.

3. Davis, *Haunted Subjects*, p.88.

4. Cua Lim, Bliss, 'Spectral Times: the ghost film as historical allegory' in *Positions* Vol. 9, No. 2 (2001) (pp.287–329) p.287.

5. Chakrabarty, Dipesh, 'The Time of History and the Times of the Gods' in L. Lowe and D. Lloyd (eds.), *The Politics of Culture in the Shadow of Capital* (Duke University Press: Durham NC, 1997) (pp.35–61) p.43.

6. Tanaka, Stefan, *New Times in Modern Japan* (Princeton University Press: Princeton and London, 2004) p.16.

7. Tanaka, *New Times*, p.6.

8. Yoda, 'A Roadmap', p.648.

9. Yoda, 'A Roadmap', p.649.

10. Steedman, Carolyn, *Strange Dislocations: childhood and the idea of human interiority 1780–1930* (Virago Press: London, 1995) p.7.

11. Tanaka, Stefan, 'Childhood: naturalization of development into a Japanese Space' in S.C. Humphreys (ed.) *Cultures of Scholarship* (University of Michigan Press: Ann Arbor, 1997) (pp.21–57) p.29.

12. Tanaka, 'Childhood: naturalization', pp.23–24.

13. Field, Norma, 'The Child as Laborer and Consumer: the disappearance of childhood in contemporary Japan' in S. Stephens (ed.) *Children and the Politics of Culture* (Princeton University Press: Princeton and London, 1995) (pp.51–79) p.63.

14. Tanaka, *New Times*, p.142.

15. Field, 'The Child as Laborer', pp.60–61.

16. Tanaka, *New Times*, p.182.

17. Arai, Andrea 'Recessionary Effects: the crisis of the child and culture of reform in contemporary Japan' unpublished PhD thesis, Columbia University, 2004, p.77.

18. Arai, Andrea, 'Killing Kids: recession and survival in twenty-first century Japan' in *Postcolonial Studies* Vol. 6, No. 3 (2003) (pp.367–379) pp.370–71.

19. Tanaka, 'Childhood: naturalization', p.17.

20. Arai, 'Recessionary Effects', p.53.

21. Kore-eda Hirokazu, sleeve notes to ICA Projects 2004 DVD release of *Nobody Knows*.

22. Ehrlich, Linda C., '*Nobody Knows (Dare mo shiranai)*' in *Film Quarterly* Vol. 59, No. 2 (Winter 2005–2006) (pp.45–50) p.47.

23. Ehrlich, 'Nobody Knows', p.46.

Chapter 2

1. Stern, Lesley, *The Scorsese Connection* (British Film Institute: London, 1995) p.34.

2. duCille, Ann, 'The Shirley Temple of My Familiar' in *Transition* No. 73 (1997) (pp.10–32) p.32.

3. Stern, *Scorsese Connection*, p.38.

4. Phillips, Adam, *On Kissing, Tickling and Being Bored* (Faber and Faber: London, 1993) pp.1–2.

5. Phillips, *On Kissing*, p.2.

6. Phillips, *On Kissing*, p.3.

7. Kincaid, James, *Erotic Innocence: the culture of child molesting* (Duke University Press: Durham NC, 1998) and *Child Loving: the erotic child and Victorian culture* (Routledge: New York and London, 1992).

8. Lesage, Julia, 'Artful Racism, Artful Rape: Griffith's *Broken Blossoms*' in *Jump Cut* No. 26 (1981) reprinted in Christine Gledhill (ed.) *Home Is Where the Heart Is: studies in melodrama and the women's film* (British Film Institute: London, 1987) (pp.235–254) p.251.

9. Studlar, Gaylyn, 'Oh, "Doll Divine": Mary Pickford, masquerade, and the pedophilic gaze' in *Camera Obscura* Vol. 16, No. 3 (2001) (pp.197–226) p.220.

10. Lesage, 'Artful Racism', pp.243–244.

11. Temple Black, Shirley *Child Star: an autobiography* (Headline: London, 1989) p.23.

12. duCille, 'The Shirley Temple', p.21.

13. Merish, Lori, 'Cuteness and Commodity Aesthetics: Tom Thumb and Shirley Temple' in Rosemarie Garland Thomson (ed.) *Freakery: cultural spectacles of the extraordinary body* (New York University Press: New York, 1996) (pp.185–203) p.190.

14. These include: *Kid 'n' Africa*, *Dora's Dunkin' Donuts* and *Pardon my Pups*.

15. Merish, 'Cuteness and Commodity Aesthetics', p.197.

16. Temple Black, *Child Star*, p.23.

17. Merish, 'Cuteness and Commodity Aesthetics', p.199.

18. Merish, 'Cuteness and Commodity Aesthetics', pp.188–189.

19. Eckert, Charles, 'Shirley Temple and the House of Rockerfeller' in *Jump Cut* No. 2 (1974) reprinted in Christine Gledhill (ed.) *Stardom: industry of desire* (Routledge: London, 1991) (pp.60–73).

20. Temple Black, *Child Star*, pp.184–185.

21. duCille, 'The Shirley Temple', pp.17–18.

22. Stanley Kubrick quoted in Hughes, David *The Complete Kubrick* (Virgin: London, 2000), p.100.

23. Kincaid, James, *Child Loving: the erotic child and Victorian culture* (Routledge: London and New York, 1992) p.126.

24. Morrison, Toni, *Playing in the Dark: whiteness and the literary imagination* (Harvard University Press: Cambridge, MA, 1992) pp.46–47.

25. Belletto, Steven, 'Of Pickaninnies and Nymphets: race in *Lolita*' in *Nabokov Studies* Vol. 9 (2005) (pp.1–17) p.16.

26. Belletto, 'Of Pickaninnies', p.5.

27. Coviello, Peter, 'Poe in Love: pedophilia, morbidity, and the logic of slavery' in *ELH* Vol. 70, No. 3 (Fall, 2003) (pp.875–901) p.896.

28. Coviello, 'Poe in Love', p.888.

29. Morrison, *Playing in the Dark*, p.32.

30. Coviello, 'Poe in Love', p.878.

31. Coviello, 'Poe in Love', p.887.

32. Coviello, 'Poe in Love', p.897.

33. Stern, *The Scorsese Connection*, p.33.

34. Stern, *The Scorsese Connection*, p.62.

35. Butler, David, 'The Days Do Not End: film music, time and Bernard Herrmann' in *Film Studies* No. 9 (Winter, 2006) (pp.51–63) p.56.

36. Stern, *The Scorsese Connection*, p.58.

37. Stern, *The Scorsese Connection*, p.61.

38. Temple Black, *Child Star*, p.90.

39. Morrison, *Playing in the Dark*, p.47.

40. Morrison, *Playing in the Dark*, p.46.

41. Williams, Linda, *Playing the Race Card: melodramas of black and white from Uncle Tom to O.J. Simpson* (Princeton University Press: Princeton NJ, and London, 2001) p.300.

Chapter 3

1. Thompson, John O., 'Reflexions on Dead Children in the Cinema and Why There Are Not More of Them' in Gillian Avery and Kimberley Reynolds (eds.) *Representations of Childhood Death* (Palgrave Macmillan: Hampshire, 1999) (pp.204–215) p.208. Original citation is from André Bazin, 'Germany Year Zero' in Bert Cardullo (ed.) *Bazin at Work: major essays & reviews from the forties and fifties* (Routledge: London and New York, 1997) (pp.121–4) p.121.

2. Bazin, 'Germany Year Zero', p.121.

3. Youngblood, Denise, 'Post-Stalinist Cinema and the Myth of World War II: Tarkovskii's *Ivan's Childhood* (1962) and Klimov's *Come and See* (1985)' in *Historical Journal of Film, Radio and Television* Vol. 14, No. 4 (1994) (pp.413–419) p.416.

4. Hardcastle, Anne, 'Ghosts of the Past and Present: hauntology and the Spanish Civil War in Guillermo del Toro's *The Devil's Backbone*' in *Journal of the Fantastic in the Arts* Vol. 15, No. 2 (2005) (pp.120–132) p.127.

5. Kinder, Marsha, 'The Children of Franco in the New Spanish Cinema' in *Quarterly Review of Film Studies* (Spring, 1983) (pp.57–76) pp.59–60.

6. Smith, Paul Julian, *The Moderns: time, space and subjectivity in contemporary Spanish culture* (Oxford University Press: Oxford, 2000) pp.35–36.

7. Steedman, Carolyn, *Past Tenses: essays on writing, autobiography and history* (Rivers Oram Press: London, 1992) p.12.

8. Davis, Colin, 'Can the Dead Speak to Us?: De Man, Levinas and Agamben' in *Culture, Theory & Critique* Vol. 45, No. 1 (2004) (pp.77–89) p.82.

9. Howe, Susan, 'Sorting Facts; or, Nineteen Ways of Looking at Marker' in Charles Warren (ed.) *Beyond Document: essays on non-fiction film* (Wesleyan University Press: Middletown CT, 1995) (pp.295–343) p.301.

10. de Ros, Xon, 'Innocence Lost: sound and silence in *El espíritu de la colmena*' in *Bulletin of Hispanic Studies* Vol. 76, No. 1 (1999) (pp.27–37) p.34.

11. de Ros, 'Innocence Lost', p.35.

12. Nelson, Tollof, 'Sculpting the End of Time: the anamorphosis of history and memory in Andrei Tarkovsky's *Mirror* (1975)' in *CiNeMas* Vol. 13, No. 3 (Spring, 2003) (pp.119–147) p.131.

13. Nelson, 'Sculpting the End of Time', p.136.

14. Nelson, 'Sculpting the End of Time', p.139.

15. Smith, Lindsay, 'Lewis Carroll: stammering, photography and the voice of infancy' in *Journal of Visual Culture* Vol. 3, No. 1 (2004) (pp.95–105) p.104.

16. Horowitz, Sara R., *Voicing the Void: muteness and memory in Holocaust fiction* (State University of New York Press: New York, 1996) p.8.

17. Levi, Primo, *If This Is a Man/The Truce* trans. S. Woolf (Abacus, new edition, 1991, first pub. Penguin: London, 1979) p.197.

18. Levi, *If This Is a Man*, p.198.

19. Agamben, Giorgio, *Remnants of Auschwitz: the witness and the archive* trans. Daniel Heller-Roazen (MIT Press: Cambridge, MA, 2000) p.39.

20. Nancy, Jean-Luc, *Listening* trans. Charlotte Mandell (Fordham University Press: New York, 2007) pp.5–6.

21. Zipes, Jack, 'The Enchanted Forest of the Brothers Grimm: new modes of approaching the Grimm's fairy tales' in *Germanic Review* Vol. 62, No. 2 (Spring, 1987) (pp.66–74) p.66.

22. Sorlin, Pierre, 'Children as War Victims in Postwar European Cinema' in Jay Winter and Emmanuel Sivan (eds.) *War and Remembrance in the Twentieth Century* (Cambridge University Press: Cambridge, 2008) (pp.104–125) p.109.

23. Luthi, Max, *Once Upon a Time: on the nature of fairytales* (Indiana University Press: Bloomsbury and Indianapolis, 1976) p.47.

24. See Haase, Donald, 'Children, War, and the Imaginative Space of Fairy Tales' in *The Lion and the Unicorn* Vol. 24, No. 3 (2000) pp.360–377.

25. Haase, Donald, 'Overcoming the Present: children and fairy tales in exile, war, and the Holocaust' in Viktoria Herling (ed.) *Mit den Augen*

eines Kindes: children in the Holocaust, children in exile, children under fascism (Rodopi: Amsterdam, 1998) (pp.86–99) p.99.

26. Bachelard, Gaston, The Psychoanalysis of Fire (Routledge & Keagan Paul: London, 1964) p.7.

27. Bachelard, The Psychoanalysis of Fire, p.7.

28. Luthi, Once Upon a Time, p.34.

29. Lingis, Alphonso, 'Mirages in the Mud' in Journal of Visual Culture Vol. 3, No. 1 (2004) (pp.107–117) p.110.

30. Lingis, 'Mirages in the Mud', p.113.

31. Wilson, Emma, 'Children, Emotion and Viewing in Contemporary European film' in Screen Vol. 46, No. 3 (Autumn, 2005) (pp.329–341) p.334.

32. Wilson, 'Children, Emotion and Viewing', p.332.

33. Wilson, 'Children, Emotion and Viewing', p.330.

34. Wilson, 'Children, Emotion and Viewing', p.337.

35. Bosmajian, Hamida, 'Memory and Desire in the Landscapes of Sendak's Dear Mili' in The Lion and the Unicorn Vol. 19, No. 2 (1995) (pp.186–210) p.200.

36. Benjamin, Walter, 'The Storyteller' in Illuminations Hannah Arendt (ed.) (Fontana: London, 1992) p.89.

37. Stargardt, Nicholas, Witnesses of War: children's lives under the Nazis (Pimlico: London, 2006) p.375.

38. Stargardt, Witnesses of War, p.375.

39. Byatt, A.S. 'Happy Ever After', in Guardian 3 January 2004, http://books.guardian.co.uk/print/o,,482121–110738,00.html [accessed 20 March 2008].

40. Steedman, Carolyn, Dust (Manchester University Press: Manchester, 2001) p.150.

41. Stargardt, Witnesses of War, p.17.

Chapter 4

1. 2007 Eureka DVD release of Little Red Flowers (2006).

2. Ridout, Nicholas, Stage Fright, Animals and Other Theatrical Problems (Cambridge University Press: Cambridge, 2006) p.100.

3. Roach, Joseph, 'It' in Theatre Journal Vol. 56 (2004) (pp.555–568) quoting George Meredith, Beauchamp's Career G.M. Young (ed.) (1876, Oxford University Press: Oxford, 1950) p.331.

4. Roach, 'It', p.561.

5. Vincente Minnelli quoted in Fordin, Hugh, The Movies Greatest Musicals: produced in Hollywood USA by the Freed Unit (Ungar: New York, 1984) p.97.

6. Schechner, Richard, Performance Theory (Routledge: London, 1988) p.248 quoted in David Williams 'Performing Animal, Becoming Animal'

in Peta Tait (ed.) *Body Shows: Australian viewings of live performance* (Rodopi: Amsterdam, 2000) (pp.44–60).

7. Varty, Anne, *Children in Theatre in Victorian Britain* (Palgrave Macmillan: Hampshire, 2007) p.13.

8. Jefferson, S., 'Junior Miss Miracle' in *Photoplay Magazine* (August, 1943) p.70.

9. Alexander Mackendrick quoted in Kemp, Philip, *Lethal Innocence: the cinema of Alexander Mackendrick* (Heinemann: Oxford, 1991) p.70.

10. The confusion is carried over between the child and character through the fact they are both called Mandy. Although I cannot say whether Mackendrick changed the name of the character to be the same as his chosen child actor, it is perhaps worth noting that Margaret O'Brien changed her name from Angela Maxine O'Brien to the name of the first major child character she played in a *Journey for Margaret*.

11. Baron, Cynthia and Carnicke, Sharon Marie, *Reframing Screen Performance* (University of Michigan Press: Ann Arbor, 2008) p.3.

12. Baron and Carnicke, *Reframing Screen Performance*, p.28.

13. Fanning says this in an interview for a documentary on the making of Tony Scott's *Man on Fire* which is available as an extra on the two-disc special edition Twentieth Century Fox Home Entertainment 2004 DVD release.

14. Temple Black, Shirley, *Child Star: an autobiography* (Headline: London, 1988) p.49.

15. Kemp, *Lethal Innocence*, p.71.

16. Interview with Luchino Visconti reprinted in booklet to accompany recent 2007 'Masters of Cinema' DVD release of *Bellissima* (1951).

17. Balázs, Béla *The Theory of Film* trans. Edith Bone (Dennis Dobson: London, 1952) p.80.

18. Balázs, Béla *The Theory of Film*, pp.80–81.

19. Kirby, Michael, 'On Acting and Non-Acting' in *The Drama Review* Vol. 16, No. 2 (pp.3–15) p.3.

20. Kirby, 'On Acting', p.5.

21. Encreve, Marie-Helene, essay on sleeve for the 1998 Tartan release of the VHS for *Ponette* (1996).

22. Kirby, 'On Acting', p.7.

23. Kirby, 'On Acting', p.7.

24. Jodie Foster interviewed in documentary available on the two-disc Sony special edition DVD 2007 for *Taxi Driver* (1976).

25. Kirby, 'On Acting', p.11.

26. Kelleher, Joe, 'Face to Face with Terror: children in film' in Karin Lesnik-Oberstein (ed.) *Children in Culture: approaches to childhood* (Palgrave Macmillan: Hampshire, 1998) (pp.29–55) p.41.

27. Read, Alan, *Theatre, Intimacy and Engagement: the last human venue* (Palgrave Macmillan: Hampshire, 2007).

28. Read, *Theatre, Intimacy and Engagement*, p.92.

29. McGrath, Charles, 'At the World's End: honing a father-son dynamic' in *New York Times*, 27 May 2008, http://www.nytimes.com/2008/05/27/movies/27road.html [accessed: 10 September 2009].

30. Fudge, Erica, *Pets* (Acumen Publishing: Stocksfield, 2008) p.27.

31. Fudge, *Pets*, p.23.

32. Caughie, John, 'The Bill Douglas Trilogy', essay published in booklet accompanying the BFI 2008 DVD release of *The Bill Douglas Trilogy* (1972–1978) p.7.

33. Read, *Theatre, Intimacy and Engagement*, p.120.

34. Read, *Theatre, Intimacy and Engagement*, p.126.

35. Goodwin, Christopher, 'Taking Candy from a Baby' in *The Sunday Times Magazine*, 27 August 2006 (pp.26–31) p.28.

36. Read, *Theatre, Intimacy and Engagement*, p.149.

37. Katz, Jack, *How Emotions Work* (University of Chicago Press: Chicago, 1997) p.197.

38. Nowell-Smith, Geoffrey, essay published in booklet accompanying the 'Masters of Cinema', Eureka 2007 DVD release of *Bellissima* (1951) p.19.

Bibliography

Agamben, Giorgio, *Remnants of Auschwitz: the witness and the archive* trans. Daniel Heller-Roazen (MIT Press: Cambridge MA, 2000).

Arai, Andrea, 'Killing Kids: recession and survival in twenty-first century Japan' in *Postcolonial Studies* Vol. 6, No. 3 (2003) (pp.367–379).

Arai, Andrea, 'Recessionary Effects: the crisis of the child and culture of reform in contemporary Japan', unpublished PhD thesis, Columbia University, 2004.

Bachelard, Gaston, *The Psychoanalysis of Fire* (Routledge & Keagan Paul: London, 1964).

Balázs, Béla, *The Theory of Film* trans. Edith Bone (Dennis Dobson: London, 1952).

Baron, Cynthia and Carnicke, Sharon Marie, *Reframing Screen Performance* (University of Michigan Press: Ann Arbor, 2008).

Bazin, André, 'Germany Year Zero' in Bert Cardullo (ed.) *Bazin at Work: major essays & reviews from the forties and fifties* (Routledge: London and New York, 1997).

Belletto, Steven, 'Of Pickaninnies and Nymphets: race in *Lolita*' in *Nabokov Studies* Vol. 9 (2005) (pp.1–17).

Benjamin, Walter, 'The Storyteller' in Hannah Arendt (ed.) *Illuminations* (Fontana: London, 1992).

Bond Stockton, Kathryn, 'Growing Sideways, or Versions of the Queer Child: the ghost, the homosexual, the Freudian, the innocent and the interval of animal' in Steve Bruhm and Natasha Hurley (eds.) *Curiouser: on the queerness of children* (University of Minnesota Press: Minneapolis and London, 2004) (pp.277–317).

Bosmajian, Hamida, 'Memory and Desire in the Landscapes of Sendak's *Dear Mili*' in *The Lion and the Unicorn* Vol. 19, No. 2 (1995) (pp. 186–210).

Butler, David, 'The Days Do Not End: film music, time and Bernard Hermann' in *Film Studies* No. 9 (Winter, 2006) (pp. 51–63).

Byatt, A.S. 'Happy Ever After' in *Guardian* 3 January 2004, http://books. guardian.co.uk/print/o,,482121-110738,00.html [accessed 20 March 2008].

Chakrabarty, Dipesh, 'The Time of History and the Times of the Gods' in L. Lowe and D. Lloyd (eds.) *The Politics of Culture in the Shadow of Capital* (Duke University Press: Durham NC, 1997) (pp.35–61).

Coviello, Peter, 'Poe in Love: pedophilia, morbidity, and the logic of slavery' in *ELH* Vol. 70, No. 3 (Fall, 2003) (pp. 875–901).

Cua Lim, Bliss, 'Spectral Times: the ghost film as historical allegory' in Positions Vol. 9, No. 2 (2001) (pp.287–329).

Davis, Colin, 'Can the Dead Speak to Us?: De Man, Levinas and Agamben' in Culture, Theory & Critique Vol. 45, No. 1 (2004) (pp. 77–89).

Davis, Colin, Haunted Subjects: deconstruction, psychoanalysis and the return of the dead (Palgrave Macmillan: Hampshire, 2007).

de Ros, Xon, 'Innocence Lost: sound and silence in El espiritu de la colmena' in Bulletin of Hispanic Studies Vol. 76, No. 1 (1999) (pp.27–38).

duCille, Ann, 'The Shirley Temple of My Familiar' in Transition No. 73 (1997) (pp.10–32).

Eckert, Charles, 'Shirley Temple and the House of Rockerfeller' in Jump Cut No. 2 (1974) reprinted in Christine Gledhill (ed.) Stardom: Industry of Desire (Routledge: London, 1991) (pp. 60–73).

Ehrlich, Linda C. 'Nobody Knows (Dare mo shiranai)' in Film Quarterly Vol. 59, No. 2 (Winter 2005–2006) (pp. 45–50).

Field, Norma, 'The Child as Laborer and Consumer: the disappearance of childhood in contemporary Japan' in S. Stephens (ed.) Children and the Politics of Culture (Princeton University Press: Princeton and London, 1995) (pp.51–79).

Fordin, Hugh, The Movies Greatest Musicals: produced in Hollywood USA by the Freed Unit (Ungar: New York, 1984).

Fudge, Erica, Pets (Acumen Publishing: Stocksfield, 2008).

Goodwin, Christopher, 'Taking Candy from a Baby' in Sunday Times Magazine August 27 2006 (pp.26–31).

Haase, Donald, 'Children, War, and the Imaginative Space of Fairy Tales' in The Lion and the Unicorn Vol. 24, No. 3 (2000) (pp. 360–377).

Haase, Donald, 'Overcoming the Present: children and fairy tales in exile, war, and the Holocaust' in Viktoria Herling (ed.) Mit den Augen eines Kindes: children in the Holocaust, children in exile, children under fascism (Rodopi: Amsterdam, 1998) (pp.86–99).

Hardcastle, Anne, 'Ghosts of the Past and Present: hauntology and the Spanish Civil War in Guillermo del Toro's The Devil's Backbone' in Journal of the Fantastic in the Arts Vol. 15, No. 2 (2005) (pp.120–132).

Hoban, Russell, Riddley Walker (Bloomsbury: London 2002, first pub. 1980).

Honeyman, Susan, Elusive Childhood: impossible representations in modern fiction (Ohio State University Press: Columbus, 2005).

Horowitz, Sara R., Voicing the Void: muteness and memory in Holocaust fiction (State University of New York Press: New York, 1996).

Howe, Susan, 'Sorting Facts; or, Nineteen Ways of Looking at Marker' in Charles Warren (ed.) Beyond Document: essays on non-fiction film (Wesleyan University Press: Middletown CT, 1995) (pp. 295–343).

Hughes, David, The Complete Kubrick (Virgin: London, 2000).

Jackson, Kathy Merlock, The Image of the Child in American Film (Scarecrow Press: New York, 1986).

Jefferson, Susan, 'Junior Miss Miracle' in Photoplay Magazine (August, 1943) (pp. 53, 70).

Jones, Owain, ' "True Geography [ ] quickly forgotten, giving away to an adult-imagined universe". Approaching the otherness of childhood' in Children's Geographies Vol. 6, No. 2 (May 2008) (pp. 195–212).

Katz, Jack, How Emotions Work (University of Chicago Press: Chicago, 1997).

Kelleher, Joe, 'Face to Face with Terror: children in film' in Karin Lesnik-Oberstein (ed.) Children in Culture: approaches to childhood (Palgrave Macmillan: Hampshire, 1998) (pp.29–55).

Kemp, Philip, Lethal Innocence: the cinema of Alexander Mackendrick (Heinemann: Oxford, 1991).

Kincaid, James, Child Loving: the erotic child and Victorian culture (Routledge: New York and London, 1992).

Kincaid, James, Erotic Innocence: the culture of child molesting (Duke University Press: Durham NC, 1998).

Kinder, Marsha, 'The Children of Franco in the New Spanish Cinema' in Quarterly Review of Film Studies (Spring, 1983) (pp. 57–76).

Kirby, Michael, 'On Acting and Non-Acting' in The Drama Review Vol. 16, No. 2 (pp.3–15).

Lebeau, Vicky, Cinema and Childhood (Reaktion Books: London, 2008).

Lesage, Julia, 'Artful Racism, Artful Rape: Griffith's Broken Blossoms' in Jump Cut No. 26 (1981) reprinted in Christine Gledhill (ed.) Home is Where the Heart Is: studies in melodrama and the women's film (British Film Institute: London, 1987) (pp. 235–254).

Levi, Primo, If This is a Man/The Truce trans. S. Woolf (Abacus: London, new edition, 1991, first pub. Penguin: London, 1979).

Lingis, Alphonso, 'Mirages in the Mud' in Journal of Visual Culture Vol. 3, No. 1 (2004) (pp.107–117).

Luthi, Max, Once Upon a Time: on the nature of fairytales (Indiana University Press: Bloomsbury and Indianapolis, 1976).

McGrath, Charles, 'At the World's End: honing a father-son dynamic' in New York Times, 27 May 2008, http://www.nytimes. com/2008/05/27/movies/27road.html [accessed 10 September 2009].

Merish, Lori, 'Cuteness and Commodity Aesthetics: Tom Thumb and Shirley Temple' in Rosemarie Garland Thomson (ed.) Freakery: cultural spectacles of the extraordinary body (New York University Press: New York, 1996) (pp. 185–203).

Morrison, Toni, *Playing in the Dark: whiteness and the literary imagination* (Harvard University Press: Cambridge MA, 1992).

Nancy, Jean-Luc, *Listening* trans. Charlotte Mandell (Fordham University Press: New York, 2007).

Nandrea, Lorri, 'Objectless Curiosity: *Frankenstein, The Station Agent,* and other strange narratives' in *Narrative* Vol. 15, No. 3 (October 2007) (pp.335–356).

Nelson, Tollof, 'Sculpting the End of Time: the anamorphosis of history and memory in Andrei Tarkovsky's *Mirror* (1975)' in *CiNeMas* Vol. 13, No. 3 (Spring, 2003) (pp.119–147).

Perec, Georges, *W* trans. David Bellos (David R. Godine: Boston MA, 1988).

Phillips, Adam, *On Kissing, Tickling and Being Bored* (Faber and Faber: London, 1993).

Read, Alan, *Theatre, Intimacy and Engagement: the last human venue* (Palgrave Macmillan: Hampshire, 2007).

Roach, Joseph, 'It' in *Theatre Journal* Vol. 56 (2004) (pp.555–568).

Smith, Lindsay, 'Lewis Carroll: stammering, photography and the voice of infancy' in *Journal of Visual Culture* Vol. 3, No. 1 (2004) (pp.95–105).

Smith, Paul Julian, *The Moderns: time, space and subjectivity in contemporary Spanish culture* (Oxford University Press: Oxford, 2000).

Sorlin, Pierre, 'Children as War Victims in Postwar European Cinema' in Jay Winter and Emmanuel Sivan (eds.) *War and Remembrance in the Twentieth Century* (Cambridge University Press: Cambridge, 2008) (pp.104–125).

Stargardt, Nicholas, *Witnesses of War: children's lives under the Nazis* (Pimlico: London, 2006).

Steedman, Carolyn, *Past Tenses: essays on writing, autobiography and history* (Rivers Oram Press: London, 1992).

Steedman, Carolyn, *Strange Dislocations: childhood and the idea of human interiority 1780–1930* (Virago Press: London, 1995).

Steedman, Carolyn, *Dust* (Manchester University Press: Manchester, 2002).

Stern, Lesley, *The Scorsese Connection* (British Film Institute: London, 1995).

Studlar, Gaylyn, 'Oh, "Doll Divine": Mary Pickford, masquerade, and the pedophilic gaze' in *Camera Obscura* Vol. 16, No. 3 (2001) (pp.197–226).

Tanaka, Stefan, 'Childhood: naturalization of development into a Japanese Space' in S.C. Humphreys (ed.) *Cultures of Scholarship* (University of Michigan Press: Ann Arbor, 1997) (pp.21–57).

Tanaka, Stefan, *New Times in Modern Japan* (Princeton University Press: Princeton NJ, and London, 2004).

Temple Black, Shirley, *Child Star: an autobiography* (Headline: London, 1989).

Thompson, John O., 'Reflexions on Dead Children in the Cinema and Why There Are Not More of Them' in Gillian Avery and Kimberley Reynolds (eds.) *Representations of Childhood Death* (Palgrave Macmillan: Hampshire, 1999).

Varty, Anne, *Children in Theatre in Victorian Britain* (Palgrave Macmillan: Hampshire, 2007).

Williams, David, 'Performing Animal, Becoming Animal' in Peta Tait (ed.) *Body Shows: Australian viewings of live performance* (Rodopi: Amsterdam, 2000) (pp.44–60).

Williams, Linda, *Playing the Race Card: melodramas of black and white from Uncle Tom to O.J. Simpson* (Princeton University Press: Princeton NJ, and London, 2001).

Wilson, Emma, 'Children, Emotion and Viewing in Contemporary European Film' in *Screen* Vol. 46, No. 3 (Autumn, 2005) (pp.329–341).

Yoda, Tomiko, 'A Roadmap to Millennial Japan' in *The South Atlantic Quarterly* Vol. 99, No. 4 (2002) (pp.629–668).

Youngblood, Denise, 'Post-Stalinist Cinema and the Myth of World War II: Tarkovskii's *Ivan's Childhood* (1962) and Klimov's *Come and See* (1985)' in *Historical Journal of Film, Radio and Television* Vol. 14, No. 4 (1994) (pp.413–419).

Zipes, Jack, 'The Enchanted Forest of the Brothers Grimm: new modes of approaching the Grimm's fairy tales' in *Germanic Review* Vol. 62, No. 2 (Spring, 1987) (pp.66–74).

Index

Adorno, Theodor, 122, 123
Agamben, Giorgio, 6–7,
    123–124, 195n
AI, 35
Alice Doesn't Live Here Anymore, 94
Aoyama, Shinji, 45, 46
Apicella, Tina, 158, 180, 183, 186,
    187, 188, 189
Arai, Andrea, 25, 28, 29, 40, 192n
Archibald, Steven, 173, 174, 176,
    177, 178, 179
Arendt, Hannah, 196n
Au Revoir Les Enfants, 109
Avery, Garth, 164
Avery, Gillian, 194n

The Baby Burlesks, 6, 66, 67, 70
Bachelard, Gaston, 127, 129, 196n
Balazs, Bela, 161, 197n
Barefoot Gen, 114
Baron, Cynthia, 154, 155, 156, 197n
Barrymore, Ethel, 59
Barrymore, Lionel, 147
Barthelmess, Richard, 58
Bazin, Andre, 106, 181, 194n
Beauchamp's Career, 147
Beecher Stowe, Harriet, 84
Belletto, Steven, 79, 80–81, 83, 194n
Bellissima, 12, 158, 159, 160,
    182–189
Benjamin, Walter, 141, 196n
Bettleheim, Bruno, 136
Bicycle Thieves, 160
Big, 149
Birth of a Nation, 59, 61
Blasetti, Alessandro, 183, 184, 188
Bloch, Ernst, 136
Bond Stockton, Kathryn, 5, 191n
Bosmajian, Hamida, 137, 138, 196n
Bow, Clara, 147
Bowen, Dong, 145, 163, 180
Brando, Marlon, 95, 147

Breslin, Abigail, 150, 151
Broken Blossoms, 4, 58–64, 69, 78, 86,
    87, 99
Brooks, Albert, 93
Bruhm, Steve, 191n
Bugsy Malone, 94
Bulger, James, 29
Burke, Thomas, 58
Butler, David, 90, 194n
Byatt, A. S, 143, 196n

Captain January, 71
Cardullo, Bert, 194n
Carnicke, Sharon Marie, 154, 155,
    156, 197n
Carroll, Lewis, 57, 121
Carter, Angela, 60
Caughie, John, 174, 198n
Chakrabarty, Dipesh, 22, 192n
Chiari, Walter, 184
child
    bride, 83, 86
    ghosts, 29, 40, 46, 98
    nation dynamic, 25, 28, 51
    sexuality, 56, 70,
    strange-changed child (kodomo ga hen
        da), 29, 41
child as
    freak, 40, 66, 67, 159, 186
    other, 1–2, 24, 106, 185
    savage, 56, 161
    thing, 66, 72
    witness, 110, 144
children
    and animals, 11, 66, 105–106,
        146, 161, 166, 167–180
    crying, 11–12, 180–189
    as victims', 27, 105, 136
The Children Are Watching Us, 160
Chopin, 103
Chouraqui, Elie, 95
Clemm, Virginia, 83

Come and See (*Idi I Smotri*), 114, 116, 125, 127, 130, 135, 139, 140
Coveillo, Peter, 83–85, 194n
Cria Cuervos (*Cry Ravens*), 108, 114
Cruikshank, George, 136
Cua Lim, Bliss, 21, 192n
'cute', 69–70, 156

Dare mo Shiranai, 3, 30, 41–45, 46, 49, 50, 51
see also *Nobody Knows*
Dark Water, 3, 17, 21, 32, 33–36, 39
see also *Honogurai mizo no soko kara*
Davis, Colin, 2, 19, 111, 191n, 192n, 195n
de Niro, Robert, 76, 95, 164
de Ros, Xon, 118, 195n
de Sica, Vittorio, 160
Dear Mili, 137–138
Dekalog, 17
del Toro, Guillermo, 107
The Demon, 30, 49–51
see also *Kichiku*
Derrida, Jacques, 2, 19–20
The Devil's Backbone, 107, 114
Diamonds of the Night, 109, 114, 116, 125, 127, 130, 135, 136, 139
Doillon, Jacques, 162
Don't Look Now, 17, 36
Dore, Gustave, 136
Douglas, Bill, 171, 176, 178
duCille, Ann, 53, 65–66, 71, 193n
duLac, Edmund, 136

Eckert, Charles, 70, 193n
Ehrlich, Linda C, 43, 192n
El Espiritu de Colmena, 7, 108, 110,114, 118–119, 126, 128, 136, 138, 140, 162
see also *Spirit of the Beehive*
El Laberinto del Fauno, 7, 110, 114, 126, 127, 128, 130, 135, 138, 140
see also *Pan's Labyrinth*
Empire of the Sun, 7, 109, 113, 129, 130, 135, 140

Encreve, Marie-Helen, 162–163, 197n
Erice, Victor, 162
Eureka, 3, 30, 45–47, 48, 49
The Evil Dead, 17
The Exorcist, 19

Fairytales, 1, 52, 125, 126–127, 135–144
Fanning, Dakota, 4, 59, 60, 76, 95, 98–99, 104, 147, 149, 157, 180, 197n
Fateless, 109
Fetchit, Stepin, 66
Field, Norma, 25, 27, 192n
Fields, W. C, 146, 147
Fordin, Hugh, 196n
Forte, Fabrizo, 168, 169,170, 171
Foster, Jodie, 4, 88, 164, 197n
Frank, Anne, 138
Frankenstein, 118
Freaky Friday, 149
The Front Page, 64
Fudge, Erica, 171, 172, 198n

Garland, Judy, 12
Germany Year Zero, 12, 126, 160
Gerrard, Lisa, 103
Gish, Lillian, 4, 58, 59, 60, 65
Gledhill, Christine, 193n
Glenn, Scott, 95
Gone with the Wind, 105
Goodwin, Christopher, 198n
Grave of the Fireflies, 105, 114
Greenberg, Jill, 180
Greene, Graham, 71
Griffith, D. W., 58, 59, 63, 96
The Grudge, 3, 17, 20, 36
see also *Ju-On*
The Grudge 2, 37–39,

Haase, Donald, 126, 127, 195n
Hardcastle, Anne, 108, 194n
The Haunting, 17
Helgeland, Brian, 97
Herling, Viktoria, 195n

Herrmann, Bernard, 49, 89
Hide and seek, 76
Hirokazu, Kore-da, 41, 192n
Hitchcock, Alfred, 49, 89
Hoban, Russell, 14, 191n
Honeyman, Susan, 3, 191n
Honogurai mizo no soko kara, 3, 17, 21,
    32, 33–36, 39
    see also *Dark Water*
Hope and Glory, 109
Horowitz, Sara R, 122, 195n
Howe, Susan, 115, 195n
Hue and Cry, 126
Hughes, David, 193n
Hurley, Natasha, 191n

I am Sam, 147
The Innocents, 17, 19
Irons, Jeremy, 148
'It', 10, 147–148, 153, 158, 167
It Happened in Europe, 106
Ivan's Childhood, 107, 113, 114, 125,
    136, 138

'J-Horror', 2, 3, 17–18, 30, 39, 40,
    44, 46, 50
Jefferson, S, 197n
La Jetee (The Pier), 7, 112,
    113–114, 126
Jones, Owain, 2, 191n
Journey for Margaret, 152, 197n
Ju-On, 3, 17, 20, 36
    see also *The Grudge*

Katz, Jack, 181, 184, 198n
Kawakami, Ryoichi, 29, 41
Keitel, Harvey, 91
Kelleher, Joe, 166, 197n
Kemp, Philip, 157, 197n
Kichiku, 30, 49–51
    see also *The Demon*
Kikujiro, 3, 30, 47–49
Kincaid, James, 57, 77–78, 193n
Kinder, Marsha, 108, 194n
Kinky, 103

Kirby, Michael, 161–162, 164–165,
    168, 182, 197n
Kitano, Takeshi, 47
Kubrick, Stanley, 4, 53, 89, 193n
Kwaidan, 17, 39

Lamont, Charles, 64, 68
Lassie Come Home, 171, 172
'latent sexuality', 77–78
Lebeau, Vicky, 191n
Les Jeux Interdits (Forbidden Games), 110
Lesage, Julia, 60, 63, 193n
Lesnik-Oberstein, Karin, 197n
Levi, Primo, 123, 124, 195n
Levinas, Emmanuel, 111, 112
Lilya 4 Ever, 133
Lingis, Alphonso, 131–133, 135, 196n
'little black girl', 53–54
The Little Colonel, 96, 147
Little Miss Sunshine, 150–151
Little Rascals, 65
Littlest Rebel, 69
Little Red Flowers, 145, 146, 163
'little white girl', 4,6, 53–54, 57, 60,
    65, 66, 72, 87, 94
Lloyd, D, 192n
The Locker (I & II), 17, 20
Lolita, 4, 6, 53, 73–87, 88, 89, 91
Lowe, L, 192n
Lustig, Arnost, 116, 117
Luthi, Max, 126, 127, 130,
    195n, 196n
Lyons, Sue, 73

Mackendrick, Alexander, 153, 157,
    158, 197n
Magnani, Anna, 183, 186, 188
Man on Fire, 6, 86, 95–104, 197n
Mandy, 153, 197n
Marker, Chris, 112
Mason, James, 53, 73
McCarthy, Cormac, 167
McGrath, Charles, 198n
Meet me in St. Louis, 12, 151
Meredith, George, 147, 196n

Merish, Lori, 67, 69, 193n
Merlock Jackson, Kathy, 191n
'Method' acting, 147, 155–156
Miller, Mandy, 153, 157, 158, 180, 197n
Minnelli, Vincente, 151, 196n
Mirror, 7, 109, 113, 119–122, 125, 127, 136, 138
Monroe, Marilyn, 147
Moodyson, Lukas, 133
Morrison, Toni, 4, 79, 84, 100, 101, 193n, 194n
The Mummy, 85
Muselmann, 123
My Ain Folk, 11, 171, 172, 173
My Childhood, 172
My Way Home, 176, 177

Nabokov, Vladmir, 4, 75–76,
Nakata, Hideo, 31
Nancy, Jean Luc, 124, 195n
Nandrea, Lorri, 13–14, 191n
Nelson, Tollof, 120, 121, 195n
Nemec, Jan, 116
Night and Day, 71
Nightmare on Elm Street, 17
Nijushi no hitomi (Twenty-Four Eyes), 26
Nine Inch Nails, 103
Nobody Knows, 3, 30, 41–45, 46, 49, 50, 51
   see also Dare mo Shiranai
Nomura, Yoshitaro, 49
Nowell-Smith, Geoffrey, 188–189, 198n
Nussbaum, Martha, 134

O'Brien, Margaret, 12, 151, 152, 153, 160, 180, 197n
O'Neal, Tatum, 148
'objectless curiousity', 13–14
The Ogre, 126, 127, 130, 135
The Others, 19
Our Gang, 65

Padre Padrone, 11, 167, 176
Paedophilia, 63, 83

Pan's Labyrinth, 7, 110, 114, 126, 127, 128, 130, 135, 138, 140
   see also El Laberinto del Fauno
Paper Moon, 148
Paquin, Anna, 148
Penn, Sean, 147, 149
Perec, George, 8–9, 191n
Philips, Adam, 56–57, 193n
The Piano, 148
Pickford, Mary, 59, 60
Poe, Edgar Allen, 83
Poltergeist, 19
Ponette, 162

Quinnell, A. J , 95

Rackham, Arthur, 136
Radvanyi, Geza, 106
Read, Alan, 166, 179, 181, 198n
Reynolds, Kimberley, 194n
Riddley Walker, 14–15
Ridout, Nicholas, 146, 196n
Ring 2, Ring O, The Birthday, 17, 30 , 31–33, 39
Ringu (or The Ring), 3, 17, 20, 30, 31–33
Roach, Hal, 65
Roach, Joseph, 147–148, 149, 153, 196n
The Road, 167
Robinson, Bill, 67, 69, 72–73, 81, 96, 98
Rome, Open City, 126, 160
Rondstadt, Linda, 103
Rossellini, Roberto, 12, 160
Rourke, Mickey, 100
Runt Page, 64

Schechner, Richard, 152, 180, 196n
Schindler's List, 107
Scorsese, Martin, 87, 89, 91, 92, 164
Scott, Tony, 95, 197n
The Searchers, 46, 53, 87
Sellers, Peter, 53, 74
Sendak, Maurice, 137, 138
Shoeshine, 160

The Shining, 36
Sivan, Emmanuel, 195n
The Sixth Sense, 19
Smith, Lindsay, 121, 195n
Smith, Paul Julian, 108, 109, 195n
Sorlin, Pierre, 126, 195n
Spartacus, 75
Speilberg, Steven, 35, 107, 130
Spirit of the Beehive, 7, 108, 110,114,
    118–119, 126, 128, 136, 138,
    140, 162
    see also El Espiritu de Colmena
Stanislavski, Constantin, 155
Stargadt, Nicholas, 142, 144, 196n
Steedman, Carolyn, 24, 30, 110,
    191n, 192n, 195n, 196n
Stern, Bert, 89
Stern, Lesley, 53, 54, 87, 88, 91, 94,
    192n, 193n,194n
Strasberg, Lee, 155
Studlar, Gaylyn, 60–61, 193n

Tait, Peta, 197n
Tanaka, Stefan, 22, 25, 26, 28, 30,
    192n
Tarkovsky, Andre, 113, 119, 120
Taxi Driver, 6, 86, 87–95, 164
Temple, Shirley, 4, 53, 59, 60, 61,
    64–73, 74, 81, 98, 147, 149,
    155, 180
Temple-Black, Shirley, 64, 68, 71, 96,
    157, 193n, 194n, 197n
Thivisol, Victoire, 163, 180
Thomson, Rosemarie Garland, 193n
Thompson, Emma, 148
Thompson, John O , 106, 194n
'tickling', 56–57
Tin Drum, 110, 115, 127

Torrent, Ana, 13, 108–109,
    138, 162
'touch', 54–55, 77, 92–93, 102–103

Ugetsue Monogatori, 17
Ullalume, 83
Un Chien Andalou, 139
'Uncle Tom', 72, 81, 101
Uncle Tom's Cabin, 84

Varty, Anne, 152, 197n
Vertigo, 89
Vice Versa, 149
Visconti, Luchino, 12, 158–159,
    160, 182, 187, 197n

Walken, Christopher, 100
War Babies, 64, 86
Washington, Denzel, 95, 98–99
Wayne, John, 46, 53
Wee Willie Winkie, 71
Whale, James, 118
Williams, David, 196n
Williams, Linda, 102, 104, 194n
Wilson, Emma, 133, 134, 196n
Winnicott, Donald, 97
Winter, Jay, 195n
Winters, Shelley, 73
The Wizard of Oz, 47
Wood, Natalie, 46, 53
Wood, Robin, 12

Yoda, Tomiko, 18, 23, 26, 191n,
    192n
Young, G. M , 196n
Youngblood, Denise, 107, 194n

Zipes, Jack, 126, 195n